What is Social Work?

What is Social Work?

Context and Perspectives

Fourth Edition

NIGEL HORNER

Series Editors: Jonathan Parker and Greta Bradley

SAGE | LearningMatters

Los Angeles | London | New Delhi
Singapore | Washington DC

Learning Matters
An imprint of SAGE Publications Ltd
1 Oliver's Yard
55 City Road
London EC1Y 1SP

SAGE Publications Inc.
2455 Teller Road
Thousand Oaks, California 91320

SAGE Publications India Pvt Ltd 150
B 1/I 1 Mohan Cooperative Industrial Area
Mathura Road
New Delhi 110 044

SAGE Publications Asia-Pacific Pte Ltd
3 Chuch Street
#10–04 Samsung Hub
Singapore 049483

Editor: Luke Block
Development Editor: Kate Lodge
Production Controller: Chris Marke
Project Management: Deer Park Productions,
Tavistock, Devon
Marketing Manager: Tamara Navaratnam
Cover Design: Code 5
Typeset by: Pantek Media, Maidstone, Kent
Printed by: MPG Books Group, Bodmin, Cornwall

© Nigel Horner 2012

First published in 2003
Reprinted 2004 (twice)
Reprinted 2005
Second Edition 2006
Reprinted 2007
Third Edition 2009
Fourth Edition 2012 by Sage/Learning Matters

Professional Capabilities Framework diagram reproduced with permission of The College of Social Work

Library of Congress Control Number: 2012941845

British Library Cataloguing in Publication Data

A catalogue record for this book is available from the British Library

ISBN: 978 0 85725 843 4
ISBN: 978 0 85725 673 7 (pbk)

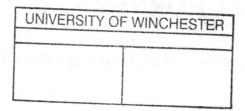

Contents

About the author

Nigel Horner is Senior Academic and Deputy Head of the School of Health and Social Care at the University of Lincoln. Nigel began his social work career as a residential child care worker in South London, before moving into community work in Sunderland, and then qualified at Glasgow University. He subsequently worked for Lincolnshire County Council in various child care and mental health settings, before becoming a Training Officer and working in policy and development, particularly in relation to children's services.

Nigel first published *What is Social Work?* in 2003, followed by *Social Work in Education and Children's Services* (2006) (also published by Learning Matters).

Dedication

For Grace, Dan, Esther, Ted and Josie, as always.

Series editors' preface

The history and development of social work is an area of focus that demonstrates the wide variations of practices, knowledge, and indeed values comprised under the umbrella-term of social work. Taking a wider view indicates social work's association with political, economic and colonial histories throughout the nineteenth and twentieth centuries in the UK and USA and the export of particular practices that did not always fit their new locations. It is important to remember the chequered and multiply layered history and development of social work in attempting to understand it for the present day. This book assists readers in the UK to locate their beginnings and to translate historical understanding into contemporary practice settings.

Such understandings are important since national and global perturbations have continued to influence and mould social and health policy developments, which often, in turn, determine the ways in which they are applied in social work practice. The UK faces numerous challenges over forthcoming years, many of which, perhaps, have been heightened following the 2007 fiscal crisis and its lasting ramifications. These include dealing with the impact of an increasingly ageing population, with its cognate health and social care needs, housing and support service needs, education and leisure services and so forth. Understanding where social work has come from in the UK, and post-devolution changes within the four administrations is central as we work with the financial implications that a changing demography, including lower fertility rates alongside population ageing, brings. This book adds to our knowledge and understanding of the complexities of social work practice in which understanding the travails of the profession help social workers to negotiate a tricky and difficult pathway.

Migration has increased as a global phenomenon and we now live and work with the implications of international issues in our everyday and local lives. Often these issues influence how we construct our social services and determine what services we need to offer. It is likely that as a social worker you will work with a diverse range of people throughout your career, many of whom have experienced significant, even traumatic, events that require a professional and caring response grounded, of course, in the laws and social policies that have developed as a result. As well as working with individuals, however, you may be required to respond to the needs of a particular community disadvantaged by world events or excluded within local communities because of assumptions made about them, and you may be embroiled in some of the tensions that arise from implementing policy-based approaches that may conflict with professional values. What is clear within these contexts is that you may be working with a range of people who are often at the margins of society, socially excluded or in need of protection and safeguarding. From this book you will gain insight into how the various fields of social work have come about, why they may have developed in the ways they have, and how policy changes and influences service development and social work responses to people with diverse issues and needs. This text provides important knowledge and information to help you become aware of the roles that social workers play, to make sense of what social work is in contemporary society, and to respond appropriately and make referrals to other professionals when faced with challenging situations.

Reflection, revision and reform allow us to focus clearly on what knowledge is useful to engage with in learning to be a social worker. The focus on 'statutory' social work, and by dint of that involuntary clients, brings to the fore the need for social workers to be well-versed in the mechanisms and nuances of legislation that can be interpreted and applied to empower, protect and assist, but also to understand the social policy arena in which practice is forged. Understanding the historical development of social work is central to this endeavour. The books in this series respond to the agendas driven by changes brought about by professional body, government and disciplinary review. They aim to build on and offer introductory texts based on up-to-date knowledge and social policy development and to help communicate this in an accessible way preparing the ground for future study as you develop your social work career. The books are written by people passionate about social work and social services and aim to instil that passion in others. The knowledge introduced in this book is important for all social workers in all fields of practice as they seek to reaffirm social work's commitment to those it serves through understanding what social work is and means.

Professor Jonathan Parker, Bournemouth University
Greta Bradley, University of York

Preface to the fourth edition

The first edition of this book was published in 2003, with the second edition being produced in 2006 and the third in 2009. Yet another three years have passed, and the book merits a further updating, not least to reflect the seismic changes that have continued to sweep across the social work and social care landscapes. I am naturally delighted to be asked to write a fourth edition of this book, particularly as it has hitherto proved to be a popular introduction to social work practice, valued by those considering a career in social work, those already engaged in social care and other allied arenas of the human services, those applying for qualifying social work programmes, those already in training, and finally for practitioners, trainers, practice assessors and service managers. I do hope this new edition will have a similarly broad appeal.

This fourth edition has been updated and wherever appropriate, facts, figures and data have been revised, as have the recommended readings and the appendices. The core message of the book is to affirm and confirm that whilst the essence of social work practice remains remarkably constant, it is the contexts within which practice takes place that continue to be radically transformed.

At the time of writing, the coalition government is processing the final confirmed findings of the Social Work Reform Board, which was established to implement the 15 recommendations of the Social Work Taskforce as published in Autumn 2009. This was intended to be 'a nuts and bolts' review of frontline social work practice and to make recommendations for immediate improvements to practice and training as well as long-term change in social work. The final chapter of this edition will examine the remit of the original Taskforce, the published recommendations, the work of the Reform Board and will offer some further thoughts as to what this all means in terms of a new vision for Social Work and Social Workers. This is particularly relevant for new entrants to Social Work: whether as applicants, students, newly registered practitioners or indeed returners to practice. In the 2009–10 period, 4082 new social workers were registered in England, having completed their qualifying programmes (the figures for Wales being 230 and for Scotland 774). Where are these former students now working and what changes are taking place in the employment landscape?

Generic teams and integrated social services departments are already becoming lost in the mist of the past that is at once very recent and yet a long time in terms of policy and political shifts. New students just embarking on their social work qualifying programmes will emerge in two or three years into organisational structures fundamentally different to those currently in existence. Children's services are becoming increasingly diverse and fragmented. Adult social services in a number of localities are retrenching into strategic commissioning authorities, with service delivery undertaken by a myriad of third-sector, not-for-profit or charitable organisations. Whether they employ qualified social workers to undertake their contacted functions remains to be seen. As we have noted in previous editions, some commentators may indeed welcome these developments, seeing them as a sign of a maturing profession that confidently plies its trade under the protected title of 'registered social worker' and operates in increasingly complex and diverse settings.

As in the previous three editions, this book is about the twin themes of continuity and change. In one sense, it is the profound difficulty of the job that remains a constant. As Rosie Varley, Chair of the General Social Care Council (GSCC) noted: *Tragedies such as the death of Baby P and other recent cases remind us how immensely challenging the role of a social worker is. We need to attract the best people into the profession with a diverse workforce that reflects the society we live in* (GSCC press release 4 February 2009). It is all too apparent that what changes are the organisational contexts of employment, the policies, the procedures, the technologies of information gathering and recording, the assessment formats and the jargon-filled narratives that impede effective communication between professions.

In 2006 we noted that Bill Utting, the former Chief Inspector of Social Services, had stated: *We must learn to do the simple things well; standards should exceed the minimum and services should be offered in spirit of generosity.* The song remains the same: these vocational and ethical qualities merit reiteration, reaffirmation and rededication. Moira Gibb, Chief Executive of the London Borough of Camden and Chair of the Social Work Taskforce, has tellingly stated that *Social Work can't be forced to be a profession, it has to choose to be* (*The Guardian*, 23 April 2009). Over the coming years, social worker practitioners and students are going to have to revisit and reflect upon the question *What is Social Work?* as we grapple with the demands of a new social work degree, as we struggle to find new ways of working with children and their families in a post-Munro Report world, as we endeavour to take forward the Personalisation/Independent Living agenda, as we brace our shoulders against the chariots of fiscal constraints that are laying waste to swathes of the welfare state landscapes and as we await the tidal wave of change that will flow from the 2012 Health and Social Care Act.

When given the opportunity, in the face of such changes, we envisage practitioners will wish to engage in the discussions with a confident exposition of social work's distinctive and indispensable purpose. We ask applicants to our programmes to tell us what social work is. A recent applicant for the post graduate qualifying social degree wrote in her essay: *the goal of social work is to positively affect lives, to improve lives, to protect lives and in the most extreme cases, to save lives.* I wish I had written that: it says so much, so eloquently and so succinctly. It is an answer the question: 'What is Social Work?'

I humbly hope that this edition will help you, the reader, develop your own confident understanding of Social Work so you can play your part in taking it forward.

The Professional Capabilities Framework

This book has been carefully mapped to the new Professional Capabilities Framework for Social Workers in England and will help you to develop the appropriate standards at the right level. These standards are:

- **Professionalism**

  Identify and behave as a professional social worker committed to professional development.

- **Values and ethics**

  Apply social work ethical principles and values to guide professional practice.

- **Diversity**

  Recognise diversity and apply anti-discriminatory and anti-oppressive principles in practice.

- **Rights, justice and economic well-being**

  Advance human rights and promote social justice and economic well-being.

- **Knowledge**

  Apply knowledge of social sciences, law and social work practice theory.

- **Judgement**

  Use judgement and authority to intervene with individuals, families and communities to promote independence, provide support and prevent harm, neglect and abuse.

- **Critical reflection and analysis**

  Apply critical reflection and analysis to inform and provide a rationale for professional decision-making.

- **Contexts and organisations**

  Engage with, inform, and adapt to changing contexts that shape practice. Operate effectively within your own organisational frameworks and contribute to the development of services and organisations. Operate effectively within multi-agency and inter-professional settings.

- **Professional leadership**

  Take responsibility for the professional learning and development of others through supervision, mentoring, assessing, research, teaching, leadership and management.

References to these standards will be made throughout the text and you will find a diagram of the Professional Capability Framework in Appendix 1 at the end of the book.

Nigel Horner
Lincoln, 2012

Acknowledgements

I would like to thank the students and my colleagues at the University of Lincoln for helping me develop ideas that have contributed to the further updating of this text, particularly new friends and colleagues in three Russian universities, with whom we have been engaged in a European Union funded TEMPUS project. This work has continually forced us to reflect on 'What is Social Work?' in a British sense, as practitioners from other countries and cultures have such a different understanding of its role, function and purpose. This new edition hopefully reflects a slightly wider gaze in trying to answer the eternal question of What is Social Work? I also wish to thank members of the Lincolnshire Excellent Ageing team, with whom it has been such a pleasure to work – and finally I particularly wish to thank my colleague Janet Walker for help in applying the Professional Capabilities Framework to this new edition.

Chapter 1
Introduction and the core themes

What is social work? The purpose of the book

As you are reading this book, you may have some ideas about how to answer the question 'What is Social Work?', but presumably you are motivated to explore the subject further. This book is written for student social workers who are beginning to develop their skills and understanding of the subject in order to meet the requirements for practice. Whilst it is primarily aimed at students in their first year or level of study, it is hoped that the material will be useful for subsequent years, depending on how your programme is designed, what you are studying and especially as you move into practice learning. The book is also intended to appeal to people considering a career in social work or social care, but who are not yet studying for a social work degree. It will assist students undertaking a range of social and health care courses in further education; nurses, occupational therapists and other health and social care professionals will be able to gain an insight into the new requirements demanded of social workers. Finally, experienced and qualified social workers, especially those contributing to practice learning, will also be able to use this book for consultation, teaching, revision and to gain an insight into the expectations raised by the qualifying degree in social work.

Whatever your situation or your motivation to read further, we hope this book will achieve its purpose – to equip you with a greater understanding of social work, in all its forms and in all of its complexities.

Beginning to answer the question

It has to be acknowledged from the outset that the question 'What is Social Work?' is not an easy one to answer. If we had started with the question 'What is social care?' we might have felt on a little firmer ground. After all, 'social care' has emerged as the preferred term to encompass the range of personal interactions and services – including caring, supporting, assisting, tending, enabling – that are offered to people to promote and further their well-being, but which do not fit under the umbrella of 'health care'. According to Thomas and Pierson (2001, p347) social care is defined as

assistance given to people to maintain themselves physically and socially. This type of care is usually provided in residential and day care centres and by domiciliary staff at home; it is distinguished from other forms such as health care and the care given by one member of a family to another.

A huge number of people are engaged in this business of social care, that in Britain today has an estimated 1.4 million workforce (as stated by the Secretary of State for Health in the House of Commons on 11 July 2005), employed in private, statutory and voluntary organisations, and amounting to over 5 per cent of the entire working population. There are about 284,000 staff employed by local authority children's services and adult care services, with about 550,000 people working for independent sector care homes and domiciliary care providers. *The State of Care Report 2010/11* (CQC, 2011) states there are 4,608 care homes with nursing and 13,475 care homes without nursing (the number of residential care services fell by 10 per cent between 2004 and 2010, while during the same period, the number of agencies offering care in people's homes went up by more than a third).

For the general public, social care – which includes such activities as caring for older people in a residential care home, or providing home care, or working in a day care setting with people with learning disabilities – generates generally positive images, allied as it is to other caring professions, such as nursing. But our primary concern here is with social work, and those who do social work – social workers – and with actions undertaken by them in the course of fulfilling others' expectations of the social work role.

The number of whole-time equivalent (WTE) registered social workers rose throughout the first decade of the twenty-first century: in September 2010, the figure was 45,800 (24 per cent higher than the 36,900 in 2000 although this was an increase of less than 0.5 per cent on the 2009 figure of 45,700. Of this figure, women continued to account for 80 per cent of WTE staff and this proportion has changed little since 2000.

Overall in September 2010, councils with adult social services responsibilities (CASSRs) in England employed 197,400 WTE staff. This is a drop of 3 per cent from 202,600 in September 2009 and a drop of 9 per cent from 217,500 in September 2000. The total number of people employed in social care in 2010 was 249,300, a decrease of 2 per cent from 2009. (In the wake of the cuts in local government expenditure throughout 2011, it was anticipated that the September 2011 figures would reflect significant reductions in the current number of employees in the sector).

Social work sits within the broader range of the social care sphere, but generates significantly different reactions. In this book we will see that, by its very nature, social work is a controversial business, and that this controversial nature often arises from the operation of power as sanctioned by legislation. By being invested with such powers and duties, it is inevitable that social work attracts public opprobrium when it is seen to do too little, or to do too much. Little notice is taken of what it does 'right', whilst public outcry inevitably follows when social work is seen to get it 'wrong'. As an activity, it has come to sit at the interface between the rights of the individual and the responsibilities of the state towards its citizens. It is an evolving, complex and dynamic arena of social intervention. As Parton (1997, p6) argues, social work is in *an essentially contested and ambiguous position*. It is also very confusing. We cannot help but agree with Thompson (2005, p12), who suggests that anyone *looking for a simple, non-controversial answer should (therefore) prepare to be disappointed!* Yet the original motivation for this book resides, in part, in the requirements for social work education that were issued by government in 2002, and therefore we shall begin to examine the nature of social work by considering the definitions enshrined in these new requirements.

Requirements for social work education

The *Modernising Social Services* agenda (Department of Health, 1998b), and the ensuing Care Standards Act of 2000 have seen social work education undergoing a major transformation, since the beginning of the twenty-first century, designed to ensure that qualified social workers are educated to honours degree level and develop knowledge, skills and values which are common and shared. A vision for social work operating in complex human situations has been adopted as part of the degree requirements (Quality Assurance Agency for Higher Education (QAA), 2000, updated in 2008). This is reflected in the following definition from the International Association of Schools of Social Work and International Federation of Social Workers, 2001 (QAA, 2000, 2008, p1).

Definition one

> *The social work profession promotes social change, problem solving in human relationships and the empowerment and liberation of people to enhance well-being.*
>
> *Utilising theories of human behaviour and social systems, social work intervenes at the points where people interact with their environments. Principles of human rights and social justice are fundamental to social work.*

Whilst there is a great deal packed into this short and pithy definition, it encapsulates the notion that social work concerns itself both with individual people and with wider society. Social workers engage with people who are vulnerable, who are struggling in some way to participate fully in society. Social workers walk that tightrope between supporting and advocating on behalf of the marginalised individual, whilst being employed by the social, economic and political environment that may have contributed to their marginalisation.

Given the dual functions, social workers need to be highly skilled and knowledgeable to work effectively in this context. The former Minister for Health, Jacqui Smith, who led the reform of social work education, was keen for social work education and practice to improve, to be more effective, more efficient, more accountable. But in order to improve the quality of professional social work in all its complexity, it is crucial that you, as a student social worker, develop a rigorous grounding in and understanding of theories and models for social work. Such knowledge helps social workers to know what to do, when to do it and how to do it, whilst recognising that social work is a complex activity with no absolute 'rights' and 'wrongs' of practice for each situation, and that what is being seen as 'good practice' is not a 'truth', but is a function of political, moral and economic trends and fashion.

When introducing the reform of social work education, the former Minister championed the practical focus of social work, whilst appearing to be sceptical of the value of theory, of critical thinking and analysis.

Definition two

> *Social work is a very practical job. It is about protecting people and changing their lives, not about being able to give a fluent and theoretical explanation of why they got into*

difficulties in the first place. New degree courses must ensure that theory and research directly informs and supports practice.

The Requirements for Social Work Training set out the minimum standards for entry to social work degree courses and for the teaching and assessment that social work students must receive. The new degree will require social workers to demonstrate their practical application of skills and knowledge and their ability to solve problems and provide hope for people relying on social services for support.

(Jacqui Smith, Department of Health 2002b)

When considering the two definitions above – from the International Federation and from Jacqui Smith – some commentators and theorists might criticise the former for its failure to emphasise the 'control' element of social work practice, which involves the use of statutory powers to intervene in relation to offending behaviour, to protect vulnerable children and young people, to enforce mental health treatment and services, and to protect vulnerable older people; whilst others would question the simplistic pragmatism of the latter, with its emphasis on the appeal to 'common sense', its focus on social work as a rational-technical activity, and its inherent anti-intellectualism.

Definition three

One of the outcomes of the Social Work Taskforce (2009), as referred to in the Preface, and examined in detail in Chapter 9, was to produce a Public Description of Social Work, which provides us with a third definition, as follows:

Social work *helps adults and children to be safe, so that they can cope and take control of their lives again.* **Social workers** *[can] make life better for people in crisis who are struggling to cope, feel alone and cannot sort out their problems unaided.*

(See Appendix 8 for the full text definition)

The Executive Summary of the Task Force report further comments on the description, by stating that:

This description makes a strong case for the value of the profession not only for the individuals who use social work services, but also for the whole of society. If they are to be able to live up to these expectations, social workers need to be able to demonstrate high quality professional skills and judgement, and they need education and a work environment which enables them to exercise those skills and judgement.

(Social Work Reform Board, 2010, p5)

When we compare and contrast the three definitions above, we can thus see that trying to define social work is complex and controversial, and it is this very contested nature that will be explored throughout this book.

Let us explore the contested nature of social work by way of a practice example.

CASE STUDY

Anne is a 20-year-old woman, who is visually impaired and has mild learning disabilities. She is of dual heritage, with an African Caribbean mother (Esther) and a white father (Geoff). She currently lives in rented accommodation with her 18-year-old boyfriend Simon. Anne and Simon attended the same special school. Anne is seven months pregnant.

Anne says she is looking forward to having her baby and feels very positive about being a mother. Simon acknowledges that he did not want to be a parent (yet), and fears the future. He has talked about splitting up with Anne. Esther feels her daughter will not cope with having a baby, and wants to look after the baby herself. Geoff is very angry with Anne and Simon, and says the baby should be adopted. He will not contemplate looking after the baby with Esther.

ACTIVITY **1.1**

You are Anne's social worker. What do you think should be done? Note down your initial thoughts.

COMMENT

As a social worker in this case, it can be seen from the outset that your work is – as we have said – controversial and complex. There are numerous competing and conflicting positions here. But this situation is made more complex by acknowledging your role. After all, this is not a family asking for advice from a friend or relative. They are not accessing private mediation or counselling to help them resolve their difficulties. You are involved as a social worker employed by the local authority, on behalf of the state, working within the confines and constraints of the law. As such, your paramount consideration, under the 1989 Children Act, is with the welfare of the (unborn) child. But there are also issues of human rights here. There are matters of cultural sensitivity. There are questions of values and ethics. Before you even begin to assess Anne's capacity to be a parent – with or without the support of the other 'key players' – the controversial nature of social work is revealed by an acknowledgement that the 'general public' would largely look askance on the idea that a disabled person should be allowed to bring up a baby. Such might be considered the 'common sense' view. Yet social work is not just about doing the public's bidding (if by 'public' we mean the majority). We will see in this book that social work's historic contribution, in relation to many service user groups, has often been to challenge public prejudices and assumptions about what is 'right' or 'normal'. The 'common sense' world has often been very punitive and disempowering to vulnerable and oppressed groups. We will see, therefore, that social work – as a profession responding to Anne's situation – has to sit on the painful fence of both promoting the rights of all people to choose to fulfil themselves through parenting (thus challenging society's prejudices and stereotypes), whilst carrying out the state's need to protect all vulnerable people, sometimes by restricting the rights and liberty of others. This is the 'moral maze' of social work practice.

As Banks (1995, p11) observes:

> *Most decisions in social work involve a complex interaction of ethical, political, technical and legal issues which are all interconnected*

and furthermore Thompson (2005, p71) states that:

> *in working with other people we enter a complex world of interactions and structures. This can lead to a positive outcome for all concerned or it can lead to a serious exacerbation of the situation. Consequently, we have to recognise the potential for social work to do harm as well as good.*

It is the fact of social work's potency – being replete with assumed and ascribed power – that, to a large degree, explains its contested and controversial identity.

In the case of Anne and her pregnancy, the initial task of the social worker is to undertake an assessment of Anne's circumstances, her hopes and aspirations, her family situation, the risks associated with the situation. But an assessment is not a hands-off laboratory activity. It is dynamic and interactive. It is based upon the worker's capacity to communicate and engage with the key players, to enable all to feel included and heard in the process. It requires networking skills and inter agency cooperation across professional and non-professional groups (see Parker and Bradley, 2007). Yet, at the end of the process, a judgement has to be made – how are the child's needs to be met? What is the optimum arrangement for the unborn child?

In such decisions the complexity of social work resides.

The scope of social work

Whilst social work's reputation continues to suffer in the wake of the seemingly inexorable list of child death tragedies, including in recent years Peter Connolly, Khyra Ishaq and Ryan Lovell–Hancox, and the parallel exposure of inhumane and abusive practices in the health and social care domain, such as at Winterbourne View, near Bristol, all of which contributes to a critique and crisis of confidence in and about the personal social services, it is worthwhile pausing for a moment to identify the number of people currently receiving support as service users.

- In 2010–11, the number of contacts from new clients of adult care services was 2.2 million.

- Of these new referrals, 25% were self-referrals, 22% came from secondary health services (such a hospitals), 14% came from primary/community health services and 14% were referrals from family, friends or neighbours.

- Of those with completed assessments, 74% had a physical disability, 21% a mental health problem, 2% had a learning disability, 1% a substance misuse problem and 3% another source of vulnerability.

- 1.6 million people received a service in 2010–11. Of this number, 1.3 million received community-based services, 213,000 received residential care services and 88,000 received residential nursing care provision.

- 6 million people are identified as carers, of whom 1.5 million are over 60 and 350,000 are aged 75 or over (Glendinning and Arksey, 2008, p220).

- The number of carers receiving support in 2010–11 was 380,000.

- Each week, over 4 million contact hours are provided to 328,600 households (or 340,000 service users). Of these, 81% are provided by the independent sector.

- There were 615,000 referrals to children's social care services in the year ending 31 March 2011.

- There were 382,400 children in need at 31 March 2011, which was a rate of 346.2 per 10,000 children (or 3.46% of all children under 18).

- At 31 March 2011, there were 42,700 children who were the subject of a child protection plan.

- There were 65,520 looked after children on 31 March 2011 (an increase of 2% from the previous year and a rise of 9% since 2007), which equates to 0.5% of all children and young people.

- 74% of those looked after were in foster care settings.

- Of the 26,830 children and young people who started to be looked after in 2010–11, 54% received services because they had been subject to abuse or neglect.

What is apparent is that society expects social workers – and their colleagues engaged in the broader related field of social care – to both protect and care for those citizens deemed in need of such protection and care. Such an expectation begs the question as to how some individuals – and not others – become deemed to be the focus of such attention, and therefore receive the services that flow from being defined as 'service users'. Common sense would suggest that services are apportioned rationally to those in greatest need, but that would be too simple. Sociological theory helps us to locate social work as a socially constructed activity, in which certain people become defined as 'clients' or 'service users' or 'customers', thereby meriting the attention of practitioners assuming the role of 'social workers'. Such social interactions have not just appeared. Indeed, current social work practices and systems have evolved fitfully and erratically over a long period of time.

Therefore, in order to begin to address the question of what is social work, we need to spend some time exploring the development of social work in Great Britain, by locating it within the historical context of broader welfare history. We will see that in British history, people such as Anne would have been living in institutions, designed – in no small part – to control and prevent their reproductive capabilities. Were Anne to have become pregnant, her baby would probably have been forcibly removed. Moral dilemmas would have been apparently absent, in that this course of action would have been undertaken without question. We will see that in many ways, social work has developed to address these complex moral issues, as the glue between the other building blocks of the welfare state.

Social work and the welfare jigsaw

To Walker (1984, p15), the personal social services amount to the fifth social policy arena, alongside social security, health, housing and education. The evolution of all of these service sectors needs to be considered, as the remit of social work is, in many respects, a function of the constraints and limitations of the other services. In fact, social work can be seen as the safety net, catching those in greatest need as they fall through the provision of health, education, housing and social security, and employment, which is seen by the current government as the route to social inclusion and independence.

Health	Education	Employment	Housing	Social Security
<<<<<Contemporary integrated social inclusion policies >>>>>				
**********The safety net: social work and social care**********				

There has emerged a sense that the vision of social inclusion, if successful, will render social work unnecessary, or perhaps a residual service. These fears are not new, and have echoes whenever there appear to be significant social policy developments, such as in the creation of the 'modern' welfare state after the Second World War. In this sense, we believe that an understanding of the profession's past is a necessary prerequisite to being able to engage in the current debates about the role and purpose of social work in the landscape of modernised and reformed public services.

The value of historical analysis

Many experienced practitioners refer to the apparent circularity of trends, even though these trends never form neat circles, and we do not return to the same starting point. Collectively, as a profession, we may revisit certain 'places' – for example, today's exhortation from government to expand, simplify and speed up adoption as a 'solution' for the permanent care of young people has been championed at various times in social work's history – but new values, new perspectives, new knowledge and new evidence will inform our practice. We may appear to be back on the adoption 'bandwagon', which has traditionally been based upon the sanctity of 'family values', but this time around our ideas of 'family' are radically different, as gay, lesbian, and unmarried couples are in the frame, and recent adoption legislation has resulted in a different form of adoption – one that is more inclusive, less secretive and even more child-centred.

So, broad trends and themes are revived, making an historical perspective all the more necessary to grasp. Parker states:

> *Today's problems, policies and controversies cannot be understood without reference to their historical backgrounds. The slate is rarely, if ever, wiped clean.... However far-reaching change may appear to be, their origins lie in what has gone before. The present is constructed from the past.*

> (Parker, 1990, pp108–9)

We will see that social work and its practice partner – social care – have progressively emerged out of the shadows, as an alternative to the policies and practices of institutional containment, of punishment, of control. By way of reinforcing the value of taking the long view, of being aware of the responses to perceived problems that have gone before the present service landscape, Hayden et al. (1999, p30) refer to the assertion of Newsome (cited in Hayden et al., 1999), that:

> *many issues are not new, but firmly rooted in the historical development of institutions. Many of the social attitudes and personal motives which existed in the past are far from dead issues, though most practitioners are unlikely to be conscious of the fact.*

> (Newsome, 1992, p155)

It is the primary objective of this book to enable you to become 'conscious of the fact', to be at the same time aware of the enormous changes that have occurred in the social work and social care world, and yet be cognisant of how little has changed, of the persistence of some key elements of what is social work. Fundamentally, the purpose of engaging in an historical review of social work's origins *is not to think historically about the past but rather to use that history to rethink the present* (Foucault, 1977, p31).

The structure of the book

This ever-expanding series of course books was initially developed to support the learning of students undertaking a social work degree, in accordance with the Requirements for Social Work Training (Department of Health, 2002b). The advent of the New Award for qualification in social work forms one part of a raft of major developments in the institutional structures that define, regulate and lead social work, and it is important for you, the student, to consider why these elements of the *Modernising Social Services* agenda (Department of Health, 1998b) have come to be seen as necessary.

It is also essential, at this stage in its history, to appreciate the significant meaning being attached to the creation of a College of Social Work, the impending reform of social work education and introduction of the Professional Capabilities Framework that defines behaviours and attributes required within the professional system.

An overview of the historical phases of social work development will enable you to have an understanding of the nature of the contemporary social work task. In turn, you will be able to reflect upon the required knowledge, skills and values deemed necessary for the modern social worker to be able to carry out the modern social work role.

In Chapter 2 you will briefly consider the beginnings of social work and social care in the medieval period, through to the development of charitable institutions in the Georgian and Victorian eras. You will be invited to discuss the major influences that shaped personal welfare systems at the end of the nineteenth century, including religious movements, philanthropy, social reform, labour movements and government policy.

In Chapter 3 we will look at social work with children, young people and families, by illustrating the historic responses to Anne and her son Jack. You will be presented with an overview of trends of child welfare policy and practice, an introduction to the current legal framework for working with children and families, and consider some of the key debates in contemporary practice in relation to the new children's services framework.

In Chapter 4 you will be introduced to George, a 25-year-old man with mild learning disabilities. As in Chapter 3, you will be given the opportunity to understand social work and modern learning disability services in the context of historical and critical perspectives, leading up to current practice issues within a legal and policy framework.

In Chapter 5 mental health practice and policy will be discussed in relation to the experiences of Mary, a 40-year-old woman with mental health problems, drawing upon historical responses to those defined as 'mentally ill' and reflecting upon major shifts in service provision in recent decades.

Lastly in this sequence, Chapter 6 will consider contemporary social work through the responses to Hannah, a 70-year-old woman with specific care needs. The 'care' of older people accounts for the largest number of service users within the social care/social work orbit, and current changes in practice thinking are introduced.

In Chapter 7 we move away from service user groups, and return to social work as a generic business, whereby you will reflect upon social work as a professional activity. The earliest formalisation of both training and practice which led to the emergence of social work being defined as *The Newest Profession* (Younghusband, 1981) will be examined. You will consider the post-1945 landscape, and locate the personal social services alongside the major institutions of the welfare state as part of the post-war reconstruction, leading on to the Seebohm Report of 1968 and the emergence of unified social services departments in the 1970s. We will chart the series of events that led to a crisis in confidence surrounding social work, and to the perceived need for legal reform, particularly in relation to child care and to adult services, which resulted in the Children Act 1989, the NHS and Community Care Act 1990 and the Mental Health Acts 1983 and 2007, all of which shape and determine the modern social work mandate for practice.

In Chapter 8 we will reflect upon the Modernising Social Work agenda, the reign of the General Social Care Council (GSCC) for over a decade, and then preview the transfer of social work into the regulatory arms of the Health Professions Council (HPC) at the same time as the College of Social Work comes into being as the body that should be best placed to answer the question 'What is Social Work?' and to advance the cause of social work as we enter an era of seismic change in the meaning of society, community and the structures that support the most vulnerable citizens in our midst.

Finally, in Chapter 9, we will attempt to read the runes about the future directions for social work and social care, and consider where you – as a student embarking upon a course of professional training – might be working in the future, when qualified and beyond.

Aids to learning: Character case studies

As we have already noted, we will examine the changing function of social work by considering the social and community responses to four characters, namely:

- Jack, an infant, whose mother Anne is unable to care for him;
- George, a 25-year-old man with mild learning disabilities/difficulties;

- Mary, a 40-year-old woman experiencing mental health problems;

- Hannah, a 70-year-old woman, unable to care for herself.

These characters are explored using a TARDIS or time-travelling approach – by considering their situations in different time periods and examining their relationships with welfare agencies, including what we now think of as social work. These people, in the literary tradition of 'Everyman', now represent Everyone. At certain times, it is reasonable to assume they would have been white, but they could just as easily have been Jewish, or Romany, or Huguenot, or of Celtic origin. For the purposes of learning, they need to be seen as equally likely to be black, or Asian, in spite of their Anglophone names. An essential requirement for achieving competence in social work practice is to value difference, and to work in a manner that respects different cultures, faiths, beliefs and traditions. Such a values perspective needs, therefore, to be applied to all of the case examples in the following text.

Learning features

The book is interactive. You are encouraged to work through the book as an active participant, taking responsibility for your learning, in order to increase your knowledge, understanding and ability to apply this learning to practice. You will be expected to reflect creatively on how immediate learning needs can be met in the area of understanding social work within a broad context and how your professional learning can be developed in your future career.

Case studies throughout the book will help you to examine theories and models for social work practice. We have devised activities that require you to reflect on experiences, situations and events and help you to review and summarise learning undertaken. In this way your knowledge will become deeply embedded as part of your development. When you come to undertake practice learning opportunities in an agency, the work and reflection undertaken here will help you to improve and hone your skills and knowledge.

Professional development and reflective practice

Great emphasis is placed on developing skills of reflection about, in and on practice. This has developed over many years in social work. It is important also that you reflect prior to practice, if indeed this is your goal. This book will assist you in developing a questioning approach that looks in a critical way at your thoughts, experiences and practice and seeks to heighten your skills in refining your practice as a result of these deliberations. Reflection is central to good social work practice, but only if action results from that reflection.

Reflecting about, in and on your practice is not only important during your education to become a social worker; it is considered key to continuing professional development. As we move to a profession that acknowledges life-long learning as a way of keeping up-to-date, ensuring that research informs practice and in honing skills and values for practice, it is important to begin the process at the outset of your development. The importance of professional development is clearly shown by its inclusion in the Professional Capabilities Framework and reflected in the GSCC Code of Practice for Employees.

A pause for reflection: Beginning with the self

Before we begin to examine the evolution of modern social work practice from its historical antecedents, it is instructive to reflect upon your own motivation for being 'a social worker'. After all, social work is not a conscripted activity in our society: every social work student, beginning and long-serving practitioner has made a free choice to engage in such an occupation, in spite of its generally agreed poor public image. Social work is routinely acknowledged to be a socially devalued activity, involving working with socially devalued people, often in a less than encouraging climate, and with diminishing or threatened resources. So, why are you doing it?

Before trying to answer this question, it is instructive to consider another definition of social work, this time taken from the British Association of Social Workers (BASW, 2002):

> *The task of the social worker is to facilitate the resolution of social problems and conflicts at the personal level. It is different but not separate from social care, which is looking after individuals on behalf of the community.*

So, if becoming engaged in social work necessitates involvement in difficult situations of a personal nature, often containing conflict and the exercising of power, a consideration of our motivation for such activity merits examination.

ACTIVITY **1.2**

Spend a few moments reflecting upon your personal motivation to become a 'social worker'. Note down some key factors that have influenced your choice.

1.
2.
3.
4.
5.

COMMENT

Vivien Cree's book Becoming a Social Worker *(2003, p155) asks a number of practitioners, researchers, academics and managers to do the same thing as you have just done – to reflect upon how they became social workers, and why. In summary, she identifies clusters of motivations amongst those contributing to the book, including:*

- *childhood and family background;*

- *experiences of education and work;*

- *the influence of significant individuals;*

- *the perceived value base of social work;*

- *the urge to 'do something', to make a contribution to society.*

Cree (2003, p157) further notes that, for many, the process of becoming a social worker has multiple starting points:

> *in childhood, in voluntary work undertaken...(and) as adults go through the process of building relationships, having children, and the looking after their own parents in older age.*

Becoming and being a social worker is a journey of personal and professional discovery, and as in all journeys, it might help to know where we – collectively – have come from.

It is likely that you will have answered the question by reference to one or more of the following four position statements. These have been taken from responses to interview questions asked of candidates for qualifying social work courses.

(a) Knowledge about social work's roles and responsibilities and a desire to 'do the job' – *I'm attracted to what the work entails. I want the variety. I couldn't stand doing a desk job.*

(b) Ideas about the skills needed to 'do the job', and belief that you possess those skills – *Everyone comes to me with their problems – I'm a good listener. I'm just made for this kind of work. I like being with people.*

(c) An attraction to the value base of social work: an identification with the community of social work and social workers – *I've always taken the side of the victim. I can't stand seeing people bullied, or oppressed, I want to make a difference and challenge oppression.*

(d) A range of experiences (past and present) that engender an identification, understanding or empathy with those using services – *My younger brother was born with a learning disability. He gets discriminated against by people in the street, in shops, everywhere. I've seen how the social worker helped my parents and my brother.*

Social work, like any other human services activity, operates through an amalgam and integration of knowledge, skills, values and experience, and it is these you will have identified in terms of your own personal motivation to be part of the social work world. In the next chapter, through the process of a beginning exploration of social work's historical legacies, the motivations, principles and beliefs of those instrumental in the shaping of social work will also be revealed. In the arena of child welfare, Holman (2001) offers biographies of a number of famous 'Champions for Children', and identifies their different backgrounds, starting points, beliefs, motivations and convictions. Social work practice should always value diversity amongst service users, and a thriving social work profession needs to equally value the different roads travelled by its members into training and practice.

The following pages will suggest that, whilst the structures within which social work takes place have profoundly altered – along with the associated language, terminology, jargon and culture – the motivations of practitioners and the location of social work between the individual and their social circumstances are more often than not characterised by consistency rather than change.

Beckett, C (2006) *Essential theory for social work practice*. London: Sage.

This text is particularly helpful in exploring the roles of social workers: advocacy roles; direct change agent roles; and executive roles.

Cree, V (2003) *Becoming a social worker*. London: Routledge.

An interesting account of social workers' backgrounds, experiences and motivations to enter the profession.

Cree, V and Myers, S (2008) *Social work: Making a difference*. Bristol: The Policy Press.

This excellent study examines social work's history and its capacity to make a difference through practice interventions.

Konrad, G (1975) *The caseworker*. London: Hutchinson.

A social work novel set in Eastern Europe, which stimulates reflection about the meaning of social work, and the boundaries between the professional and the personal self.

Thompson, N (2005) *Understanding social work*. 2nd edition. Basingstoke: Palgrave.

A core introductory text, which explores the knowledge, skills and value bases of practice.

Chapter 2

The beginnings of social work: 'The comfort of strangers'

Plus ça change, plus c'est la même chose
(The more things change, the more they are the same)

Alphonse Karr, *Les Guepes*, 1849

Indeed, history is nothing more than a tableau of crimes and misfortunes

Voltaire (1694–1778)

The past is another country. They do things differently there

LP Hartley, *The Go Between* (1953)

A C H I E V I N G   A   S O C I A L   W O R K   D E G R E E

This chapter will help you to develop the following capabilities, to the appropriate level, from the **Professional Capabilities Framework**.

- **Professionalism.** Identify and behave as a professional social worker committed to professional development.
- **Values and ethics.** Apply social work ethical principles and values to guide professional practice.
- **Diversity.** Recognise diversity and apply anti-discriminatory and anti-oppressive principles in practice.
- **Rights, justice and economic well-being.** Advance human rights and promote social justice and economic well-being.
- **Knowledge.** Apply knowledge of social sciences, law and social work practice theory.
- **Judgement.** Use judgement and authority to intervene with individuals, families and communities to promote independence, provide support and prevent harm, neglect and abuse.
- **Critical reflection and analysis.** Apply critical reflection and analysis to inform and provide a rationale for professional decision-making.
- **Contexts and organisations.** Engage with, inform and adapt to changing contexts that shape practice. Operate effectively within your own organisational frameworks and contribute to the development of services and organisations. Operate effectively within multi-agency and interprofessional settings.
- **Professional leadership.** Take responsibility for the professional learning and development of others through supervision, mentoring, assessing, research, teaching, leadership and management.

See Appendix 1 for the Professional Capabilities Faremwork diagram.

This chapter will also introduce you to the following standards as set out in the 2008 social work subject benchmark statement.
4.3 Defining principles.
5.1 Subject knowledge and understanding.
5.1.2 The service delivery context.
5.1.3 Values and ethics.

Social work and pre-social work

Dame Eileen Younghusband, whose working life almost matched that of the activity we call social work, published her account of its evolution in 1981, and entitled it *The Newest Profession*. The title is significant in that it acknowledges social work's relatively recent arrival on the welfare stage, yet at the same time clearly sees social work as a professional activity. To many commentators, the hallmark of the claim to any professional status lies in the satisfaction of a set of specific criteria – a code of ethics, often based upon ideas of altruism; a specialist body of knowledge; control over processes of qualification, recruitment and expulsion; protected title status – and it might be said that the current *Modernising Social Services* agenda (Department of Health, 1998b) indicates that, at last, social work is engaged in a determined push to acquire the status of a profession after all these years. In Chapter 7 we will look at these aspects of professionalisation that could mean that social work has finally arrived on the professional stage. If the relatively recent award in social work is indeed to signify a consolidation of status for social work, then we need to reflect upon the tradition in British society whereby personal ills became public concerns, and whereby the responses of certain concerned individuals evolved into the caring role – by offering the comfort of strangers.

Why does social work exist?

In this chapter we need to ask ourselves the basic question: do all societies need to have social workers? We take it for granted, perhaps erroneously, that other professions – teachers, doctors, architects, lawyers – are social necessities, yet concede that social workers are not automatic members of the list, a point made by Jordan (1997, p8):

> *Whereas there were doctors and lawyers, pharmacists and engineers, in Classical Greece and Rome and throughout the medieval period, social workers did not appear until the nineteenth century.*

In an earlier book Bill Jordan had offered – using now rather out-of-date language – a wider perspective on the evolution of professional social work:

> *In simple societies there are no social workers. Orphans, widows, handicapped people and the elderly are looked after within the extended family or tribe. Unconventional behaviour is either tolerated, venerated or punished by retributive methods. The notion of having specialists in planning the care of dependants, or in changing the non-conformist behaviour of other people is largely the creation of modern industrialised societies.*

> (Jordan, 1984, p1)

The two quotes from Jordan invite the student of social work to question why western societies developed a model of personal social services, which has to be seen as an historical, social construct. The same author (Jordan, 1997), in his article *Social Work and Society*, goes on to note the absence of social workers amongst non-westernised societies, in the People's Republic of China, and amongst the Soviet Bloc countries prior to the collapse of Communist regimes after 1989. This observation leaves us to pose and reflect upon the question: what is it about the modern western free market democracies that produces the demand for social work as an activity?

In part, this question can be answered by reference to an analysis of western ideology. Modern western social democratic capitalist societies are committed to ideals of citizenship, whereby the state offers equality of opportunity but not equality of experience. It is seen to be essentially up to each individual citizen to determine to what extent she or he wishes to take advantage of these opportunities. Whilst such a model is based upon the 'freedom' of the presumed rational adult to make such choices, it is recognised that some citizens – such as children – are dependent upon the attitudes and efforts of those people responsible for them (such as parents). Therefore, it follows that if the parents or carers fail to exercise their freedoms in the best interests of the child, then the state has a choice: it can do nothing, and accept that some vulnerable, dependent beings – such as children – will be harmed, neglected, or abandoned; or it can reserve the right to respond, by intervening on behalf of the child, through the exercising of the law. If it chooses the latter, the modern state needs to create a civil servant group, a set of officials, who will carry out such interventions and provide the necessary care that logically follows from the state assuming responsibility for a vulnerable person. To this end, western societies have created a state role – social workers – to carry out such protective and intervening functions in relation to children, young people and other such vulnerable people. We will see, in the following historical summary, that the state has assumed such responsibilities for a variety of vulnerable groups, taking over from the earlier responses of voluntary, religious and philanthropic bodies.

Of course, the state also has a third choice – to engage with potentially vulnerable families, groups and communities – to prevent the need for statutory intervention and to address the causes of their difficulties, which may be located in discrimination, oppression, marginalisation, poverty and deprivation.

Our historical overview of social work will enable us to note that, from the earliest years, social workers had begun to aggregate the experiences of those people for whom the state developed concern, and to recognise collective factors. If those whom the state sought to 'rescue' came disproportionately from the poorest and most deprived communities, then would it not be better for social work to try to change these communities rather than rescue each individual 'casualty'? By addressing such questions, social work has always connected to community work, to community action and indeed to political activism.

We will attempt in this chapter to explain the emergence of social work – to look at its historical antecedents in Britain and elsewhere. We will also seek to examine social work's claims for itself – what it has set out to do. According to Younghusband (1981, p9):

> *it has been accused, and sometimes accused itself, of being moralistic, authoritarian, knowing best what was good for other people, permissive, soft, manipulative, ineffective, damaging, essential, or a waste of public money.*

It may be all or none of these things, but without doubt modern social democratic societies seem to agree that some form of social work is both necessary and desirable.

Before examining the historical evidence, it is useful to reflect upon our own assumptions, by reflecting upon our own hunches and beliefs about the origins of social work. Such ideas amount to our personal 'theory' or 'model', and reveal our assumptions about why social work has evolved in certain societal structures.

ACTIVITY 2.1

Based upon your own experiences, or your ideas of politics, note down your own beliefs and ideas as to why western societies defined for themselves the need for social work and social care.

COMMENT

You might have thought about a number of reasons, including:

- *to fill a gap left by families, communities, social groups;*
- *to control unacceptable behaviour or threats to social order;*
- *to protect the most vulnerable people in society from oppression and abuse;*
- *to express a moral obligation to those in greatest need;*
- *to promote change to the social system on behalf of those with least power.*

In fact, all of these possible explanations may have some element of truth to them. We now need to turn to historical sources to identify the key factors that have served to shape the evolution of the activity presently conceived as social work and social care.

The Middle Ages and post-Elizabethan welfare

It may be an agreed fact amongst most historians of the subject that social work, as so named, is a nineteenth-century concept. However, we need to consider what preceded it. After all, the need for societies to create some form of structures that engender the twin goals of regulation and care of some of its most vulnerable members would appear to be a universal imperative. Such measures may not have been called 'social work', but they served similar functions. When we deconstruct 'social work', we discover a range of activities with much longer pedigrees.

What preceded formalised social work in western societies is subject to historical debate. It is very difficult to determine the origins of care, compassion and concern for others, although we can see that all of the world's major religions uphold ethics of duty and mutual responsibility. What is easier to discern are the enactments by the state that amount to control and regulation. (The timeline of legislation can be found as Appendix 5.) Laws to control able-bodied vagabonds stem from as early as 1383, and by the Tudor period a range of punitive statutes is designed to control beggars and the roving poor, including university students, who are considered a significant nuisance (Ridley, 2002). Yet at the same time, a range of charitable institutions and foundations sought to care for those in need. Some historians have focused on the role played by women and, in particular, by widows in medieval society. Leyser (1995) cites studies attesting to the harbouring of strangers by widows. Whilst the imperative to directly 'care' may well have arisen out of economic necessity, there is also evidence that *women were more likely to give charitably than men* (Cullum, cited in Leyser, 1995, p237), and that this may be seen as a reciprocity between the desperate need of many women to receive charity and the manifest willingness of others to provide it (Bennett, cited in Leyser, 1995, p237).

More commonly, historians have focused on the role played by monasteries, convents and other religious houses, and Moulin (1978) argued that the equivalent of modern social services was *dispensed completely by religious people* in medieval times. As evidence, Moulin cites the monastic Rule of St Benedict, which states that there are four categories of people with whom the greatest care should be taken: the sick, children, guests and the poor. Whilst the degree of genuine charitable activity in Christian monasteries has been questioned (Brandon, 1998), there is little doubt that the number of vagrants increased with the decline of the medieval church leading to the Dissolution of the Monasteries (Hibbert, 1987), with the ranks of the new destitute including monastic servants and the poor who had previously been accommodated, and possibly cared for, within the religious institutions.

Guy (1990, p43) sees the events of the Tudor period as a watershed between traditional attitudes – in which the poor's function was to furnish others with opportunities for acts of charity – and secular relief systems based upon the allegedly rational distinction between 'deserving' (the aged, sick, disabled, abandoned) and 'undeserving' (work-shy, lazy, feckless, criminal) supplicants. Such distinctions were identified in 1536 by the first Poor Law and, in 1572, by legislation authorising weekly parish collections 'for the relief of poor and impotent persons'. Contemporary commentators of the day, such as Hugh Latimer in the *Sermon of the Plough* (1548), lamented the decline in charitable action:

> In times past, men were full of pity and compassion; but now there is no pity...in times past, when a rich man died in London, they...would bequeath great sums of money towards the relief of the poor...Charity is waxen cold.

> (Guy, 1990)

(The history of welfare always reveals a tendency for harking back to the golden age – meaning that people think society was more cohesive, more responsible, more compassionate and more caring in past times than it is in the present.)

By the end of the sixteenth century in Britain, the ruling elites and government were most concerned about the spiralling levels of public destitution, and the perceived risks to private property and public order, resulting in the first Elizabethan Poor Laws (1598 and 1601). (*Hark, hark, the dogs do bark, the beggars are coming to town.*) According to Robert Pinker (1971) the state started to intervene after the disintegration of feudal and local networks, and fused the twin objectives of 'deterrence and therapy'. Responsibility for the care of individuals outside of family structures fell to parishes, who soon developed strategies to 'move people on', and thereby reduce the burden on the local rate payers.

Of course, the fear of a mobile mass of people is a recurring historical theme, which has informed welfare policy up to the present day, in terms of poverty, unemployment, welfare dependants, immigrants, asylum seekers and refugees.

Summary points linked to contemporary social work

- Religious organisations played a significant part in the development of care for social 'outsiders'. Today, many services for refugees, asylum seekers, people with drug and substance use problems, those who are homeless and roofless are provided in large measure by voluntary sector organisations, many of which have their origins in the established and non-conformist churches and in various faith-based organisations.

- Although no longer based on the Poor Law parish structure, modern social work is delivered through local government structures, and similar tussles about handovers, demarcations and financial responsibility for people have an enduring Poor Law 'echo'.

- The government is concerned about the 'postcode lottery' – whereby people with the same needs receive different quality of services in different parts of the country. Such differences have their roots in local parish arrangements for the poor, the destitute and the sick.

- The gendered nature of caring, as noted in historical studies, remains a persistent theme – workers in care settings with all service user groups are overwhelmingly female.

Georgian welfare models

During this period social welfare systems continued to be most concerned about the threat to public order posed by those in poverty. As a response, the eighteenth century witnessed the marked expansion of workhouses across Britain, mainly as generic institutions housing those with a range of needs. By 1776 there were nearly 2,000 workhouses in Britain (stemming from a general Workhouses Act of the 1720s). These workhouses, like the later lunatic asylums and special hospitals, were more in evidence in rural rather than urban settings.

The impoverished that were not deemed able-bodied had to go to the workhouses, with the parish providing jobs outside the workhouse for those able to work.

Henry Fielding, in his text *An Inquiry into the Causes of the Late Increase of Robbers (1751)*, recommended dividing the poor into:

- such poor as are unable to work (the responsibility of private charity);

- such poor as are able and willing to work (to be put in workhouses and set to work);

- such poor as are able but not willing to work (for whom criminal sanction should be invoked).

According to Picard (2000, p57), in her study of mid-eighteenth century London,

> parishes sometimes paid indigent bachelors in other parishes a small fee – 40s – to marry some of their poor women, effectively taking them off their books and adding them to the husbands' parishes.

However, whilst efforts to offload costs from the parish are to be expected, Picard (2000, p86) also records numerous examples of charitable impulse giving during the period, such as paying off debts to release prisoners, giving to the Lord Mayor's Christmas collection, contributing to hospital funds. This latter activity explains the growth of institutions, which stood as edifices of charity and philanthropy – an activity that reached a level of near mania in the nineteenth century, more of which we will examine later.

Summary points linked to contemporary social work

- The eighteenth century established the emphasis on self-reliance through work, which has particular resonance with the current 'Welfare to Work' policy and the desire to reduce the number of people receiving incapacity benefits.

- The growth of philanthropy through the endowment of institutions has little contemporary equivalence, and modern benefactors are far more likely to endow universities, the arts and public buildings. We will note in later chapters that this is, in part, attributable to the challenge of the patronage by such forces as the disability movement. Nevertheless, the persistence of such events as Children in Need attests to the resilience of the philanthropic or charitable impulse, irrespective of the service user critique of such patronage.

Nineteenth-century reforms and the mania for institutions

The most significant nineteenth-century development in social work's history was the Poor Law Report, leading to the 1834 Poor Law Amendment Act, which adopted and endorsed the system in operation in Southwell, Nottinghamshire since 1818, whereby all out-relief was virtually abolished, and the regime of the workhouse was set to become harsh and deterring: *uninviting places of wholesome restraint* (Edwin Chadwick, 1800–1890).

Workhouses, particularly in rural communities, absorbed a whole range of those in greatest need who were unable to care for themselves or to be supported by others. Of the 200 pauper inmates in the Louth (Lincolnshire) workhouse in 1847, 111 were under the age of 15, and of these children 11 were orphans; 35 were illegitimate; 10 were with their mothers in the workhouse; 27 had been abandoned, and 22 were children of widows or widowers unable to look after them (Painter, 2000, p51). Here we also find people with learning disabilities, each then defined as 'an idiot', and with – as yet – nowhere else to go. Similarly, people with mental health problems might still be in the workhouse – in 1858 James Wilkes, Commissioner for Lunacy, visited the Louth Workhouse and found five inmates of unsound mind – although county asylums had been established since the early 1800s. Destitute older people would have been in the workhouse, or, if more fortunate, in the almshouses to be found in many small towns.

Our modern ideas of separate service user groups in part stem from the segregation of 'inmates' that arose towards the end of the nineteenth century, as newly formed professional groups developed specialist areas of practice, in separate institutions. The separation of individuals into specialist services resulted from the emerging realisation that the one-size-fits-all approach of the workhouse was not acceptable, and this resulted in a mania for different and distinctive institutions.

To Roy Parker (1988, p8) *the history of institutions in this country has been dominated by destitution, madness and criminality.* Foucault (1961) identifies that there had been a 'great confinement' across Europe from the mid-seventeenth century, but this trend accelerated significantly after 1800. The Victorians expressed civic pride through the erection of grand buildings, often on the outskirts of the newly industrialised conurbations. Whilst nothing in the pre-nineteenth century period would be described as 'social work' at the time, the demand for out-of-home care – for the aged, and for those defined contemporaneously as lunatics, idiots, imbeciles – had greatly increased, resulting in a flourishing private and charitable sector. According to Murphy (1991), the proprietors' creed was definitely one of 'low cost, high volume', and she cites the pamphlet published by the visiting apothecary John Rogers in 1816, graphically entitled *A Statement of the Cruelties, Abuses, and Frauds which are Practised in Madhouses.* Such publications, and the following Select Committee Reports, resulted in the Act for the Regulation of Madhouses in 1828, covering issues of medical supervision, rules for committing patients and licensing systems. Public bodies grew increasingly concerned about this unregulated trade in human misery, and ultimately the small, semi-regulated madhouses were replaced by the establishment of voluntary hospitals – catering for respectable local citizens and the 'deserving' poorer classes. Asylums were built to house and control the mentally ill and disturbed (people with learning disabilities and mental illnesses were indiscriminately incarcerated in institutions); and hospitals were founded; boarding schools emerged to 'care for' unwanted children. As a result, the censuses of 1881 and 1891 record an increasing number of male and female inmates in all institutions as idiot or imbecile, deaf, dumb or paralysed. We need to ask the fundamental question: *what lay behind this rush to incarceration and institutional building?*

In the opinion of a number of critical theorists (such as Scull, 1979; Ryan and Thomas, 1980) the motivating factors were not philanthropy, care or compassion, but professional imperialism, whereby the care of people with learning disabilities, physical disabilities and mental health issues became the exclusive concern of the medical profession. The creation of the treatment of 'madness' as a medical specialism – to the exclusion of educationalists, moralists, rationalists and humanists – defined the 'medical model' that has shaped the experiences of those with mental health problems and learning disabilities ever since (or at least until the very recent past).

Payne (1998) identifies four distinct phases in the development from institutions towards community care.

Period	Phase	Comment
To end of nineteenth century	Institutional	Main response to social need is to 'incarcerate' people in institutions
First part of twentieth century	Commitment	Increasingly committed development of community response to social need
1960s and 1970s	Community/collective	Ideological commitment to 'community' in response to social need
1980s and 1990s	Individual	Shift from 'community' to emphasis on responding to individualised definitions of need

Payne's model identifies a shift in the early part of the twentieth century, from institutional to a commitment towards a community response to need, particularly through the provision of early forms of social welfare, such as old age pensions. However, the response to those with mental health issues, or people with learning disabilities, remained an essentially institutional one.

Summary points linked to contemporary social work

- The nineteenth century witnessed the mass incarceration of vulnerable individuals into firstly generic workhouses and then into segregated specialist institutions. Decarceration from mainly Victorian institutions has been a dominant feature of recent and current community care developments.

- The 'professionalisation' of such institutional containment was predicated upon the 'medical model' of treatment, control and restraint, and the creation of specialist roles that separated those in need of care from their families, neighbourhoods, communities and societies.

- Whilst decarceration has occurred, many critical commentators would state that the medical model of disability/mental health/older people still dominates over relevant social models even within a community care framework, and that the model has merely shifted from control in institutions to control in the community.

- The current collaborative arrangements between health, social work and social care (explored in Chapter 8) reflect the ongoing struggle between medical and social models of need assessment and intervention.

We have thus seen that social care, in the later part of the nineteenth century, was subsumed into hospitals, asylums, workhouses, colonies and other institutions. However, we need to turn our attention to the emergence of 'friendly' or charitable visiting – which amounts to the beginnings of field social work.

The age of change in social relations: 'Perfect friendship' and the beginnings of casework

So far, we have necessarily considered social work in terms of social care provision – where people lived, whether in religious institutions, in madhouses, workhouses, hospitals or asylums. But a new activity began to emerge in the mid-nineteenth century, which can be seen as more directly linked to social casework practice, namely the development of the charity or mission worker. The administration of charitable funds was an extensive part of the Victorian economy. By the mid-1880s, the income of London charities exceeded that of the entire Swedish state. In the period between 1818 and 1840 there were 28,880 endowed charities, with a total income of £1.2 million. To regulate this economy, the Charity Commissioners were established in 1853. We will first consider the scope and purpose of these charitable foundations, and then reflect upon the possible factors driving the development of the activity that would later be called 'social work'.

Let us first consider the characteristics of the earliest 'social workers'. According to Hannah More (quoted in Walvin, 1987, p100):

> It would be a noble employment, and well becoming the tenderness of their sex, if ladies were to consider the superintendence of the poor as their immediate office.

Such sentiments clearly identify 'care of the poor' as a female function, although records show, not surprisingly, that the charitable funds were mainly administered by men. Contemporary literature shows that the dominant thesis to explain poverty resided in the lax morality of the poor themselves, who were seen as the architects of their own misfortune due to drink, gambling, ill health, promiscuity and a general lack of Christian discipline. As with all eras, a particular 'moral panic' would dominate the discourse at any one time, ranging from the eighteenth-century concern with gin consumption, through to nineteenth-century concerns about prostitution, incest, child labour, the plight of prisoners and the fear of deviant behaviours (from the 'hooligans') (Pearson, 1983).

The nineteenth century threw up a number of middle-class reformers – Elizabeth Fry, Florence Nightingale, Mary Carpenter, Octavia Hill, Dr Barnardo, General Booth, Edwin Chadwick, Edward Foster, Dr Thomas Arnold, Lord Shaftesbury – seen by a bourgeois reading of history as almost 'saintly' men and women, shaping the emerging welfare systems. Many of these were associated with child welfare, resulting in the emergence of dedicated organisations: the Methodist National Children's Home (1869), Dr Barnardo's (1870), the Church of England Waifs and Strays Society (1881), the National Society for the Prevention of Cruelty to Children (NSPCC) (1884) and the Catholic Children's Society (1887). As various charitable groups began to undertake 'social work' with individuals (as distinct from the institutional management of groups, or the management and disbursement of charitable funds), a debate emerged amongst the early professional 'pioneers' as to the precise role, function and purpose of this activity. The Charity Organisation Society (COS) was founded in 1869, in part as a response to the proliferation and duplication of charities, and to discipline charities themselves: *to be beneficent, charity should assist adequately, i.e. so as to produce self-help in the recipient.* Many writers, such as Jones (1983), have associated the beginning of state social work with the emergence of the COS, which held great sway in the period from its inception up to 1908. Like other late Victorian institutions, the COS was concerned about the threat to social order caused by poverty and destitution, leading to disorder and the threat to the established order. However, rather than a punitive or repressive response, the distinctive contribution of the COS lay in its conviction that solutions to public ills lay in the development of moral character within the poor themselves, and therefore *the COS developed casework* as the *method of social reform* (Jones, 2002, p43). By adopting this approach, the COS set itself against other bodies which advanced a more structural perspective, and which thereby saw the root of private ills as lying in the destructive consequences of capitalism itself.

A comparative case example: From charitable volunteers to architects of social welfare

Let us consider, for a moment, the emergence of social work in the United States of America, and note the similarities with Great Britain. At the end of the nineteenth century the US witnessed the uneasy union between the 'scientific charity' movement, with its emphasis on friendly visiting and individual case diagnosis on the one hand, and the settlement movement, with its stronger orientation towards social reform and social survey, on the other. 'Scientific charity', working through the Charity Organisation Society (founded in Buffalo, New York, in 1877), attempted to apply rational principles to the distribution of funds, and offered a diet of moral persuasion, friendship and personal example to those in greatest need. The Settlement Movement – best exemplified by Hull House in Chicago – focused on environmental causes of poverty, on expanding working opportunities for poorer communities and campaigning for social reform. Similar beliefs had informed the thinking of Canon and Mrs Barnett, founders of the Toynbee Hall Settlement in London (although the Barnetts' motto of 'one by one' revealed a social work commitment to the uniqueness of the individual). The Stepney Council on Public Welfare, initiated by the Barnetts in 1894, was concerned with administration of charity and *all matters affecting the welfare of the district* (Barnett, 1918, p633).

According to the historical account offered by the University of Michigan (2001):

> *while the settlements focused on what later became group work and community organisation, social work in the COS increasingly focused on casework with individuals and families.*

Such a division in perspectives is reflected and mirrored by the debate in the UK about casework, welfare reform and the future of the Poor Law. The story is, in fact, more complex than at first sight. It is easy to characterise the COS – in Britain and the USA – as spearheading morally based casework, focusing exclusively on the failings and salvation of the individual, yet the COS thought that to 'organise the district' was more important than casework with individuals. In fact, Younghusband believed that both the COS and the Settlement movements sought to integrate casework, groupwork and community work.

> *Why the three disastrously fell apart and only casework was conceptualised is a mystery, a failure for which we paid and continue to pay dearly.*

(Younghusband, 1981, p13)

Summary points linked to contemporary social work

- As we will see later, social work is still predominately carried out by women, and managed by men.

- The COS was focused upon the best use of available funds by distinguishing between the 'deserving' and 'undeserving'. In a similar vein, current community care practices are essentially based upon the operation of 'eligibility criteria' – assessments that determine which applicants are to receive various services. Systems of best value support this process.

- An individual casework model – with its roots in early charitable visiting – dominates contemporary field social work. Community-based approaches and groupwork remain secondary to the casework principle, now rebranded as 'care management'.

- However, the current policies of social inclusion, of building strong communities and of community regeneration, the localism agenda and the 'Big Society' concept, all offer an opportunity for social work to balance casework with an involvement in addressing the broader social structures that contribute to the continued social exclusion of most service users – and therefore might link to the ideology of the Settlement Movements.

The *fin de siècle* debate

In the 1890s, 3 per cent of those under 60 were dependent upon poor relief, whilst over half of those over 65 were on the parish. Thus the stimulus for debate in fact focused upon the high percentage of retired, older people unable to care for themselves.

To the protagonists in this debate – on both sides – the great concern was poverty. To almost all contemporary observers, poverty was the root of homelessness, drunkenness, ignorance, immorality, apathy and despair, which in turn lead to mental illness, child maltreatment and neglect, domestic violence, the destitution of older people, the sick, infirm and disabled – in other words, the issues that were to become the primary concerns of statutory social work in the following century. The agreed thesis was that the eradication of poverty would lead to the eradication – or at least the reduction – in the consequent social ills. What was not agreed upon was the means towards the eradication of poverty itself.

The debate, therefore, centred on the possible responses to deprivation. The COS leaders – Charles Loch, Helen and Bernard Bosanquet, Octavia Hill and others – believed in a deterrent Poor Law. They opposed all forms of state financial provision, on the grounds that such measures would pauperise and undermine incentives to work. They argued for self-reliance, the organisation of the district, the development of self-help groups, community education, thrift, prudence and mutuality. They embodied the link between philanthropic concerns and disciplinary ends.

Sidney and Beatrice Webb and their Fabian colleagues, on the other hand, were convinced of the need for state intervention with regard to employment rights, pensions, housing conditions, income support and public health. Accordingly, their view of social work included such issues as housing management, youth employment, and education in a wider sense than education welfare.

The 1905–9 Royal Commission on the Poor Laws included Loch, Hill, Bosanquet and Beatrice Webb. The COS leaders signed the Majority Report, advocating the retention of modified Poor Laws. Webb and her supporters put forward the Minority Report, recommending the complete break up of the Poor Laws, and their replacement with comprehensive state-run services for health, education and employment. (The Minority Report recommendations, of course, became the cornerstone of the welfare state system as established after 1945.)

Significantly, the Webb camp paid little attention to the *personal* social services, being convinced that personal ills could be completely addressed through the provision of public welfare. However, an irony must be acknowledged here. The Webbs believed that the necessity and rationale for social work would fade away with the advent of social insurance, free medical care, pensions, rights, benefits – in fact the raft of measures that were to define the welfare state after the Second World War. Their concession to a residual social work function would be – and here is the irony – that of a social control nature, as they saw a need for enforcement, recommending detention colonies for a residual group of the 'work-shy and lazy'. The acknowledgement of such a necessity was lamented:

> If families which prefer dirt, disorder and disease are to be forced by persistent pressure to mend their ways, what a terrible restriction on the liberty of the individual.

> (Webb and Webb, 1911)

Summary points linked to contemporary social work

- The Fabians – perhaps unwittingly – foresaw the paramount and residual role of social work as being statutory, an enforcing role working primarily with 'involuntary clients' (Trotter, 1999).

- With its emphasis on individualism, self-determination, the role of voluntary associations, of mutual support, and its critique of state structures, the COS heralded the alternative side of social work – with the focus being on promoting, enabling, supporting excluded groups – that ironically has resonance with the Third Way vision of New Labour (Jordan and Jordan, 2000), and with the 'Big Society' concept.

- The contested debate between the COS and the Fabians, through twists and turns, has ended up in the complexities of modern social work practice.

- To the 'left' of the Fabian position lay that of some early social work educators, such as John MacCunn at Liverpool University: *the purpose of social work is to emancipate the poor from oppression* (cited in Holman, 2001, p3). The radical, critical tradition in social work has long roots, although it often appears periodically dormant. Whilst the concern with 'poverty' has been replaced by issues of diversity and difference, the role of social work as being engaged with challenging oppression merits re-examination.

We will end this chapter, in the early years of the twentieth century, by considering the emergence of social work in more theoretical terms.

ACTIVITY **2.2**

How do we explain the emergence of social work in Britain from the mid-nineteenth century? Try to think of the possible factors that might explain this development.

> **COMMENT**
>
> *To Payne (1998) there are certain key 'drivers' in the emergence of social casework in Britain. Clearly, as we have seen from the debate between the Fabians and the COS, the concept of social work emerges from the key nineteenth-century phenomena:*
>
> - *the Temperance Movement, and its belief that social 'evils' were associated with the excessive use of alcohol, spearheading the moral reforming tradition;*
>
> - *the Christian evangelical movements, that sought to 'rescue' orphaned or abandoned children from their 'feckless' or incompetent parents;*
>
> - *the commitment to moral welfare with prostitutes, unmarried mothers, and others seen as in need of moral and spiritual guidance and support;*
>
> - *the Settlement Movement, committed to developing neighbourhood responses to poverty and deprivation, and thus being a forerunner of community development, community work and neighbourhood regeneration strategies;*
>
> - *the beginnings of the state taking an enforcing role, particularly in relation to children – such as the development of compulsory elementary education – and the need for a professional role to enforce such legislation.*

There are clearly broad theoretical themes to explain the development of social work. To Jordan (1997, pp9–10) social work:

> *arises where communities (either of the traditional type, based on kinship and geographical proximity, or of the twentieth-century compulsory kind, forged by state regulation and coercive inclusion, as in the former communist countries) begin to break up under pressure from market forces... There is a contradiction at the heart of social work, because it is spawned by market-oriented economic individualism, yet its values are those of a caring, inclusive, reciprocal community that takes collective responsibility for its members. In this sense, social work substitutes 'professional friendship' (or 'targeted intervention' in present day 'business speak') for the inclusive membership rights provided by those disintegrating systems, thus seeking to shore up the social relations of disrupted communities, and shield the vulnerable and excluded.*

Such ideas are taken up by Oliver (1990, p28) in relation to people with disabilities:

> *Changes in the organisation of work from a rural based, co-operative system where individuals contributed what they could to the productive process, to an urban, factory-based one organised around the individual waged labourer, had profound consequences...As a result of this, disabled people came to be regarded as a social and educational problem and more and more were segregated in institutions of all kinds including workhouses, asylums, colonies and special schools, and out of the mainstream of life.*

If we accept this theoretical model, it is not surprising that social work as currently understood began to emerge with force by the mid-nineteenth century, when industrialised Britain was in the throes of its greatest social upheaval: mass urbanisation; high levels of labour migration; extreme exploitation of labour; religious turmoil; high levels of illness, disease, infant mortality; the disintegration of traditional social relations of mutual obligation and care.

Summary points linked to contemporary social work

- Contemporary social work can be seen to have a significant role to play in relation to current social crises: concerns about wide-spread substance use and misuse; problems of social disintegration; a significantly ageing population creating challenges in terms of caring roles and responsibilities; changing social structures in families and networks.

- Social work has always had to balance 'care and control' functions: it is expected to fulfil the state functions of controlling problem phenomena in terms of mental illness, offending behaviours, the regulation of families.

- Current responses to the urban/suburban/rural balance of power have echoes with the power dynamics of the nineteenth century.

- Victorian racism directed towards Irish and East European Jewish immigrant groups is replicated by contemporary challenges in multi-cultural Britain, with social work being engaged in anti-racist strategies.

In Chapter 3 we will explore the developments towards contemporary social work practices in relation to specific service user groups, beginning with working with children, young people and families.

CHAPTER SUMMARY

In Chapter 2 you have briefly considered the beginnings of social work and social care in the medieval period, through to the development of charitable institutions in the Georgian and Victorian eras. You have been invited to discuss the major influences that shaped personal welfare systems at the end of the nineteenth century, including religious movements, philanthropy, social reform, labour movements and government policy.

FURTHER READING

Alcock, C, Payne, S and Sullivan, M (2004) *Introducing social policy*. 2nd edition. Hemel Hempstead: Prentice Hall.

This book includes a very accessible introduction to the welfare state and its antecedents.

Jordan, B (1984) *Invitation to social work*. Oxford: Robertson.

A very helpful introduction to social work – its origins, traditions, values and beliefs.

Payne, M (2005) *The origins of social work*. Basingstoke: Palgrave Macmillan.

This thoroughly readable yet comprehensive text charts the development of social work within European, North American and broader global traditions.

Pierson, J (2011) *Understanding social work: History and context*. Maidenhead: Open University Press

A rich, vibrant source for those committed to developing a further understanding of social work's varied and dynamic historical antecedents and first flowerings.

Chapter 3

Social work with children, young people and families

This chapter will help you to develop the following capabilities, to the appropriate level, from the **Professional Capabilities Framework**.

- **Professionalism.** Identify and behave as a professional social worker committed to professional development.
- **Values and ethics.** Apply social work ethical principles and values to guide professional practice.
- **Diversity.** Recognise diversity and apply anti-discriminatory and anti-oppressive principles in practice.
- **Rights, justice and economic well-being.** Advance human rights and promote social justice and economic well-being.
- **Knowledge.** Apply knowledge of social sciences, law and social work practice theory.
- **Judgement.** Use judgement and authority to intervene with individuals, families and communities to promote independence, provide support and prevent harm, neglect and abuse.
- **Critical reflection and analysis.** Apply critical reflection and analysis to inform and provide a rationale for professional decision-making.
- **Contexts and organisations.** Engage with, inform and adapt to changing contexts that shape practice. Operate effectively within your own organisational frameworks and contribute to the development of services and organisations. Operate effectively within multi-agency and interprofessional settings.
- **Professional leadership.** Take responsibility for the professional learning and development of others through supervision, mentoring, assessing, research, teaching, leadership and management.

See Appendix 1 for the Professional Capabilities Faremwork diagram.

This chapter will also introduce you to the following standards as set out in the 2008 social work subject benchmark statement.
4.3 Defining principles.
5.1 Subject knowledge and understanding.
5.1.2 The service delivery context.
5.1.3 Values and ethics.

Introduction

The general public, through the pervasive influence of the mass media, could be forgiven for seeing social work with children, young people and families as defining the image of the whole profession. When things go wrong in child protection cases, the denigration of social work and social workers ripples through all service sectors. The Peter Connolly case (London Borough of Haringey) is a classic example of this dynamic. A case could be made for redressing the balance, and for this book not to begin with a consideration of child care. But social work is a 'cradle-to-the-grave' activity, and it makes sense, therefore, to work through the life course, beginning with children.

We will begin with a statement from an adult survivor of the care system, offering an oft-stated indictment of the lack of consistency and continuity on offer:

> *With children in care, they need to always know they have someone they can turn to and talk to. I never felt that. I ended up in and out of prison and felt like I had no support. The longest I had a social worker was three months, then from there I've had 14 different social workers. It's hard because you get to know and trust one and it leaves.*

> (Department for Children, Schools and Families (DCSF), 2009a, p10)

Before we begin to critically explore the child welfare system, we need to get a sense of its reach.

Children in the social work arena

It is important to identify contemporary social work practice with children, young people and their families by beginning with statistical data.

- There were 615,000 referrals to children's social care services in the year ending 31 March 2011.

- The number of children subject to a section 47 inquiry (Children Act 1989) into concerns about potential significant harm was 111,700.

- Of these, 53,000 (47.5%) were subject to an initial stage child protection conference.

- At 31 March 2011, there were 42,700 children who were the subject of a child protection plan.

- In the year ending 31 March 2011, 49,000 children became the subject of a child protection plan. Of these, 6,500 (13.3%) became the subject of a plan for the second or subsequent time.

- On 31 March 2011, 42,300 children were the subject of a Child Protection Plan (a significant rise from 39,100 at 31 March 2010 and from 27,900 in 2007)

- Of this number, 18,600 were categorised as subject to neglect, 4,400 subject to physical abuse, 2,300 subject to sexual abuse, 12,100 to emotional abuse and 5,000 to multiple abuse categories.

- There were 382,400 children in need at 31 March 2011, which was a rate of 346.2 per 10,000 children (or 3.46% of all children under 18).

- There were 65,520 looked after children on 31 March 2011 (an increase of 2% from the previous year and a rise of 9% since 2007), which equates to 0.5% of all children and young people.

- 74% of those looked after were in foster care settings.

- Of the 26,830 children and young people who started to be looked after in 2010–11, 54% received services because they had been subject to abuse or neglect.

- 3,050 looked after children were adopted during the year ending 31 March 2011, a decrease of 5 per cent from 2010 and a decrease of 8 per cent since 2007. Similarly, there has been a decrease in the number of looked after children placed for adoption. This figure has fallen from 2,720 in 2007, to 2,500 in 2010 with a further fall to 2,450 in 2011.

The characteristics of children within the public care system

As we noted in the previous chapters, a number of the social work pioneers were engaged in social surveys, looking at whole population groups and identifying those in greatest need. This work continues, and recent research evidence identifies a number of significant factors concerning children and young people in public care.

- There were 5,750 children looked after continuously for 12 months at 31 March 2011. Of these 5,750 children, on 30 September, 70.5% were in full-time education, 4.6% were in full-time training, 7.4% were in either full-time or part-time employment and 17.5% were unemployed.

- Of the looked after children, a quarter leave care with no qualifications and a quarter leave care with fewer than five GCSEs or equivalent.

- A third of previously looked after young people are not in employment, education or training at age of 19.

- Of the 30,230 children looked after continuously for 12 months at 31 March 2011 who were aged between 10 and 17 years, 2,210 (7.3 per cent) had been convicted or subject to a final warning or reprimand during the year. (This compares with 7.9 per cent in 2010.) Offending was higher in older children and more frequent in boys.

- For children aged 13 to 15 who had been looked after continuously for 12 months, 8.7% of boys and 5.4% of girls had been convicted or subject to a final warning or reprimand during the year.

- Of the children looked after continuously for 12 months at 31 March 2011, 1,960 children (4.3%) were identified as having a substance misuse problem during the year. As expected, substance misuse was more common among older children; 1,340 children identified as having a substance misuse problem were in the 16- to 17-year-old age group.

The outcomes for children and young people who have spent a substantial period of time in public care are a cause of particular concern for all those involved in children's services. The life chances and opportunities of those for whom the state has assumed some form of parental responsibility are absolutely and relatively very poor. The organisational structures of state agencies – from the Poor Law Guardians through to public assistance departments, children's departments and social services departments – would appear to have made little progress in terms of the outcomes for children and young people in public care, but the picture, as always, is more complicated. At present, children's services are still being developed as a new structure, bringing together health, social care and educational services (to which we will return at the end of this chapter and in Chapter 9). In addition, apart from the short-term objectives of improving the life opportunities of those children and young people within the looked-after arena, the challenge facing those working in 'joined up' children's and families' services is to consider, evaluate and embrace new ways of working that will minimise the use of a public care system that clearly does not work effectively for many of its service users.

The persistent dynamics of child welfare

Before beginning to consider current innovations in child welfare practices, it is important to locate these trends within an historical context. From the outset, the contested nature of social work can be evidenced by child welfare models.

In their historical overview of state child care, Hayden et al. (1999, p29) identify three particular and recurring themes.

1. *The tension between family-based and institutional care*. Expressed another way, this debate centres on whether children should always be found a 'family', or whether group care could be a viable and even preferred option for some children in need of care. Each has its merits but each also has its ideological as well as its practical defenders.

2. *The tension for children's services departments between intervening too early or too late in child protection cases*. Sometimes referred to a 'damned if you do, and damned if you don't' view, social work operates on the high wire between being seen to interfere in family life, or not doing enough to protect children from abuse. Either approach can be, and has been, heavily criticised by politicians and the media.

3. *The perception in some quarters of important links between childhood deprivation, delinquency and later criminality*. 'Tough on crime and tough on the causes of crime' means that the government of New Labour began to acknowledge significant correlations between those formerly looked after by the local authority and the population in the secure estate (prisons, young offender institutions, secure units). On the other hand, the 'No More Excuses' doctrine emphasises the personal responsibility of the criminal for his or her actions, rather than seeing offending behaviour as a consequence of material deprivation and emotional distress.

The assertion that these themes have a persistent resonance means that an historical perspective will enable us to contextualise current theory and practice in the child welfare arena.

Early child welfare responses

As we have already seen in Chapter 2, the eighteenth-century state – through Poor Law officials – began to assume responsibility for 'foundling' children, by placing them in workhouses, although we will see that to a large extent early protection and welfare responses were orchestrated by the burgeoning charitable bodies. Let us return to the case of Anne, whom we met in the first chapter, but we will this time turn back the clock and consider Anne's situation in retrospect.

ACTIVITY **3.1**

The year is 1750. Anne is a 20-year-old woman, of dual heritage, with an Irish Protestant mother and an English father. Anne is working in London as a domestic servant, although she comes originally from the small village of Castor, in Northamptonshire. She is seven months pregnant, and feels unable to care for her unborn infant.

What options are available to her? Using your imagination, try to list down what these might be.

COMMENT

You might have noted the following options available to Anne.

- *Risk abortion, via the local 'wise woman'.*

- *Marry the child's father, if possible.*

- *Return to Northamptonshire, and ask for the baby boy, who is to be called Jack, to be brought up by members of her family.*

- *Abandon Jack in a public space.*

- *Leave him with those of means (this option represents a long tradition of hope for the poor and desperate – after all, Moses was left in a basket to be found by those more able to care for him; in Henry Fielding's book* A History of Tom Jones: A Foundling, *the eponymous hero is left as a baby in the bed of Squire Allworthy).*

- *Take Jack to the local parish – but Anne would need to disclose her identity and admit her 'sin'.*

- *Take the child to the newly opened Thomas Coram Foundling Hospital.*

RESEARCH SUMMARY

The care of infants and children by those other than parents and families

Following the example already set by Rome, Florence, Lisbon and Paris, the Hospital for the Maintenance and Education of Exposed and Deserted Children, soon to be known as the Foundling Hospital, was started by Thomas Coram in London, in 1741. Parliament subsidised the Hospital, so long as all babies offered were accepted (a universal service),

Continued

and between 1756 and 1760 almost 15,000 babies were admitted, but over 10,000 of them died. Yet this survival rate was superior to the parish workhouse, and only four babies were lost in the paperwork. After 1760, admission reverted to being by petition only. Admission criteria reveal its philosophy: admission was restricted to war orphans, children of deserted wives and, from 1801, only illegitimate children. To place her child, the unmarried mother had to show that her good faith had been betrayed, and that:

she had given way to carnal passion only after a promise of marriage, or against her will...and that her conduct had been irreproachable in every other respect.

(Barret-Ducrocq,1989, p41)

Infants were sent to the country to be breast-fed and generally looked after for two to four years (by wet nurses engaged, in effect, as early examples of foster parents), and then returned to the Hospital, to begin an apprenticeship for domestic service. In the same period Jonas Hanway, a campaigner for the protection of children, brings our attention to current themes, such as the abuse and neglect of children in public care.

We ought no more to suffer a child to die for want of the common necessities of life, though he is born to labour, than one who is the heir to a dukedom. One thousand or 1,200 children have annually perished under the direction of parish officers. I say under their direction, not that they ordered them to be killed, but that they did not order such means to be used as are necessary to keep them alive.

(Jonas Hanway, 1766: An Earnest Appeal for Mercy to the Children of the Poor)

By the nineteenth century, if we assume that Anne was unable to care for Jack, he would have become a 'child of the parish', and would have been admitted to the workhouse. However, after 1850, workhouse patterns changed, particularly characterised by the reduction in child inmates. In the Louth Union, for example, the boarding-out system (now known as 'foster care') was adopted in 1869.

A ladies boarding out committee of visitors was formed. They actively sought homes for children, especially the girls, visited any children after they had been placed... they submitted a quarterly report on each child, and an annual report on their own endeavours.

(Painter, 2000, p68).

Summary points linked to contemporary practice

- An emerging commitment to children being brought up in families rather than in institutional settings (as currently expressed in the Children Act 1989).

- Quality control exercised by case workers, visiting the child in the family (current Foster Care Regulations determine frequency of contacts and the holding of reviews).

- The importance attributed to the keeping of effective and accurate case records (the Looking After Children Action and Assessment Records, introduced in 1995, emphasise the importance of record-keeping for identity development and posterity).

- The accountability of the visitors/practitioners to a public committee (foster care services are routinely inspected and audited).

- A recognition that care by others needed to be recompensed by the payment of fees from the public purse (the payment of foster carers remains contested and controversial).

- The gendered nature of the role, revealing family care to be a female responsibility (foster care and child care working generally remains a gendered, mainly female activity).

The 1908 Children Act

This Act – described by Lord Shaftesbury as representing a *quickened sense on the part of the community at large of the duty it owes to the children* (Hansard, 1908, p1251, cited in Cameron, 2003, p81) – contributed to the social construction of childhood, by setting up juvenile courts and seeing juvenile offenders as distinct from adult criminals. The distinction was not merely based upon sentimentality, or the idea that children should receive lesser sentences. The separation of children was predicated on the need for support, for moral guidance, for social intervention. It is instructive to note that British society instituted social welfare in relation to young offenders earlier than it did with regards to those children experiencing neglect, abuse or maltreatment. The care of abandoned or neglected children remained the concern, primarily, of the voluntary organisations identified in the previous chapter, apart from those being received into the workhouse. State social work, at least in relation to children, can therefore be said to be founded upon the need for control of the delinquent rather than care of the child in need.

Children, such as Jack, if received into public or voluntary care, would have been part of the 'child rescue' movement, that saw its purpose and mission as being to rescue children from 'bad parents' and give them a completely fresh start – only achievable by the complete separation from their original parents, families and communities (see Fox-Harding, 1997). If Jack had come under the auspices of charities such as Dr Barnardo's, he may well have been ultimately sent abroad, along with thousands of others, to Canada, Australia and New Zealand (Holman, 1988). Alternatively, children like Jack might have spent their early years with foster carers, as was the Thomas Coram policy, but they were separated from their substitute family at the age of five or six, and were moved to the Foundling Hospital site in London, and, from 1926, to their premises at Redhill, Surrey. The extract below tells of the pain and suffering resulting from such a policy.

For the majority of children in public care under the auspices of the Poor Law, institutional life was the norm. According to Hendrick (1994, p76), between 1900 and 1914, 70,000–80,000 children were in various forms of residential care under the Poor Law, while only 10,000 were boarded out.

CASE STUDY

Thomas Coram between the wars

And the next memory after all that was getting to Redhill and this very big building and having our hair shaved off. I remember Bill saying to me, Don't cry. I had this in my mind. Don't cry. I can remember this big stone room that had iron beds and there were two bed heads put together like that. And there was this little boy in the other bed and he was crying all the time: I want my mummy. I want my mummy. And I remember putting my hand through and holding his hand and thinking I must not cry. I had promised Bill I would not cry. May, aged 72 (cited in Oliver, 2003, p49).

From care to social work: The lure of achieving change

As Parker notes, with reference to child care policy:

One powerful nineteenth-century conviction, born of middle-class prosperity, self confidence and optimism, was that behaviour could be altered and improved... Poor law officials (especially the inspectorate) believed that the cycle of pauperism could be broken by giving the children in the Homes the right education and training...

(Parker, 1988, p7)

The essential point in Parker's quote relates to the conviction that the cycle of deprivation could be broken if children were completely separated from the perceived negative influences of their families, communities and cultures. This is a recurring theme in child welfare policies: is the purpose of the child welfare system to 'rescue' children from inadequate parents, or to provide support services that amount to the *defence of the birth family* (Fox-Harding, 1997)? Child care policy after 1945 followed a twin track model of beginning to offer family support systems whilst seeking to improve the care and welfare of children and young people in public care.

Post-war welfare – The 1948 Children Act

According to Douglas and Philpot (1998, p11), when surveying the Second World War, *the welfare of children was the motor which drove reform*. The evacuation of children had highlighted two distinct but interrelated issues. First, as Marwick noted:

it brought to middle- and upper-class households a consciousness for the first time of the deplorable conditions endemic in the rookeries and warrens that still existed in Britain's industrial cities...'

(1976, p75)

Secondly, it enabled many to witness the stark effects of separation and loss, through the process of evacuation itself. The new children's departments inherited the care of 3,000 'homeless evacuees', left in foster homes, together with 5,000 children in the care of public assistance committees, 6,000 in the care of education departments, plus a further 2,000 evacuees in children's homes (Jordan, 1984, p78). Three significant events conspired to crystallise thinking about the welfare of children in public care.

- Following an extensive examination of children's homes, Lady Allen of Hurtwood sent a letter to *The Times* that referred to

many thousands of children [who] are being brought up under repressive conditions that are generations out of date and are unworthy of our traditional care of children. Many who are orphaned, destitute or neglected still live under the chilly stigma of 'charity'; too often they form groups isolated from the main stream of life and education, and few of them know the comfort and security of individual affection.

(15 July 1944) (cited in Holman, 2001, p35)

- The Inquiry into the death of Dennis O'Neill (a 13-year-old boy starved and beaten to death by his foster father in Shropshire, where he had been placed by Newport Borough Council) resulted in the Monckton Report (Home Office, 1945) which made the following key statements:

The 'fit person', local authority or individual, must care for the child as his own; [there was not] sufficient realization of the direct and personal nature of the relationship between a supervising authority and a boarded-out child...The administrative authority should be improved and informed by a more anxious and responsible spirit.

- In 1946 the Curtis Committee Report reported on the care of children away from home, particularly in residential child care settings.

The child in these Homes was not recognised as an individual with his own rights and possessions, his own life to live and his own contribution to offer. He was merely one of a large crowd, playing and eating with the rest, without any place or possession of his own or any quiet room to which he could retreat. Still more important, he was without the feeling that there was anyone to whom he could turn who was vitally interested in his welfare or who cared for him as a person.

(Curtis Committee, 1946, para 418, p134)

These events served to highlight, in contrast with the less flamboyant welfare departments, the idealistic basis of the new children's departments (Jordan, 1984). This reforming zeal attracted into its ranks a number of passionate and committed graduates. Jordan quotes John Stroud (1960, p8), who saw the country as *dotted with castle-like institutions in which hundreds of children dressed in blue serge were drilled to the sound of whistles. We were going to tear down the mouldering bastions. We were going to replace or re-educate the squat and brutal custodians*. The earlier extract from the Thomas Coram records illustrates perfectly the objects of their concern.

We need to understand the work of child care officers in terms of the role of the children's departments. Why were children being received into public care? *The Duties and Functions of Child Care Officers* (Association of Child Care Officers, 1963, p2) stated that:

> *Some children are committed to the care of the local authority by court orders, but the majority are received into care at the request of the parents...the most frequent reasons for admission at the request of parents are the confinement of the mother, physical and mental illness, desertion, illegitimacy and homelessness.*

Such an account explains why Jack would still be coming into public care in this post-war era. He would fit the criteria in terms of being 'illegitimate'; his mother might be homeless; and Jack might be seen as 'deserted'.

In all probability, Jack would be placed in a residential nursery or be boarded out with foster 'parents'.

The beginnings of family support, prevention and promotion: The City of Sheffield as an example

In 1963 the Children and Young Persons Act provided, for the first time, for 'preventive and rehabilitative' social work with families – to remove conditions that might result in children coming into care or remaining in care or being brought before the juvenile court. This is the first legal imperative for *preventive* social work to be undertaken. As the City of Sheffield Children's Department Annual Report (1967, p16) states: *Emphasis (therefore) should be on trying to improve home circumstances rather than the removal of the child.*

This would be achieved through the provision of advice, guidance and assistance. These were interpreted to mean: the establishment of Family Advice Centres; guidance in *household management* and support for homeless families; assistance in terms of cash grants or loans in *exceptional circumstances*.

Let us imagine that, in the 1960s, Jack and his mother were in Sheffield, and Jack was now in public care on a voluntary basis. The City of Sheffield Children's Department Annual Report (1967) shows that there were the following establishments in the city.

- A residential nursery (12 beds), staffed by a matron, deputy matron and nursery nurses.

- 16 family group homes (average size nine beds), each staffed by a housemother in charge, housemother and assistant housemother (part-time) (of the 51 staff in total in this sector, only two were male).

- A boys' remand home (30 beds), with an all-male staff group, apart from the matron.

- A girls' remand home (22 beds), with an all-female staff group.

- An Approved School for senior girls (70 beds), with 48 staff members (of whom six were male).

In total, the city had 19 establishments, with 189 children and young people in residence.

The report identifies the reasons for children being received into public care during the preceding year.

Mother's illness or confinement	Illegitimacy	Deserted by mothers	Homeless or living in unsatisfactory conditions	Committed to care by the juvenile court usually due to neglect	Various reasons, including death of mother, or beyond parental control
41%	13%	12%	12%	4%	18%

When considering this breakdown, it is instructive to note the number of cases that relate to poverty, stigma, social exclusion and structural oppression. Significantly, no mention is made in the summary of child abuse – whether physical, emotional or sexual – apart from the issue of neglect. (In the report, the term 'child protection' is used only in relation to children in situations we would now define as 'private fostering'.) The largest figure – 41 per cent arising from mother's confinement or illness – was usually very short term. Of the total ongoing number of children in Sheffield's care, 30 per cent had been committed by the courts – the long-term cases. Altogether, the Report notes that 33 per cent of children in care were illegitimate, and suggests that preventive help should be provided for *unsupported mothers*.

So, let us imagine that Jack's mother, having had her baby, requested help with his care. What would be offered? At a social level, being an unmarried mother would still carry an enormous stigma in the 1960s, so Jack's mother might be considering adoption as an option for her son. However, as already noted above, Section 1 of the Children and Young Persons Act 1963 had established, for the first time, a duty on social workers to help any family whose children were in need but were not in their care. Many local authorities offered free full-time day care in a nursery for women such as Jack's mother, to enable her to be financially independent through employment.

However, if Jack had been permanently separated from his mother, he might have been placed under the 1958 Adoption Act. The City of Sheffield *Report* (1967, p18) gives a fascinating insight into the perspective on permanent family care at the time:

> *The theory behind the adoption law is the idea of conferring the privileges of parents upon the childless and the advantages of having parents upon the parentless.*

Summary points linked to contemporary practice

- The grounds for concern about children and young people have significantly shifted from poverty and the absence of available parental/family care to the focused nature of 'significant harm', based upon various forms of abuse and neglect.

- The threshold for being 'looked after' is much higher, and there is now rigorous gate-keeping to keep children out of the care system.

- Residential nurseries have closed, as have most of the children's homes that were open in the 1960s, with an emphasis on effectively supporting children in their own families, or placing them in foster care or kinship care.

- The 1960s emphasis on 'trying to improve the home rather than remove children' links to the current equivalent services of Sure Start, Homestart Children's Centres and a range of family support services.

- The City of Sheffield assumed corporate responsibility for children in its care – an attitude critically absent in much subsequent local authority practice.

The 1969 Children and Young Persons Act

The Children and Young Persons Act of 1969 reflected the optimism associated with the children's departments and social work practice. Children and young people would come under the care and control of social workers for a host of reasons: due to concerns about their welfare; because they were not attending school; because they were in moral danger; and, most significantly, because they had committed an offence. As Colton et al. (2001, p4) suggest, delinquency was clearly defined as a consequence of deprivation, and thus families needed assistance, advice, guidance and support – and the new social services departments were charged with this duty.

The death of Maria Colwell (1973) and subsequent child protection concerns

Maria Colwell was a 6-year-old girl who was removed from her foster carers, reunited with her birth mother and then subsequently killed by her step-father. This particular case proved to be a watershed in the self-confidence of the new social services departments (SSDs) in their formative years, and set in motion the still-continuing transition from 'child care to child protection', whereby the broad conception of service for children and their families, first established in the children's departments and reinforced by the Seebohm reforms, were *reconstructed around the axis of child protection* (Parton, 1991, p203).

The key findings of the Colwell Inquiry were:

- a questioning of professional judgement of social workers and their managers;
- the assertion that social workers were not listening to the wishes of the child (Maria) to stay with her foster carers;
- concern about excessive attention being paid to the importance of blood ties between children and natural parents;
- a finding of a failure of communication between new SSDs and other agencies.

In summary:

> *What has clearly emerged, at least to us, is the failure of a system compounded of several factors of which the greatest and most obvious must be that of lack of effectiveness of communication and liaison.*

> (DHSS, 1974, para 240)

The Maria Colwell case led directly to the advent of tighter managerial control of practice, and the eventual establishment of inter-agency child protection systems, firstly structured as Area Review Committees and then Area Child Protection Committees. In terms of broader child care policy, the allegation of social worker adherence to the *rule of optimism* in the case of Maria Colwell, with its emphasis on 'blood ties', led directly to the 1975 Children Act, with the resulting formation of Permanency Policy: the removing of those children seen to be at risk more rapidly from their birth families, the severing of parental links whilst in residential or foster care with the explicit goal of establishing permanent placements, and ultimately the adoption of the child. Colton et al. cite the work of Holman (1988) which suggests the consequence of such a (permanency) policy was that:

> *a higher proportion of parents had lost their say in their children's lives by the end of the 1970s than at any other time, including the reign of the Poor Law.*

(Colton et al., 2001, p6)

Yet, in spite of the ever-increasing professional and financial effort being dedicated to child protection procedures, training and management, the 1980s witnessed the seemingly constant procession of high-profile inquiries into the circumstances of children killed by parents or other family members, such as Jasmine Beckford (London Borough of Brent, 1985), Tyra Henry (London Borough of Lambeth, 1986) and Kimberley Carlile (London Borough of Greenwich, 1987). This sequence was – almost ironically and para-doxically – to be followed by the events in Cleveland, when during the first part of 1987 there was *an unprecedented rise in the diagnosis of child sexual abuse* (Butler-Sloss, 1988, p1), raising concerns about the welfare of 121 children and leading to the compulsory separation of the majority from their families. The subsequent report was highly critical of the lack of inter-agency cooperation, and introduced the notion of *system abuse* whereby the modes of examination, interviewing, removal and separation of the children from their families was seen to be an abuse in itself. Butler-Sloss exhorted practitioners to remember that *the child is a person and not an object of concern.*

The Cleveland Inquiry, together with the preceding inquiries into the deaths of children, epitomised the dilemma for social workers, representing the most visible and notable agency within the child protection system, when faced with the decision as to whether children need to be removed – that they are *damned if they do and damned if they don't*. As Franklin and Parton (1991) recorded, social workers were variously pilloried in the media as lacking in intelligence and common sense, as being too liberal or casual, or indifferent and unrepentant.

CASE STUDY

Rikki Neave, a six-year-old, died in November 1994, whilst in the care of his mother. She herself had been brought up in local authority care, having given birth to Rikki when aged 16 and living in a children's home. The Inquiry suggested that social workers were so committed to supporting Rikki's mother Ruth – a laudable aim in itself, given the all too frequent examples of young people who had been formerly in public care being abandoned by their 'parenting' authority – that they lost sight of their primary duty as being assuring the welfare of her child, Rikki.

The case example of Rikki Neave graphically and tragically illustrates the accumulating crisis in public confidence in the capacity of social work, as a profession, to assure the welfare of vulnerable children and young people.

Personal comment

I remember driving home, listening to the evening news on the radio, when the Rikki Neave Inquiry findings were being discussed. The interviewer challenged the Chief Executive of the Council to guarantee that such tragedies would never occur again. I found myself willing the respondent to say that, as a profession, we can never make such a promise. Children will continue to be killed by their parents, their carers, by friends, neighbours and sometimes, but rarely, by strangers, and the validity of the question needed to be refuted.

Unfortunately, the answer given talked of tighter procedures, better inter-agency cooperation, more staff training and, rightly, referred to the fact that:

> staff are currently working to secure the safety and support of over 340 children recorded on the Cambridgeshire child protection register.

> (Submission by the Director of Cambridgeshire SSD to the
> Bridge Child Care Consultancy, 1996.)

Nevertheless, the impression given was that such tragedies could be prevented. It was a matter of will, resources, management skill and expertise. If these could be sorted, then presumably children could be assured protection.

Of course, such assurances and guarantees cannot and should not be made. What does need to be recorded and proclaimed is that the UK child protection system is renowned internationally (Douglas and Philpot, 1998, p65), and that the number of children killed by a parent has progressively fallen over the past decades. That said, the cases of Victoria Climbié and Peter Connolly have again been used to question social work's capacity to protect children.

By charting the sequence of child abuse Inquiries up to the mid-1990s, we have identified the persistence of impossible expectations laid at the door of the social work profession (and repeated in the Climbié Inquiry, Department of Health, 2003a). However, we need to retrace our steps to the government sponsored report of the early 1980s, which revealed contemporary concerns about the social work task only ten years after the advent of generic social services departments.

The case for child welfare reform

Apart from the concerns about child protection (as already mentioned), a number of other concerns emerged during the 1980s about the system of child welfare in general. Firstly, the raft of legislation relating to children and their families seemed to be piecemeal, contradictory and cumbersome, and therefore in need of review and consolidation. Secondly, it was perceived (by the unlikely alliance of New Right thinkers in the conservative government and organisations committed to defending the rights of parents and families, such as the Family Rights Group) that the balance of the law had tilted too far in favour of the state and that a new balance needed to be established. Thirdly, the Social Services Committee of the House of Commons, chaired by Renee Short MP (House of Commons, 1984) had supported the above demand for reform, arguing that the emphasis on 'permanency' (terminating child contact with families and the push towards adoption planning) had resulted in local authorities lessening support for families of either a preventative nature, or which would enable children to be reunited with their families and carers. Finally, the Department of Health and Social Security (DHSS) published a summary of nine research projects (*Social Work Decisions in Child Care*, DHSS, 1985), which showed that with appropriate support, care episodes could either be prevented or reduced in duration if action was targeted and focused appropriately. In summary, all sides in the fraught debate concerning the triangular relationship between the child, the family and the state were unified in one respect – the need for legal reform. As Parker commented (1990, p96), taking a longer view:

> *The conviction and self-confidence of the nineteenth-century child-savers has been replaced by the doubts and uncertainties of the latter part of the twentieth. Once justification of severance came to be questioned, it was only a matter of time before a fundamental dilemma in child care policy and practice became agonisingly apparent.*

The 1989 Children Act

What is remarkable is the extent to which the Children Act was consensual, commanding cross-party support for the change in the law and seeming to satisfy all sides in the debate. Described by Lord Mackay, the then Lord Chancellor, as *the most far-reaching reform of the law in living memory*, the Act was structured around a series of principles.

- In all matters, the child's welfare should be the paramount consideration.

- There should be a new balance of responsibilities for children between parents/carers and the state.

- The former concept of *parental rights* was replaced by responsibilities and duties, with parental responsibility agreements allowing for a broader definition of parenting.

- Children are best brought up in their own families.

- The state should offer support to enable families to bring up their own children, who would be defined as *in need*, and including children with disabilities.

- If it is not possible to maintain a child at home, then children should be 'looked after' by the state on a *temporary basis*, on the basis of a partnership between the state and parents, with a presumption of family reunification, and ideally on the basis of no court orders being made (via the provision of *accommodation* for the child).

- Local authorities have a duty to promote and support contact between the child and her/his family.

- Children are no longer to be seen to be *in care*, but to be *looked after* by the local authority.

- The state should intervene as little as possible and court proceedings should be based on the presumption of *no order* being made.

- Due consideration should be given to the child's wishes and feelings, and to the child's religious, cultural, racial and linguistic background when making any decisions or planning any intervention.

Following implementation in 1991, it was hoped that the Children Act would herald a new dawn for social work with children and families. Whilst the Act required local authorities to redefine and renew their approaches to supporting families, to intervening in child protection cases and to court orders in the broadest sense, it required little action in relation to children and young people already within the system (those in care).

ACTIVITY 3.2

Review of learning activity

In the light of your previous learning, what would be happening to Jack in the post-1970 period?

COMMENT

So where would Jack be in this period? That would depend – the period spans less than 40 years, yet the changes in trends, policy and practice have been numerous.

- *Before the death of Maria Colwell, the new social services departments are likely to have tried to offer support to Jack and his mother, in accordance with the spirit of the Children and Young Persons Acts of 1963 and 1969.*

- *After the Colwell Inquiry, with the switch towards child protection, it is more likely that Jack may have been received into voluntary care if his mother Anne was seen to be failing as a 'good enough' parent, with the result that he might have been subject to the 'permanency' policy, resulting in his adoption. Following the publication of Children Who Wait (Rowe and Lambert, 1973), child welfare trends shifted towards finding permanent homes for children, be that in terms of long-term foster care or adoption. Such a policy development was buttressed by the 1975 Children Act.*

- *After the 1989 Children Act, and in response to the refocusing debate (Department of Health, 1995), much greater emphasis would have been given to family support, and thence to kinship care.*

- *Current practice is based upon the concept of parallel planning – to provide a focused, time-limited programme of intervention in the family (to achieve change that could result in the child being supported or reunited with the family of origin), whilst at the same time preparing for the possibility of this strategy not being successful, and that the child might ultimately need to be permanently placed in a foster family, or even adopted.*

Current policy is to substantially accelerate the process of adoption, in terms of the selection and approval of adopters and the care planning processes by which children become available for adoption as soon as possible, in accordance with the identified best interests of the child.

The critical literature on children in public care

The revelations of a punitive regime in Staffordshire children's homes (Levy and Kahan, 1991) led to a government-sponsored survey of residential childcare provision (Utting, 1991), and a report on the recruitment, selection, screening and monitoring of staff working with vulnerable children and young people (Warner, 1992). The publication of research findings, *Patterns and Outcomes* (Department of Health, 1991), served to highlight the deficiencies in public care, and in particular the failings of local authorities to discharge their duties as *corporate parents*.

The critical literature seemed to legitimise the action of some authorities in closing children's homes, and defining residential care as *the last resort*, although service user groups representing young people continued to argue for a full choice in placement options – including children's homes.

Nevertheless, if the 1980s can be characterised as the decade of Inquiries into the abuse and even deaths of children within their family homes, the 1990s was to become awash with revelations concerning the abuse of children within the public care system (Corby et al., 2001) – from Pindown (Levy and Kahan,1991), through the Kirkwood Report (Kirkwood, 1993) concerning Leicestershire children's homes up to the Waterhouse Report (Department of Health, 2000d), relating to the North Wales Inquiry. In summary, these Reports and Inquiries seem to assert that if social workers could not be trusted to protect children from abuse by their families and carers, then they seemed to be equally unable to protect them within their own welfare system.

An overview of contemporary child welfare practice

We will finish this chapter by reviewing the current arrangements for working with children, young people and their families, and considering the range of initiatives that have shaped the practice in the past decade. Until recently, the majority of social workers engaged in children and families practice have been employed by social services departments. The powers and duties of the Children Act 1989 are exercised by the local authority (with the exception of the NSPCC), and have been divided into the key functions:

- children in need;
- child protection;
- children 'looked after'.

In accordance with these three modes of activity with children, young people and families, some children's services departments have operated three teams, corresponding broadly to the above functions. These are:

- family support/children in need team;
- referral, access or assesment team;
- children 'looked after' team.

However, in many areas there has been a progressive return to integrated children and families teams. Again, some authorities have begun to transfer the term 'care management' across from adult service into the children and families division, often with a functional split between first contact work (assessment) and longer-term work based upon family support, or with children 'looked after' in public care.

In addition, specialist practitioners in the children, young people and families arena work in:

- fostering and adoption/access to resources/placement support teams;
- leaving care/after-care teams: personal advisers operating a pathway plan service;
- youth offending teams: based in multi-agency teams, under the auspices of the Youth Justice Board;
- children with disabilities teams;
- family centres and children's centres;
- residential child care settings;
- children and adolescent mental health services (CAMHS).

Child protection and family support

The development of child protection procedures over the past two decades – that involve a sequence of taking referrals, undertaking initial assessments on a multi-agency basis, moving (where necessary) on to core assessments and appropriate interventions, and supported by sophisticated information data, child protection registers, independent child protection conference chairs and service evaluation – all add up to a very expensive, complex system. The consequences of the perceived failings in the child protection system, resulting in the notoriety of a particular social services department for its failure to protect a particular child or children (albeit often temporary notoriety, until the next 'tragedy' occurs elsewhere), continue to drive and feed the priority status that this element of the system commands. The Department of Health publication of 1995, *Child Protection: Messages from Research*, exhorted departments to divert resources away from an exclusive child protection focus towards a family support approach, and this became known as the *Refocusing Debate*. However, the tensions between child protection and family support remain, and increasingly the service elements of systems to promote and enable families who – for whatever reason – find parenting difficult, are being provided by new organisations. For example, the Sure Start programme offers a range of services, provided on an inter-agency basis, and targeted on communities most in need by virtue of indices of deprivation (Department of Health, 1998a). Such provision by other agencies serves to reinforce the idea that contemporary children's services departments are increasingly focusing on child protection issues, and addressing the needs of looked after children and young people.

Quality Protects and Children First

Quality Protects was established as a five-year government programme of dedicated funds dispersed to their social services departments to improve the outcomes of children in public care, given the extent of the difficulties arising from research. Studies identified poor health and education prospects of children and young people within the looked after system and, as a result, particular targets were set for social services and other corporate agencies, to be achieved through management action plans. Children First was a parallel scheme for children in Wales.

Contemporary social work practice with children, young people and their families, although informed primarily by the Children Act of 1989, is largely driven by the *Framework for the Assessment of Children in Need and their Families* (Department of Health, 2000b). The framework encompasses three major headings or domains – the Child's Developmental Needs; Dimensions of Parenting Capacity; and Family and Environmental Factors. It is ecological in its approach, and increasingly social workers are exploring models of Kinship Care and Family Group Conferences as ways to promote and encourage caring responsibilities amongst a wider familial network than birth parents or the immediate nuclear family structure (see Colton et al., 2001, pp181–8).

The Children Act 1989 (Amendment) (Children's Planning) Order came into effect in 1996. It requires local authorities to assess the need for Part III (Family Support) services, to consult with other agencies, including stakeholders and service users and carers, and finally to produce and publish their plans. The emphasis is on corporate responsibility – that education, housing, health, social services and other agencies all have a combined responsibility to care for children in public care and for those in greatest need within their families (Department of Health, 2000a).

The outcomes from the Laming Report (see below) have resulted in new procedures for inter-agency collaboration and cooperation:

> *Improvements to the way information is exchanged within and between agencies are imperative if children are to be adequately safeguarded. Staff must be held accountable for the quality of the information they provide.*

> (Department of Health, 2003a, p143)

Every Child Matters and the Children Act 2004

When introducing the Children Act 2004 the then Minister for Children, Margaret Hodge, affirmed the government's commitment to assuring high-quality child care for all, to giving children a good start in life, and to supporting parents in their choices.

Let us trace the origins of these aspirations. Firstly, the appalling circumstances surrounding the death of Victoria Climbié in 2000 led to the Laming Inquiry and thence to the publication of the Green Paper *Every Child Matters* in 2003.

Significantly, it was assumed by government that this particular child abuse fatality appeared to confirm a number of assumptions, including:

(a) too many children do not reach their potential and remain socially excluded;

(b) too many children, such as Victoria Climbié, are harmed and abused;

(c) a range of human services, such as health and social work, are reactive and fragmented;

(d) the children's workforce itself is segmented;

(e) UK society remains other than child-centred.

To respond to these concerns, the Change for Children programme demands a radical transformation of services through new structures, a reframing of how children and families receive universal services, and an integration of targeted and specialist services. Significantly, a number of commentators (such as Parton, 2006, p151) suggest the Green Paper was primarily concerned with taking forward the government's proposals for reforming children's services which it had been developing for some years. This would indeed appear to be confirmed by the following quotation – pre-dating the Climbié Inquiry and the publication of Every Child Matters – and suggesting that the government's Children and Young People's Unit (CYPU) had already determined a 'vision' for young people in terms of the need to ensure that:

> *Every child and young person deserves the best possible start in life, to be brought up in a safe, happy and secure environment, to be consulted, listened to and heard, to be supported as they develop into adulthood and maturity, and be given every opportunity to achieve their full potential.*

(CYPU, 2001, p2)

Whatever the motivation, the consequence of *Every Child Matters* has been to herald the end of the social services departments, and to introduce children's services departments, bringing together child and family social work with education, together with child health, youth offending teams, youth services and the general children's workforce.

What binds this 'big vision' project is the objective of securing five outcomes for all children, namely:

- enjoying and achieving;
- staying safe;
- being healthy;
- making a positive contribution;
- economic well-being.

How are the outcomes to be achieved?

The defined outcomes are to be achieved via the ten elements of the national framework:

1. *A duty to cooperate to promote the well-being of children and young people.*

2. *A duty to make arrangements to safeguard and promote the welfare of children and young people.*

3. *The development of statutory Local Safeguarding Children's Boards (LSCBs) to replace the non-statutory Area Child Protection Committees (ACPCs).*

4. *The appointment of local directors of children's services.*

5. *The establishment of a National Service Framework for Children, Young People and Maternity Services.*

6. *The outcomes framework.*

7. *The development of an integrated inspection framework.*

8. *The appointment of a Children's Commissioner.*

9. *The development of a common assessment framework.*

10. *Workforce reform to help develop skills and to ensure appropriate staffing levels.*

(from Horner and Krawczyk, 2006, p50)

The contemporary practice system

- In relation to vulnerable children and young people, the system is as follows.

- Assessments are based upon the domains identified in the *Framework for Assessment for Children in Need and their Families* (Department of Health, 2000b).

- Agencies are required to work together under arrangements as set out in *Every Child Matters* and the Children Act 2004.

- All local authorities have now implemented the Common Assessment Framework (CAF).

- The use of CAF relates to children in second, third or fourth levels of need as outlined in the guidance. The hierarchy of need is as follows:

Level 1 *Children and young people who make good overall progress in all areas of development; broadly, these children receive appropriate universal services.*

Level 2 *Children and young people whose needs require some extra support from a targeted service.*

Level 3 *Children and young people whose needs are more complex and require integrated support from targeted services.*

Level 4 *Children and young people who have complex and enduring needs that require integrated support from statutory or specialist services*

(Barker, 2009, p13)

Essentially, the CAF should be used to enable children to make progress towards one or more of the five *Every Child Matters* outcomes by offering specific support services. The CAF offers a standardised approach to conducting an assessment of a child's additional needs. It is assumed that the early identification of need promotes coordinated service provision and reduces the need for repeated and repetitive assessments (see Sections 10 and 11 of the Children Act 2004).

The widening of the scope of intervention in relation to children, young people and their families is welcomed by some and greeted with scepticism by others. As Cree and Myers note (2008, p37):

> today, all children in England and Wales have come under heightened scrutiny through the creation of new electronic databases, and it seems likely that early intervention will draw more children (and more families) under surveillance and control 'for their own good'.

This means a widening range of activity for social workers within children's services.

That said, the death of Peter Connolly (in the London Borough of Haringey) in 2008 and the subsequent public outcry about social work's apparent failure to protect extremely vulnerable children has called into question, yet again, whether the organisation of practice is fit for purpose. We will return to these important questions in Chapters 8 and 9.

In 2010, the incoming coalition government asked Eileen Munro to examine existing child protection policies, procedures and practices, which resulted in the report, the *Munro Review of Child Protection: Final Report – A child-centred system* (published in May 2011). The key recommendations from the Munro Review are examined in the final chapter, when looking at current and future practice.

Summary

As we noted in the Preface to this edition, good practice with children, young people and their families and carers is predicated upon consistent themes that have long been the cornerstone of child care work – listening, communication, sensitivity, transparency, honesty, respect, accuracy and reflection – and such themes transcend structures. Indeed Denise Platt, Chair of the Commision for Social Care Inspection, affirms such a perspective:

> Good social care can – and does – make a real difference to children's lives, their development, opportunities and achievement. And positive outcomes for children must be the driver for all social care, regardless of what structures are put in place for its commissioning, delivery and regulation.

(Platt, 2005)

CHAPTER SUMMARY

There have been trends in child welfare in the latter part of the twentieth century, and these have been defined by Colton et al. (2001, p171) as follows.

Time	Reform	Focus	Philosophy
Before 1970	Family foster care	Foster family	Children belong in a family rather than in an institution
1970s	Permanency planning	Adoptive family	Children belong to a permanent family: no child is seen as unadoptable
1980s	Family preservation	Biological parents	Children belong with their biological parents: reasonable effort must be made to maintain the family
1990s	Family continuity	Extended family	Children belong in a family network that continues relations over time

One might add a further period, the 2000s, which we might call *relationship stability*. The focus is on the birth, extended or substitute families, with the philosophy emphasising the importance of stability, identity development, resilience and educational achievement as the best insurance against future difficulties. We will return to this theme in the final chapter when looking at the future of social work practice.

FURTHER READING

Bell, M and Wilson, K (2003) *The practitioner's guide to working with families*. Basingstoke: Palgrave.

A succinct reader that includes policy contexts and practice models for work with children, young people and families.

Chase, A, Simon, A and Johnson, S (eds) (2006) *In care and after: A positive perspective*. London: Routledge.

An excellent summary of research concerning looked after children and young people in terms of outcomes and prospects.

Hendrick, H (2003) *Child welfare*. Bristol: The Policy Press.

A comprehensive overview of child welfare history, including contemporary debates and perspectives.

Horner, N and Krawczyk, S (2006) *Social work in education and children's services*. Exeter: Learning Matters.

A summary of the Children Act 2004 and education legislation that forms the basis of practice in children's services.

Spray, C and Jowitt, B (2012) *Social work practice with children and families*. London: Sage.

This comprehensive guide to social work with children in families draws upon the practice base of its authors, with excellent legal summaries, case scenarios and research summaries.

Chapter 4

Working with people with learning difficulties (or learning disabilities)

Setting the scene

The awkward and rather lengthy title of this chapter reveals a contemporary ambivalence about labels – and their meanings – that are ascribed to people with some form of supposed variance of capacity. For Williams (2009, p7), *a person with learning difficulties is someone who has social and personal vulnerabilities associated with impairment of cognitive under-standing or of learning practical skills which has existed since childhood.*

By various definitions and organisations (see MENCAP, British Institute of Learning Disability (BILD) and the Learning Disability Coalition websites as listed in Resources and useful websites on p186), figures of 1.2 to 1.5 million in the UK are frequently offered as indicators of overall need. BILD suggests a figure of 1,198,000 people in England as have a learning disability (equating to 2 per cent of the general population). Of this figure, it is suggested that 210,000 are people with severe and profound disabilities.

The definition of any form of disability, and in particular as it pertains to intellectual difference, leads us into the recognition of this subject as a highly political and contested arena of social welfare.

The abuse of people with learning difficulties resident in the private hospital of Winterbourne View, near Bristol (identified in 2010) illustrates how that in the early part of the twenty-first century, the most vulnerable members of society continue to be subject to marginalisation, humiliation, danger and abuse. It is therefore most important to appreciate and understand the history of people with a learning disability if we are to avoid the dangers of complacency about the present.

The politics of mental handicap

The title of this section, taken from the seminal text by Ryan and Thomas (1980), highlights the essentially political and sociological processes that have determined the experiences of people with learning disabilities in modern western societies. Ryan and Thomas (1980) pinpoint the industrial revolution as creating a demand for a skilled, literate workforce, with the consequence of displacing those with different capacities and capabilities from the labour force.

As we noted in Chapter 2, such displacement coincided with the aggressive colonisation of problems by the medical profession, resulting in the pre-eminence of the medical model in its claims to explain and manage a range of 'problems', including that now defined as learning disability.

In recent years, it has been the view of a number of commentators that social work with people with learning disabilities represents, in many respects, the profession's high water mark. Writing from a residential perspective, Dick Clough reveals an enthusiasm for the enormous changes that have occurred in the lives of many people with learning disabilities:

> *In contrast to the development in residential care for children and older people, a newly found confidence pervades the service [for people with learning disabilities], promoting a positive outlook for groups of people who could formerly only look forward to a sterile lifestyle, often involving menial tasks in large institutions.*

> (Clough, 1998, p216)

Similarly, Thompson (2002b, p290) notes that the contemporary use of the terms 'learning difficulties' or 'learning disability', in itself reflects:

the struggle that we have had in trying to move away from the problematic terms such as 'mental handicap' or 'mental deficiency', terms that are profoundly stigmatising and unduly negative.

Indeed, Williams (2009, p2) notes that the term 'learning difficulty' is preferred by those in the self-advocacy movement and identifies the rationale for such a view: 'disability' means you can't do things, 'difficulty' means you want to learn and be taught how to do things.

By reviewing the history of care interventions in this sector, it can be seen that social work, supported by its own value base, and linked to significant and dynamic user movements, has participated in profound and significant developments, many of which would have seemed unthinkable only 30 years ago.

CASE STUDY

A personal perspective

In the mid-1970s I worked as a nursing assistant in a long-stay establishment, defined as a county sub-normality hospital. Containing hundreds of residents on a large, rural campus, the hospital had its own school for children, industrial workshops for adults, recreational facilities, laundry, kitchens and other necessary services. The site was divided into 'villas' (in itself seen as a progressive development from traditional wards), where a number of patients of varying needs co-existed. This was a permanent 'home' for most of the residents. Many older 'patients' had lived there all of their lives. It never occurred to me that such places would have a limited future, that change would come and that the institution would close.

Another personal perspective

Howard Mitchell was born in and grew up within sight of Lennox Castle Hospital. He subsequently worked in the hospital and later researched the experiences of both patients and nursing staff. As he stated in his reflective account

> I had witnessed and indulged in conduct which I was later ashamed of and was determined not to repeat or allow to be repeated.

(Mitchell, 1998, p28)

From incarceration to independent living: Charting the changes

How have these changes come about, and what forces produced the unthinkable – the closure of most of these institutions that had been the dominating feature of many local communities for over 100 years? We will begin to consider these developments by introducing our second character, in the early part of the nineteenth century.

COMMENT

In the eighteenth century many people such as George were in fact employed as rural labourers, undertaking various tasks and managing to sustain a role within the community. However, a combination of change in rural social patterns, due to the agricultural revolution and enclosure, and the growth of workhouses, sweeping up the poor and destitute, resulted in significantly altered circumstances for people with learning disabilities. Our example is located in 1820 precisely because this period represents the cusp of experience for those people defined at the time and thence subsequently as idiots, feeble-minded, subnormal, defective, mentally deficient or mentally handicapped.

What is often forgotten is that much welfare provision in the late eighteenth and early nineteenth centuries was 'farmed' – that is to say, the cost was contracted out, whereby the holders of the Poor Law purse purchased care from private providers. (We will return to the contracting culture in later chapters, when the 'truth' about history repeating itself will become more apparent.) The Royal Commission in 1832 visited a range of situations housing the poor, such as the workhouse in Great Grimsby, where we find someone just like George (note that he is identified by the label of *idiot*):

> *Another inmate was an unfortunate idiot lad, of about 19 or 20. I was shown the sleeping place of this poor wretch, in an outhouse in the yard, with a very damp brick floor, half of which he had pulled up…the whole presented a spectacle alike disgraceful to a civilised country, and to the parish where it exists.*

(Cited in Painter, 2000, p19)

Where would George be in the early part of the twentieth century? The end of the nineteenth century had witnessed an increasing interest – from many quarters – in the eugenics movement. Deriving from the Greek *eugenes*, meaning 'well born', this ideology sought to improve society, by deciding *who should be born, who should die, and who should reproduce* (Priestley, 2003). Whilst eugenics was to reach its apotheosis as a cornerstone of the German Third Reich's philosophical base, it had become increasingly fashionable in intellectual and scientific communities in western societies in earlier decades. According to Priestley (2003):

> *so-called 'positive' eugenics promoted the procreation of the most desirable in society…while 'negative' eugenics sought to reduce the procreation of the least desirable (through segregation, abortion, birth control or sterilisation).*

We can thus see that a central drive behind the resulting incarceration of people with learning disabilities was profoundly based upon the fear of procreation, a fear of the reproductive capabilities amongst people defined as 'abnormal'.

Summary points linked to contemporary social work

- The White Paper on genetic research *Our Inheritance, Our Future* (Department of Health, 2003b) prompted debate and concern amongst disability rights campaigners, such as Values into Action.

- Whereas, in the past, a disabled child was seen as a matter of chance, the future might see the existence of a disabled child as evidence of parental irresponsibility (by virtue of a failure to undertake appropriate screening or rejection of abortion as an option).

- Other concerns emanate from anti-abortion groups, such as Life, which fear a move towards the 'quality control' of people and the combined use of genetic screening and testing, together with terminations, to make disabled people 'unnecessary'.

The Mental Deficiency Act of 1913 – which made reference to *idiots, imbeciles and the feeble-minded* as categories of learning disability and the term *moral imbecile* as a means to control unacceptable behaviour – provided the legal framework by which an increasing number of people were incarcerated by virtue of their identity, because of who they were, rather than because of any particular problem or need. Section Two of the Act identified the circumstances under which someone's entry to an institution might occur, including at the insistence of his parent or guardian. According to Ryan and Thomas (1980, p107):

> This Act established the basis of a separate and unified service, which would exclude mental defective people from other welfare and social agencies as well as from the general education system.

> (Quoted in Means and Smith, 1994, p30)

Figures supplied by Tregold (cited in Means and Smith,1994, p31) show that the number of people with learning disabilities under the auspices of the Act rose from 12,000 in 1920 to 90,000 by 1939. Given these figures, it is inevitable that George would be in such an institution, described by the Report of the Mental Deficiency Committee (1929) as

> a large one, preferably built on a colony plan [which] takes defectives of all grades and all ages. All, of course, are properly classified according to their mental capacity and age.

CASE STUDY

George

Under the legislation, George would be seen as 'feeble-minded', the equivalent to a modern day definition of someone with a mild learning disability. The Report of the Mental Deficiency Committee (quoted by Malin et al., 1980, p43), identifies his lifestyle within an institution:

Continued

....the high-grade patients are the skilled workmen of the colony, those who do all the higher processes of manufacture, those on whom there is a considerable measure of responsibility; the medium-grade patients are the labourers, who do the more simple routine work in the training shops and about the institution; the rest of the lower-grade patients fetch and carry or do the very simple work.

Like the namesake of our case example, another George appears in the records of the Bedfordshire Mental Deficiency Committee. Aged 17, he lived on a farm with his father. The Visitor (from the Committee) believed the lad would benefit from training as there was no mother. George's father was duly persuaded it would be in his best interests to go to the local colony, Bromham, where he remained for 23 years.

(Atkinson, 1997, cited in Bytheway et al., 2002, p57)

However, contrary to our present-day assumptions (which tend to see entry to the old 'subnormality' hospitals as a one-way journey), institutional care was not always seen as an end in itself, but as a means towards instruction, training and preparation for settlement 'outside'. A contemporary text reveals the objectives, if not necessarily the reality, of 'community care', but note the moral caveat that life outside the institution can be countenanced only for those individuals who can 'behave' – particularly by curtailing sexual behaviour.

The modern aim is to restore such a person to the community provided adequate steps can be taken to avoid his falling into misconduct or becoming a parent.

(Shrubsall and Williams, 1932, p177)

Indeed, research by Walmsley and Rolph (2002) shows that in 1939 the Board of Control recorded the presence of 46,054 people in institutions, with 43,850 under statutory supervision. (This figure was to rise to 58,000 in mental deficiency hospitals by 1955.) Families and guardians who provided care for a certified 'mental defective' were subject to regular scrutiny as to their ability to care for, and most importantly, control their relative.

Furthermore, the same authors, by referring to the quote from the Somerset Mental Deficiency Committee of 1925, identify a form of 'social work' being undertaken by visitors, charged with the duty of inspecting community-based resources and regulating the care and control of those licensed to be placed within a family:

Frequent visits should be made by an experienced visitor and any tendency to form friendships likely to lead to marriage or immorality should be reported at once, in order that recall to the Institution or a charge of Guardianship can be effected in time.

Such a task conforms to the theoretical perception of Foucault (1977) that social work and care is primarily about state control – in this case the almost obsessive concern with the control and regulation of the personal, emotional and sexual behaviour of people with learning disabilities. Similarly, Walmsley and Rolph (2002, p61) remind us that:

the early twentieth-century ideology was to use community care alongside institutional care to exert control over 'defectives' and their families.

Summary points linked to contemporary social work

- The 2003 Sexual Offences Act, which made it illegal to have sex with a person with learning difficulties unless they are able to give informed consent, is part of a long line of legislation and policy that centres upon controlling the sexuality of disabled people.

- The current legislation (further discussed in Chapter 8) ostensibly seeks to protect disabled people from abuse and exploitation, yet critics of the plan see it as a further example of infantilisation and a denial of human rights.

The acceleration of decarceration

Although we have noted above the earlier practices of 'supervision' in the community, the majority of people defined as having a learning disability remained in Victorian institutions until the latter part of the twentieth century.

Referring to the 1970s and 1980s, Jordan and Jordan (2000, p106) note that:

> social work with people with learning disabilities, long-term mental illnesses and physical handicaps moved in the direction of 'normalisation' – treating service users as citizens, whose primary need was for access to the enabling facilities and resources by which all citizens sustain their lives as members of the community.

The political climate began to question the logic of maintaining such a large number of people in institutions, under the auspices of medical control. As Twigg suggests (1998, p272), *the boundary between the medical and the social is a shifting one, constructed in complex ways that reflect both institutional and ideological factors*, and there is no better illustration than the colonisation and then the subsequent decolonisation of people with learning disabilities. For the majority of 'patients', being in a hospital meant being 'cared for', or 'minded by' nursing staff, but it did not mean being treated in any formalised, technical medical sense. Given, as Twigg further notes (1998, p273), the paramount interest in medicine being in the processes of intervention, and the prospect of change and cure, then it was inevitable that in the converse situations – where there are few prospects for cure or for medical intervention – medicine would redefine the territory as 'social care'.

Such an analysis would be misleading, in that it would fail to recognise or acknowledge the significance of the challenge to the medical model that came from service user groups, carers, the broadly based disability movement and from social work itself, with its interest in the principles of normalisation.

Normalisation (or in its later guise, as Social Role Valorisation) stemmed from the work of Wolf Wolfensburger, who defined the normalisation principle as:

> *The utilisation of culturally valued means in order to establish and/or maintain personal behaviours, experiences and characteristics that are culturally normative and valued.*

> (Quoted in O'Brien, 1981, p1, and cited in Stainton, 2002, p194)

We can thus see that services continually evolve and change, emerging from the imprisonment mode, through the medical/institutional/hospital mode, to the current social mode, based upon the social model of disability that, according to Priestley (2003, p13), *tends to relocate the 'problem' from the individual to society. Disability can thus be viewed as a social problem caused by social processes.*

The context of contemporary practice

We can see that over a 30-year period there has been a significant reduction in reliance upon hospital-based or institutional services towards community-based support systems. At least three levels of support systems are involved. These are:

1. formal, through statutory agencies like social work, health and housing;

2. informal, through voluntary groups, user groups, carers groups, churches and faith-based organisations, community structures; and

3. benefits, such as financial support systems, housing benefits etc. (from Dockrell et al. 1999, p291).

Usually based in multi-disciplinary community teams or integrated service teams, and jointly managed by primary care trusts (NHS) and adult community services departments, the current focus of work is on:

- community care planning;

- assessment of need in partnership with other professionals, users and carers;

- designing packages of care;

- managing the implementation of care packages;

- service coordination;

- reviewing and monitoring service delivery;

- working in accordance with the *Valuing People* policy document (Department of Health, 2001b).

Practice teams usually comprise social workers, occupational therapists, nurses, physiotherapists and behaviour therapists.

Aspects of contemporary practice

The key issue of social work practice with people with learning disabilities centres around issues of power, control, participation, engagement and entitlements. As we noted above, the experience of people with learning disabilities, as an excluded social group, has been one of being devalued, marginalised and, in effect, dehumanised. Therefore, contemporary practice must achieve the opposite, and a key aspect in this process is the promotion of self-advocacy and empowerment.

According to People First Workers (1996), self-advocacy includes:

- speaking up for yourself;

- standing up for your rights;

- making choices;

- being independent;

- taking responsibility for yourself.

Inevitably, such principles lead to questions as to the role of social work in this process. Using the new jargon acquired from health settings, it could be envisaged that social work's new role is be a 'change agent', working with user groups, to address the disabling environments – nationally and locally – that confront those with learning disabilities, be they in relation to education, employment, housing, income, access to leisure and recreation facilities, etc. A parallel function, at the intermediate level, would be to facilitate such individual and collective development by supporting families and carers, to promote and engender rights and responsibilities, and to move away from the tendency towards over-protectiveness and infantilisation. At the micro, individual level, social work and social care services should facilitate and develop person-centred plans to address specific needs, be they about aspects of independent living, expressing choices and preferences, developing and sustaining relationships, sexuality and identity.

As Stainton suggests (2002, p196):

> *the struggle to recognise and respect the autonomy, citizenship and rights of people with a learning disability is at heart a political struggle*

and that

> *social workers' key roles as assessors and case managers are critical in determining if people are to be supported to be autonomous, rights-bearing citizens, or if they are to continue to be oppressed.*

Clearly, such a struggle needs to be carried out on a number of fronts. Simone Aspis (cited in Campbell and Oliver, 1996, p97) expresses concern about the manner in which people with learning difficulties/disabilities are discriminated against within the disability movement itself, which has tended to be synonymous with expressing the aspirations of (physically) disabled people.

From an organisational perspective, a new era is dawning, as the social specialist and segregated education centres – that were the successors to workhouses, sub-normality hospitals, mentally handicapped hospitals, and then adult training centres – are themselves subject to review and change. According to Means and Smith, there always have been periodic episodes of interest and commitment to changing the realities of marginalised, 'unseen' groups, but the key is the episodic nature of the impetus to reform.

> *Usually, the Cinderella groups return to being the concern of the committed few at the margins of political and policy influence.*

(Means and Smith, 1994, p45)

The incremental progress from medical to social model has produced a conviction about the logic of social inclusion policies with the objective of locating services in 'everyday' settings – such as schools, colleges, leisure and community centres, and disbanding 'specialist' or dedicated units for those with learning disabilities. Such developments, allied with the potential expansion of direct payments schemes, the focus on independent living and developments in involving user groups in service design and delivery all conspire to redefine the role of the social worker in this arena.

Valuing People: The contemporary policy framework

The 2001 White Paper entitled *Valuing People: A New Strategy for Learning Disability for the 21st Century* stated that:

> People with learning disabilities are amongst the most vulnerable and socially excluded in our society. Very few have jobs, live in their own homes or have choice over who cares for them. This needs to change: people with learning difficulties must no longer be marginalised or excluded. 'Valuing People' sets out how the Government will provide new opportunities for children and adults with learning disabilities and their families to live full and independent lives as part of their local communities.

By focusing on rights, independence, choice and inclusion, the *Valuing People* White Paper set out a 'cradle to the grave' vision for Britain's 1.4 million people with learning difficulties, and established specific targets for local authorities that included increasing the numbers of people taking up direct payments, moving people out of NHS long-stay hospitals into the community and modernising day services.

Valuing People set a deadline to close all the long-stay hospitals by March 2004. The *Valuing People* progress report showed that this had not been achieved and the deadline was extended.

Valuing People: The story so far

In March 2005, the *Valuing People Support Team* produced a report summarising service user perspectives on the Valuing People *project. The report highlighted things that were going well:*

- *People are listened to more.*

- *When a person-centred planning is done well, it makes a difference to people's lives.*

- *More people are living independently.*

- *Direct payments are giving people control over their lives.*

- *Organisations are working better together.*

Continued

The report also identified areas for improvement:

- *Life is not much better for many people.*

- *Many of the things* Valuing People *talks about have not happened properly yet.*

- *We have made sure that more people understand that people with learning difficulties have rights and should be treated as equal citizens.*

- *We need to keep on working hard.*

(Source: *Valuing People Support Team*, 2005)

The *Valuing People Now* document (Department of Health, 2009, p12) sets down a reaffirmation of the guiding principles of working with people with learning difficulties (or disabilities) as follows.

The four guiding principles of **Valuing People Now**

Rights *People with learning disabilities and their families have the same human rights as everyone else.*

Independent Living *This does not mean living on your own or having to do everything by yourself. All disabled people should have greater choice and control over the support they need to go about their daily lives; greater access to housing, education, employment, leisure and transport opportunities and to participation in family and community life.*

Control *This is about being involved in and in control of decisions made about your life. This is not doing exactly what you want, but is about having information and support to understand the different options and their implications and consequences, so people can make informed decisions about their own lives.*

Inclusion *This means being able to participate in all aspects of community – to work, to learn, get about, meet people, be part of social networks and access goods and services – and to have the support to do so.*

(Department of Health, 2009, p30)

In order to achieve the desired outcomes for people with learning disabilities, the *Valuing People Now* document set key priorities for 2009–10.

- To raise awareness of *Valuing People Now* across national and local government, private and voluntary sectors, and within wider society.

- To have an effective Learning Disability Partnership Board operating in every local authority area.

- To secure access to, and improvements in, healthcare, with strategic Health Authorities and Primary Care Trusts (PCTs) responsible for, and leading, this work.

- To increase the range of housing options for people with learning disabilities and their families, including the closure of campuses.

- To ensure that the *Personalisation* agenda is embedded within all local authority services and developments for people with learning disabilities and their family carers, and is underpinned by person centred planning.

- To increase employment opportunities for people with learning disabilities.

(Department of Health, 2009, p6)

The current government policy platform is entitled 'Valuing People Now'. The National Development Team for Inclusion analysis of the policy suggests that five core aspects need to be kept in focus as we move forward:

---

1. Focus on Rights and Life Outcomes. *We are still on the long journey back from institutionalised societal discrimination against people with learning disabilities and so our prime focus has to be people's rights and the quality of the life outcomes they achieve. We must develop strategies that ensure service decisions are based upon asking two key questions: (i) does this respect and promote people's rights and (ii) will this improve the life outcomes achieved by people? Any other measuring or box ticking has to take second place to these core questions.*

2. Remember 'Nothing About Us Without Us'. *How can we both protect investment in self-advocacy (and family carer support) and also ensure that the organisations (big and small) involve people and families in decision making in ways that are genuine?*

3. Use the Big Society Concept. *Without specific action (reasonable adjustment) people with learning disabilities risk being excluded from whatever Big Society turns out to be. How can we use the concept, get involved in it and exploit it for the benefit of people with learning disabilities? Are we willing to finally take risks and more wholeheartedly try out ways of working that are not based on traditional definitions of a 'service'?*

4. Get vocal and get organised. *People with learning disabilities have been marginalised because their voices are ignored by those with power, both nationally and locally. We need to be united, clear and vocal in what needs to happen – communicating defined expectations to decision makers at all levels.* Valuing People *provided a unifying focus and whatever happens to the policy, it is important that progressive voices are united and heard in the right places.*

5. Remember our history and use it well. *There has been real progress made in the last ten years. Whether that is around the increasing voice of people themselves, a new partnership with many families, greater person centred working and self-directed support or the final closure of the long stay hospitals – we must trumpet that progress and the knowledge of how that was achieved. An honest, but strong articulation of where and how we have progressed since 2001 should be a part of our daily lives.*

Extracts from Valuing People – What Now? (2010) *National Development Team for Inclusion*

Summary

In order for these current policy objectives to be achieved, the question remains as to which professional groups are best placed to make a significant contribution to their implementation. Williams (2009) locates current social work practice within Community Teams for People with Learning Disabilities (CTPLDs) as being broadly characterised by the term 'care management', and indeed adult services – whether for people with sensory impairments, with complex physical needs, with mental distress, for older people, or for those with learning difficulties – are all underpinned by the same policy platforms.

The *Personalisation* agenda as set out by the government circular *Transforming Adult Social Care* (Department of Health, 2008a) is having, and will have, the greatest impact on the shape and structure of services across the adult social care landscape. Following the Green Paper, *Independence, Well-being and Choice* (Department of Health, 2005a) and reinforced in the White Paper, *Our Health, Our Care, Our Say: A New Direction for Community Services* (Department of Health, 2006b), the circular describes the vision for development of a personalised approach to the delivery of adult social care and context in which this policy is grounded.

Personalisation, including a strategic shift towards earlier intervention and prevention, is being established as the cornerstone of public services. This means that every person who receives support, whether provided by statutory services or funded by themselves, will have choice and control over the shape of that support in all care settings.

What this means in terms of social workers' roles and functions in relation to the broad spectrum of vulnerable adults and their families remains to be seen, and will be the subject of further discussion in Chapter 8.

CHAPTER SUMMARY

In Chapter 4 you have been introduced to George, a 25-year-old man with mild learning disabilities. As in Chapter 3, you have been given the opportunity to understand social work and modern learning disability services in the context of historical and critical perspectives, leading to current practice issues within a legal and policy framework.

FURTHER READING

Gardener, A (2011) *Personalisation in Social Work.* Exeter: Learning Matters.

A very helpful overview of the dynamics surrounding personal budgets and personalisation.

Malin, N (1994) (ed.) *Services for people with learning disabilities*. London: Routledge.

An overview of history, definition and range of services in the learning disability arena.

Oliver, M (1996) *Understanding disability from theory to practice*. London: Macmillan.

Essential reading for students wishing to understand the social model of disability and user perspectives.

Williams, P (2009) *Social work with people with learning difficulties*. 2nd edition.
Exeter: Learning Matters.

A thorough and accessible overview of contemporary social practice in the learning difficulty arena.

Chapter 5
Social work with people experiencing mental distress

After the asylums

Together with child care and child protection practice, social work in the arena of mental health work exemplifies the 'dilemma' of social work itself, being situated between the powers of statutory intervention and enforcement, and the historic struggles of an oppressed group in the face of state control. The physical and metaphorical symbol of such control has traditionally been the asylum – the place where people could be taken, against their will, to receive compulsory treatment. However, the location of control has shifted, from the institutional setting into the community itself. The title of this section is taken from the text by Elaine Murphy (1991), which – like the previous chapter concerning people with learning disabilities – charts the slow and often fitful emergence of a specific group of people from the margins to the mainstream.

Whilst the objective of decarceration of thousands of people from former long-stay asylums was roundly advocated by service users/patients, social workers and carers, medical professionals and successive governments, the consequences have engendered high levels of criticism from various quarters:

> *Prisons, doss-houses and 'cardboard cities' housed a high and growing proportion of mentally ill people, many of whom had fallen through the net of the mental health services.*

> (Tilbury, 2002, pix)

Such opinion suggests that, for some patients, the asylums provided something – a home, a retreat, security – and that the 'revolving door' policy of current acute in-patient care leaves many vulnerable people prone to slipping into a cycle of rootlessness, homelessness, criminality and judicial detention.

In this chapter we will explore the processes by which the closure of asylums took place, and discuss the roles and functions of social workers practising within current mental health services. First, however, we will offer a brief overview of mental health issues, beginning with questions of definition and identification.

Who uses mental health services?

As thinking has moved from an emphasis on 'mental illness' to one of 'mental health', Tilbury (2002, pp1–2) – in summarising the theories of others – suggests that we need to develop an idea of what constitutes mental health, based upon the three elements:

1. the idea of the mature self (being satisfied with who you are, linked to ideas of self-esteem, self-worth, firm identity and personal integrity);

2. self-management in social relations (the capacity to make and sustain important relationships, including the capacity for intimacy without dependency); and

3. the discharge of social roles (based upon an understanding of performance roles, within families, groups, neighbourhoods, communities, including the capacity for adjustment and change).

Essentially, most people approximate to some satisfactory level in these three domains most of the time, although everyone will have periodic crises when usual coping mechanisms break down, either due to the sheer weight of a specific pressure, or the cumulative build-up of small pressures, or because usual support systems have become fragmented or unreliable.

Beyond concepts of mental health lie ideas of 'mental health problems' or mental distress. Again, Tilbury (2002, pp10–11) suggests there are three possible stances to consider.

(a) *The widest stance*. This perspective sees as mental health problems all breakdowns in coping, with a range of causes that include all psychoses, neuroses, relationship difficulties, bereavement, victimisation and oppression, etc.

(b) *A more limited view*. This view defines the boundaries of mental ill-health as being coterminous with the remit of psychiatry. In other words, people are mentally ill if psychiatrists treat them, and the list therefore includes personality disorders, addictive behaviours, emotional disorders as well as the obvious neuroses and psychoses, and accords with the *Diagnostic and Statistical Manual 4 (DSM IV)* (American Psychiatric Association, 1994).

(c) *The narrowest view*. This position asserts that the only certain mental illnesses are the psychoses, because they are qualitatively different from emotional difficulties, neuroses and other relationship issues.

A number of professionals advocate an adoption of the third position – precisely because they wish to target resources at those with the greatest need and to avoid locking larger numbers into the psychiatric grasp – yet much broader definitions are commonly used, often arising from a desire to 'normalise' or destigmatise mental distress. Yet further, the law in Britain defines mental disorder as having four separate component conditions: mental illness, mental impairment, severe mental impairment and psychopathic disorder (Pilgrim and Rogers, 1999). Given that mental impairment relates to the previous chapter (learning disability), and the disputed nature of psychopathic disorder, our focus here is on mental illness.

By using the widest definitions, it is not surprising that some authors assert that one in four people will consult their GP about a mental health problem at some point in their lives (Douglas and Philpot, 1998, p108). Literature from the 'Defeat Depression' Campaign, organised by the Royal College of Psychiatrists in association with the Royal College of General Practitioners, suggests that around 10 per cent of the population suffer from a depressive disorder at any one time (Moncrieff, 1997). It is therefore apparent that a large percentage of the population will engage with mental health services at some point in their lives, and a number of those will encounter social workers practising within multi-disciplinary mental health teams.

- One in four people will suffer from as mental illness at some point in their lives.

- 30 per cent of visits to GPs relate to mental health.

- Three out of ten people take mental health-related sick leave every year.

- Over 90 million working days a year are lost trough mental health problems

  (Evans and Huxley, 2012, p143)

Each year more than 250,000 people are admitted to mental health in-patient facilities and over 4,000 people take their own lives. Mental distress interfaces profoundly and significantly with many other aspects of social work practice, particularly in relation to safeguarding children and young people, and services for older people, and all practitioners need to understand the nature of mental distress.

We will briefly resume the history on institutional incarceration before considering contemporary practice issues.

From asylums to community care

Foucault (1961) describes a *great confinement* occurring across Europe from the mid-seventeenth century, and Britain was no exception. In Chapter 2 it was noted how the medical profession effectively colonised the care and control of various vulnerable groups, including people with learning disabilities, older people and those who were defined as mentally unwell. The paramountcy of the medical model was to prove particularly significant for nearly 150 years. According to Gibbins (1988), asylum occupancy rose from about 20,000 in 1850, to 86,000 in 1890, to 120,000 in 1930 (when asylums were renamed mental health hospitals), reaching a peak of 148,000 in 1954.

ACTIVITY **5.1**

It is 1930. Mary is a white woman, aged 40. She has mental health problems that manifest themselves as a form of mania, and periodically involve self-harm, such as cutting her forearms and hands. She has been living at home, with her parents, who run an alehouse. When well, Mary helps to serve in the bar, but her behaviour can be erratic and she has attacked customers in the past. Where would Mary be in the inter-war period? What would her life be like? In the light of the preceding material, try to identify the societal response to people with mental health needs.

COMMENT

Given the absence of any medication to help contain Mary's episodic 'mania', or any forms of community-based treatment, it is highly likely that she would have been admitted to an asylum. Murphy (1991, p38) provides an illustration of 'life in the asylum':

> Life was governed by a rigid timetabled regime of sleep, work, eat. Whitewashed walls; plain brick, stone or wooden floors; deal benches and tables; and two WCs for thirty or forty patients provided a fairly cheerless though roomy environment. Windows were generally barred and many wards were locked, although the better asylums gave considerable internal freedom to the inmates.

The ritualised nature of the incarceration process is poignantly illustrated by the auto-biographical notes of Marian King (*The Recovery of Myself: A Patient's Experience in a Hospital for Mental Illness*, 1931):

> *I was taken down the hall by my attendants, and found a bath awaiting me. After much unnecessary scrubbing, all done by my attendants, I was at last taken to my room. The door was closed and once more I got wearily into bed.*

(Quoted in Porter, 1991, p211)

As Parker (1988, p12) points out, *decarceration and release were not easily obtained* – a reality understood by the inmate, such as Daniel Paul Schreber who, in his *Memoirs of My Nervous Illness* (1903), said:

> *I laboured under the delusion that when all attempts at cure had been exhausted, one would be discharged – solely for the purpose of making an end to one's life either in one's own home or somewhere else.*

> (Quoted in Porter, 1991, p211)

The inexorable rise in numbers of in-patients, coupled with the emerging range and use of drug treatment options, resulted in the Percy Report (Ministry of Health, 1957), which examined mental health services, coined the term *community care* and proposed a new social work service for *mentally ill and handicapped* people, to be provided by local councils. The ideas were enacted in the Mental Health Act of 1959, and thus began the long, evolving process of transfer of service responsibility from hospital-based services towards community-based services. The progress towards decarceration was patchy and fitful. As a cleaner states (quoted by Bornatt, 1998, p23):

> *The closure of St Mary's was being talked about for 15 years and there were very few new staff taken on while I was there. Half the wards were unoccupied. Most of the patients were elderly – psycho-geriatrics. They thought they were going to be here till they died. One chap used to walk the corridors. He used to say to me, 'I don't have to go home, do I? You have to go home but I live here.' He'd been there most of his life; he was 60.*

Summary points linked to contemporary social work

- Whilst many authors have rightly warned against the nostalgic, retrospective romanticisation of the asylums, it is apparent that for many dislocated, marginalised people the asylums represented a permanent home, a source of security and a location of identity.

- The replacement of the asylums with acute in-patient psychiatric facilities addresses the problem of 'institutionalisation' but not the problem of rootlessness, social drift and dislocation.

- A comprehensive mental health strategy, therefore, has to address people's holistic needs, including housing and community membership.

The critical literature concerning asylums came from varied sources. Goffman's study of institutions in *Asylums* of 1961 and Bridget Robb's study (1967) of hospital provision for those defined as elderly mentally infirm added to the mass of critical literature concerning the institutional nature of service for a variety of service user groups. Thus, as Payne summarises (1998, p36), *the concept of community care became associated with deinstitutionalisation of patients in mental hospitals*, and the then Conservative Health Minister Enoch Powell called for *making a bonfire* of the long-stay institutions in the early 1960s.

How can the process of hospital closure be explained? Rogers and Pilgrim (1996, p79) adapt the model of Busfield (1986) and suggest four main reasons.

1. The pharmacological revolution (the use of drugs to manage and control problem behaviours).

2. Economic determinism (shifting the focus from high-cost institutions).

3. A shift to acute problems (the establishment of community-based support for less serious problems, coupled with in-patient care for acute disorders).

4. A shift in psychiatric discourse (rethinking roles and meaning in the psychiatric domain).

As has been noted by many critical authors (such as Scull, 1977, 1979) the imperative towards closing institutions was primarily driven by economic, not welfare principles. This argument is supported by a recognition of the cost of institutional care. Goodwin (1990, cited in Means and Smith, 1994, p32) revealed that in the 1950s, 40 per cent of NHS beds were located in mental and mental deficiency hospitals, although this accounted for only 20 per cent of the total hospital budget. Thus, whilst there was a demonstrable under-spend (per patient) in the mental health and learning disability sectors, the total cost was still seen as excessive – a cost that could be reduced by a shift towards a community-based service. In fact, in the period 1954 to 1974, there was a reduction of 60,000 in-patient numbers (Murphy, 1991), but this was associated with an absence of community-based services, resulting in Murphy's assessment of the 1962–90 period as *the disaster years* for those with mental health problems (Murphy, 1991, p60).

Part of the difficulties was a matter of structural and organisational constraint. Nurses, psychiatrists, occupational therapists and psychiatric social workers were employed by health authorities and were institutionally based – their own homes were in the hospital, jobs passed from one family member to another and they belonged to a semi-closed community. A transfer of patients into the community needed to be accompanied by a similar movement of the service's greatest asset and resource: the staff. This move required staff to redefine themselves from being *keepers* (Glouberman, 1990) to being members of community-based multi-disciplinary teams.

Eventually, staff, money and resources moved, spurred on by the White Papers *Better Services for the Mentally Handicapped* (DHSS, 1971) and *Better Services for the Mentally Ill* (DHSS, 1975), leading to a clear commitment to a hospital closure programme and the establishment of community-based services.

Social workers, who had been previously employed by health authorities, transferred to local authority social services departments in 1974, although most remained located in hospitals, contributing to discharge plans and community support schemes.

The context of service delivery

The current context of practice is shaped by:

(a) legislation and government policy;

(b) recent historical events, associated concerns and public 'moral panics';

(c) professional intentions and aspirations;

(d) service user expectations and demands.

Let us briefly examine one case that had a particular significance in shaping current mental health legislation and practice.

CASE STUDY

Christopher Clunis

Of a number of highly publicised cases, that of the care and treatment of Christopher Clunis attracted the greatest concern, as it pertained to the fatal attack on Jonathan Zito on a railway station platform in 1992. This case had all the hallmarks necessary for provoking a moral panic: a random attack, whereby the victim was entirely unknown to the perpetrator; a fatal killing in a public space; the fact that Christopher Clunis had been a recipient of mental health services since the mid-1980s and yet, due to poor inter-professional communication, he had become 'lost' by the authorities in the late 1980s; the fact that between 1987 and 1992 he had been admitted to four different psychiatric units yet each lost contact with him; and the absence of discharge plans (Ritchie, Dick and Lingham, 1994).

Following these reports, amendments were made in 1996 to the 1983 Mental Health Act, ushering in the powers of *supervised discharge*, which enabled psychiatric teams to have access to the patient, and to be able to enforce attendance at mental health facilities. Such changes in the law reflected the issue of the perceived threat posed to the public by those defined as having 'severe' mental health difficulties. According to the Boyd Committee, 39 homicides and 240 suicides were committed by people with serious mental health problems annually in the years up to 1995 (Boyd, 1996), yet research consistently indicates that *male gender, low social class, youth, and drug and alcohol abuse are much better predictors of violence than mental state* (Rodgers and Pilgrim, 1996, p192). It is an accepted truism that the management of disruptive and dangerous behaviour is a problem for any society, and social workers – by being part of mental health teams – play a crucial role in working within the framework of a social model of mental health to counterbalance the medical or disease model sometimes proffered by the psychiatric profession.

Social work in mental health settings – like child care work – illustrates the contested nature of the social work task. Without doubt, social work has a significant and distinctive role to play in the mental health system, which – again like child protection – operates at the border post between the state's powers to control behaviours it deems to be dangerous or risky, and the rights of the user/patient to protection from the oppressive use of the law. As Bailey (2002, p172) quotes from the work of Walton (1999, p378):

> *Social work in the mental health field has traditionally occupied an unstable, ambivalent and ambiguous position, caught between the dominant theoretical and professional discipline of biological psychiatry and the psycho-socially oriented theory and practice of mainstream social work.*

The location of practice has progressively shifted from hospitals to social services departments and has now moved into mental health trusts.

The legal context of social work practice

The inevitable public scrutiny of mental health services after the Clunis case led to changes in policy (through *Modernising Mental Health Services: Safe, Sound and Supportive* (Department of Health, 1999a), to the publication of *The National Service Framework for Mental Health (NSFMH)* (Department of Health, 1999b), and propelled forward the long overdue changes in legislation *(Reforming the Mental Health Act: Part 1 the New Legal Framework*, Department of Health, 2000c). Finally, after many years of delay and debate, the current legislation governing mental health intervention and treatment was passed as the Mental Health Act 2007 and was enacted in October 2008.

The cornerstone of legal intervention with people experiencing mental distress remains the Mental Health Act 1983, which sets out the circumstances in which a person with a mental disorder can be detained for treatment for that disorder with or without his or her consent. The Mental Health Act 2007 amends the 1983 Act and introduces Deprivation of Liberty Safeguards by amending the Mental Capacity Act 2005 with effect from April 2009.

The Mental Health Act 2007 has some features of particular note.

- **A new single definition of mental disorder**, which abolishes reference categories of disorder.

- **New criteria for detention**, which prohibit compulsory detention unless medical treatment which is appropriate to the patient's mental disorder, and all other circumstances of the case, is available to that patient.

- **Professional roles**, which widen the group of practitioners who can take on the legal functions of the Act to encompass a wide range of mental health practitioners. This particularly applies to the broadening of access for professionals being registered as Approved Mental Health Practitioners (AMHPs), replacing the exclusive Approved Social Worker role.

- **Supervised community treatment (SCT)**, which allows for some patients with a mental disorder to be discharged from detention subject to the possibility of recall to hospital if necessary;

- **Establishment of an Independent Mental Health Advocacy Service.**

- **Age-appropriate services**, determining that services to patients under 18 should be suitable for their age.

The practice context

Service delivery is often structured around multi-disciplinary community mental health teams of social workers, community mental health nurses (CPNs), occupational therapists, psychiatrists, psychologists and mental health support workers, based in mental health partnerships and trusts.

Most social work practitioners are located in one of three service settings, namely:

- early intevention teams;
- crisis resolution teams;
- assertive outreach teams.

Furthermore, social workers are employed in specialist service settings, such as CAMHS, in drugs and alcohol and forensic teams.

Practice is configured by strategic policy, legislation, guidance and standards and is centred upon the *Care Programme Approach*, first introduced in 1991, and redefined in 2008 (Department of Health, 2008b) as applying only to complex and high-risk cases, defined as those who need multi-agency support and intense intervention.

The world of mental health practice is a necessarily highly regulated arena. The Care Quality Commission (as introduced in March 2009) has assumed responsibility for all mental health matters, regulating hospital conditions, monitoring standards of safety, dignity and professional care.

Aspects of contemporary practice

Tilbury (2002, p42 *passim*) suggests the following as elements in the transactions between practitioners and mental health service users.

- Empathise with the service user's reality and the response it generates.
- Help the service user to keep in touch with reality.
- Relate to the person, not the symptoms.
- Promote the service user's skills to manage themselves and their lives.

Furthermore, the same author (Tilbury, 2002, p57) distinguishes between the skills of sustaining a relationship and the skills of operating in and effecting change in the broader system.

The sustaining process	Direct influence
Interest and concern	Using the law
Sympathetic listening	Working in multi-disciplinary teams
Acceptance	Networking across professional boundaries
Realistic resonance	Accessing other services
Encouragement	Advocacy with other agencies
Introduction of practical services	Balancing the rights of the service user and the rights of others in terms of risk and potential harm (to others or self)

Whilst recent legislation, reports and policy directives have tended to focus upon the operation of the right-hand column, very little 'official' attention has been paid to the left hand column. Yet service user research indicates the importance of engagement and relationship-building. According to Perkins and Repper (1998, p24), an *effective relationship* for people with severe and enduring mental health problems:

> *...might best be judged in terms of the extent to which the person is facilitated in living the life they wish to lead and achieving their own goals.*

Such a sentiment might apply to working with children, young people, with families, with people with learning disabilities, disabled people and the group discussed in the next chapter – older people. The rational-technical aspects of practice, as evidenced by the plethora of law, policy and procedure for each service domain, indicate the need for specialist activity. By contrast, the value base, the commitment to anti-oppressive practice and essential communication skills, indicate the generic, transferable nature of the practice elements. After all, as Sayce (1993, p3) correctly observes:

> *People with a diagnosis of mental illness face specific discrimination: it is hard to obtain work, training, a mortgage or even life insurance. A record of using psychiatric services, unlike a criminal record, is with you for life.*

Social work's distinctive contribution lies in its capacity to work with service users – both individually and collectively – to address these aspects of oppression.

Many of the systemic difficulties confronting those persons experiencing mental distress can be broadly linked to the concept of social exclusion. It is clear that mental distress is both a very obvious cause of accentuated social exclusion and a potential result of being socially excluded. It is also abundantly evident from research that there is a number of effective ways to tackle exclusion, ranging from early intervention, strengthening communities, working in partnership with service users and tackling discrimination and stigma (Social Exclusion Unit, 2004). The latter is particularly relevant in relation to those members of black and minority ethnic communities who are disproportionately recipients of Mental Health Act detentions and other forms of compulsory treatment interventions.

Socially inclusive practice is currently attempting to address a number of core issues: the complex interface between substance use and mental distress; issues of ethnicity, racism and social stress; parental mental health and the impact of child safeguarding; and coherent recovery planning.

As the government's mental health policy agenda continues to promote community-based interventions, the distinctive contribution of social work and social care has all the more to play for in terms of shaping and changing outcomes for service users. As Terry Bamford has suggested:

> *Social Work does bring something distinctive to mental health. Articulating it is more difficult. It is a constellation of values, commitment to social justice and partnership with users and carers. Social workers practised social inclusion before the term had been invented. Above all, in mental health, it challenges the traditional medical model which does not fully acknowledge the patient or client as best informed about their needs.*

> (Bamford, 2006)

One might assert that it is social work's capacity to advance the cause of integrated, holistic, inclusive, culturally competent practice that assures its role in modern responses to mental distress.

On the same theme, it is instructive to note that over a substantial period, feedback from service users (such as the Mental Health Foundation Report of 1994) has consistently suggested that a number of factors contribute to recovery and prevention of relapse. These are:

* an adequate place to live;
* an adequate income;
* a varied social life;
* employment and other daytime activity;
* help and support;
* respect and trust; and
* choice and consultation.

All of these needs reflect and represent *par excellence* the social dimension of the individual's world, whether it is in crisis or recovery. This clearly stated set of needs attests to the distinction and important contribution of social work and social care in supporting people experiencing mental distress.

The GSCC paper *Social Work at Its Best* (2008a) offers an aspirational account of all aspects of social work, including the following description of mental health settings:

> *People with mental health problems want expert help at times of difficulty, freedom from abuse, stigma and discrimination, and support to recover, get jobs and homes of their own, and take their place in society. Social work at its best can help them overcome the barriers to living full lives in the community, challenge negative stereotyping and improve public understanding of mental health matters.*

> (GSCC, 2008a)

As Goemans (2012) suggests, this quote highlights the importance of understanding the impact that social factors, such as employment, housing, and stigma can have on causing or preventing mental illness. Such a perspective is *enshrined within social work's values, which are the defining characteristic of the profession, embodying structural explanations of disadvantage through human rights and social justice discourses, translating these into practice shaped by a person centred, anti-oppressive, and empowerment based focus* (Goemans, 2012, p70).

We will consider current services and perspectives in relation to working with those experiencing mental distress in Chapter 8.

CHAPTER SUMMARY

In Chapter 5 mental health practice and policy have been discussed around the experiences of Mary, a 40 year-old woman with mental health problems, drawing upon historical responses to those defined as 'mentally ill' and reflecting upon major shifts in service provision in recent decades.

FURTHER READING

Archambeault, J (2009) *Reflective reader: Social work and mental health.* Exeter: Learning Matters.

A wide-ranging source book on mental health perspectives and practice models.

Golightley, M (2011) *Social work and mental health.* 4th edition. Exeter: Learning Matters.

This informative and clearly written text equips the beginning practitioner with an understanding of mental health policy, law and practice issues.

Jones, K (1972) *A history of the mental health services.* London: Routledge and Kegan Paul.

A definitive account of mental health services.

Pilgrim, D and Rogers, A (1999) *A sociology of mental health and illness.* Buckingham: Open University Press.

An accessible text that looks at a wide range of themes about mental health, including legal and service issues in relation to age, ethnicity and gender.

Tew, J (ed.) (2007) *Social perspectives in mental health.* London: Jessica Kingsley.

A valuable edited text that brings together a range of perspectives that explores mental distress in terms of people's social experience.

Chapter 6
Social work and older people

People do not care about organisational boundaries when seeking support or help and expect services to reflect this.

(Department of Health, 2006b)

ACHIEVING A SOCIAL WORK DEGREE

This chapter will help you to develop the following capabilities, to the appropriate level, from the **Professional Capabilities Framework**.

- **Professionalism.** Identify and behave as a professional social worker committed to professional development.
- **Values and ethics.** Apply social work ethical principles and values to guide professional practice.
- **Diversity.** Recognise diversity and apply anti-discriminatory and anti-oppressive principles in practice.
- **Rights, justice and economic well-being.** Advance human rights and promote social justice and economic well-being.
- **Knowledge.** Apply knowledge of social sciences, law and social work practice theory.
- **Judgement.** Use judgement and authority to intervene with individuals, families and communities to promote independence, provide support and prevent harm, neglect and abuse.
- **Critical reflection and analysis.** Apply critical reflection and analysis to inform and provide a rationale for professional decision-making.
- **Contexts and organisations.** Engage with, inform and adapt to changing contexts that shape practice. Operate effectively within your own organisational frameworks and contribute to the development of services and organisations. Operate effectively within multi-agency and interprofessional settings.
- **Professional leadership.** Take responsibility for the professional learning and development of others through supervision, mentoring, assessing, research, teaching, leadership and management.

See Appendix 1 for the Professional Capabilities Faremwork diagram.

This chapter will also introduce you to the following standards as set out in the 2008 social work subject benchmark statement.
4.3 Defining principles.
5.1 Subject knowledge and understanding.
5.1.2 The service delivery context.
5.1.3 Values and ethics.

A hundred years of ageing

She won't leave you anything duck...I shouldn't bother.

The above statement, made as recently as 2003 by a permanent staff member to a social work student in a residential care home for older people, illustrates the persistence of oppressive attitudes and practices within group care settings. The statement was made as the student was trying to engage a withdrawn, confused older woman in a conversation, in a relationship, in a human exchange. The message was – why bother? The persistence of such oppressive and devaluing attitudes is illustrative of the point that whilst structures, policies, financial arrangements and quality assurance/inspection regimes have changed beyond all recognition, the marginalised and vulnerable position of many older people remains as stark as ever. *Plus ça change, plus c'est la même chose*.

One hundred years ago, in spite of the earliest stirrings of welfare reform under the Asquith Liberal government – which resulted in pensions being introduced in 1908 – large numbers of older people continued to experience the 'haunt of misery' and entered the workhouse, where they increasingly became the dominant group. Yet older people made up a much smaller percentage of the population then. In 1901, 6 per cent of the population was over 65; in 2001 it was 25 per cent and it is projected to rise to 36 per cent by 2031. More significantly, the number of people aged over 85 rose from 44,000 (0.2 per cent) in 1901 to 1,058,000 (2 per cent) by 2001, with a projected rise to 1,827,000 (3.1 per cent) by 2031 (Sumner, 2002).

It is the speed of demographic change that is most remarkable and which demands the most fundamental rethink as to how we construct a society with communities able to respond effectively to the complex and diverse needs of older people. By 2022, 20 per cent of the population will be over 65. By 2027, the number of over-85 year olds will have increased by 60 per cent (Department of Health, 2007). A study conducted on behalf of the Alzheimer's Research Trust in 2007 (Department of Health, 2012) estimated that the number of people with dementia and other causes of cognitive impairment will rise by 83 per cent by 2031, that the number of people with such difficulties living in care homes will rise by 88 per cent over the same period, and that the cost of providing such long-term care for older people with dementia will increase to £16.7 billion by 2031. (The Health Commission (Department of Health, 2012) has estimated that there will be more than 1 million people with dementia by 2025). In terms of most recent data, the government currently estimates that 670,000 people have dementia in the UK, resulting in an annual expenditure of £19 billion to support them and their carers (Department of Health, 2012).

Such a demographic projection indicates that the highest area of potential growth in social work and social care will be in relation to working with older people. This is not, of course, necessarily the case – we have already shown that the roles and purposes of social work are often a function of the boundaries of other professional groups. In addition, the fact that people live longer will not necessarily mean higher levels of need or dependency – it may just mean that the onset of need will occur later in life. The current concerns about the stability and value of pensions and the early beginnings of the debate concerning a revision of the retirement age all indicate that complex social policy decisions in relation to older people are imminent.

We will begin with a brief review of the 'lot' of vulnerable older people over the past century, and identify the emerging role of social work in this service setting. Today, and often contrary to public myth, only around 5 per cent of older people live in some kind of residential or nursing care. A third live in their own home, others in public, private or voluntary (housing association) settings and a number live with relatives. More older people live alone due to divorce, separation, bereavement and family dislocation. Yet for the first half of the twentieth century, options for older people were very limited, with the fear of the Poor Law and Public Assistance never far away for many working-class elders.

CASE STUDY

Hannah in 1930

Hannah is 70 years old, a white woman apparently unable to care for herself, due to her deteriorating health problems. She lives in a private rented house in County Durham. Her husband, a former miner, died a few years ago. Her only daughter and her son-in-law moved to London two years ago. What would be the lot of Hannah in the inter-war period? Assuming Hannah could not be supported by any relatives, friends or neighbours, she might have no other option but to move into an institutional care setting. Her situation in institutional group care would probably accord with the description by Roberts (1970) whereby most elderly inmates slept ...

... in large dormitories, sat on hard chairs, looked out on cabbage patches diversified by concrete, were separated by sex and, except on one day of the week, could not pass the gates without permission.

(Quoted in Means and Smith, 1994, p20)

The same authors refer to contemporary writers in the 1930s calling for change in standards of care:

... through contact with visitors from the outside world, by providing occupations as well as entertainments and by introducing more variety into their food, clothing and surroundings.

It is fair to say that there was a complete absence of social work with older people. Those in need were either cared for at home, in the workhouse, or in the Public Assistance Hospital. There was either a medical or a moral response to need.

Challenging institutional care for older people

The commitment identified in Chapter 3 – to challenge and change the institutional arrangements for children – was sadly lacking in the arena of adult care. As Parker (1988, p106) noted:

The concern to maintain and foster family life evident in the (1948) Children Act was completely lacking in the National Assistance Act. The latter made no attempt to provide any sort of substitute family life for old people who could no longer be supported by their own relatives. Institutional provision was accepted without question.

However, the poverty of experience for older people in institutional settings was well known. The Nuffield Report of 1946 offered a damning indictment of workhouse care for older people: *there is usually acute apathy. The residents tend to sit around the walls unoccupied, merely waiting for the next meal or bedtime.* There were campaigns to highlight the desperation of older people who, as a result of being made homeless by bombing raids, and the absence of family support, ended up in Public Assistance Institutions (the renaming of workhouses after 1929).

> *But down each side of the ward were ten beds, facing one another. Between each bed and its neighbour was a small locker and a straight-backed, wooden uncushioned chair. On each chair sat an old woman in workhouse dress, upright, unoccupied. No library books or wireless. Central heating, but no open fire. No easy chairs. No pictures on the walls...There were three exceptions to the upright old women. None was allowed to lie on her bed at any time throughout the day, although breakfast was at 7am, but these three, unable any longer to endure their physical and mental weariness, had crashed forward, face downwards, on to their immaculate bedspreads and were asleep.*

> (A Workhouse Visit: letter published in the *Manchester Guardian* 1943, quoted in Means and Smith, 1994, p23)

CASE STUDY

Hannah in 1960

Given this set of circumstances, it is almost inevitable that Hannah, in the post-1945 period, would have been resident in Part III accommodation under the 1948 National Assistance Act. Adams (1996) states that, in spite of the demise of the Poor Law arrangements in 1960, 37,000 older people were still living in 309 former workhouses, although some purpose-built residential homes were being developed. The high number of geriatric wards in hospitals indicated the ease by which institutional health care was made available, rather than any form of community-based alternative.

ACTIVITY 6.1

What would have been the social work or social care role in relation to Hannah in the 1960s?

COMMENT

With regard to social work, the answer would still probably have been 'none'. Forward thinkers such as Sheldon (1948) and De Largy (1957) (both cited in Moriarty and Levin, 1998) had recognised that admissions to acute hospital (geriatric) care were occurring when carers could no longer cope, and they therefore advocated the establishment of respite care schemes. However, these were very rare. We can thus presume that Hannah and her support system either coped, or she was admitted to the geriatric ward of a general hospital. Increasingly, the critical literature of dysfunction (Jack, 1998, p17), such as Townsend's study of care for older persons (The Last Refuge, 1962), which echoed

Continued

COMMENT *continued*

the findings of Barton's study (1959), painted a depressing picture of the experiences of patients and residents in institutional settings for older people. Although Section 29 of the National Assistance Act (1948) now empowered local authorities to promote the welfare of persons who are blind, deaf or dumb and others, who are substantially or permanently handicapped by illness, injury or congenital deformity, the responses on offer continued to be of a largely institutional nature. There had been a change of ownership of establishments – from Poor Law guardians to local authorities – but beyond that, little had changed. According to Means and Smith (1994, p25), domiciliary services were seen by the post-war legislators as an 'extra frill' and consequently a patchwork of visiting services, meals services, day centres and other forms of support emerged through the efforts of the voluntary sector. Local authorities were not empowered to provide meals services until the passage of the National Assistance (Amendment) Act of 1962.

Slouching towards community care

The literature of dysfunction, linked to a general critical awareness of institutional and hospital-based care, and combined with the campaigning efforts of voluntary organisations such as Meals-on-Wheels and Age Concern, led towards an emerging community-care focus in relation to older people.

CASE STUDY

Hannah after 1970

As in the case of Jack (in Chapter 3), Hannah's circumstances would have changed significantly over the 30-year period post-Seebohm. In the 1970s Hannah would have probably still been on a geriatric ward in a hospital, or in a residential home run by the local authority. The latter were still large institutions, many based upon former workhouse sites, often with multiple occupancy bedrooms, and little by way of regulation, inspection, or checks-and-balances on the quality of the care experience. However, the National Health Service Act of 1977 made home care a mandatory responsibility rather than a discretionary power, and thus the framework to promote choice and enable older people to stay in their own homes began to be established.

By the 1980s Hannah would probably have been located in a residential home, which might have been run by the local authority, depending upon the political nature of the council, but would increasingly have been in the burgeoning private sector, where the service would have been subject to registration and inspection under the Registered Homes Act of 1984.

Rethinking social care: The challenge to state provision

To most people engaged in the worlds of social policy, administration and practice, it had been reasonable to expect that, following the Mental Health Act 1959, the Hospital Plan (Ministry of Health, 1962) and the Seebohm Report (1968) (see Chapter 7), there would have been a significant shift from institutions towards community-based services, but this had failed to materialise. In 1986 the Audit Commission analysed the lack of progress in developing community-based services, and identified the following reasons.

- Funds were not coordinated; local authorities were subject to 'rate-capping' if they over-spent and so were reluctant to invest in community services.

- There was a *perverse financial incentive* under the central government (DHSS) fee system for people to enter residential care regardless of need. After all, if people stayed at home, with community support, then social services footed the bill; if they entered residential care, the DHSS paid their fees.

- There was organisational confusion over who was responsible for coordinating strategies.

- Inadequate staffing levels and training for social care in the community were identified (Audit Commission, 1986).

Summary points linked to contemporary social work

- There is a remarkable degree of continuity concerning the challenges facing public policy, social care and older people.

- People want to maintain their independence, to remain in their own homes, neighbour-hoods and communities for as long as possible.

- Institutional care – whether in hospital, in nursing homes or residential homes – is very expensive and represents an inefficient use of available resources.

- 'Personal crises' occur as a result of sudden changes in support systems or due to acute changes in functioning capacity (e.g. a fall, a stroke).

- Policy initiatives since the mid-1980s have been focused on the redesignation of resources away from institutional resources towards the meeting of needs within community structures.

As a result of these findings the Conservative government, in 1988, charged Sir Roy Griffiths with the task of producing proposals for reform. It is instructive to be reminded of the core principles guiding the review.

- People should be helped to remain in their own homes, rather than enter residential care.

- Services should be based on the assessment of individual needs, taking account of the wishes of both client and carer.

- Social services should have the lead role in planning and organising community care services. Previously, Community Care had been *everybody's distant cousin, but nobody's baby* (Griffiths, 1988, piv).

- Case managers would have a role in coordinating packages of care.

- Services should be delivered in a *mixed economy* of care, with greater emphasis on the private/voluntary sector.

It is important to note that in the same year, the Green Paper on Social Security had stated:

State provision has an important role in supporting and sustaining the individual, but it should not discourage self-reliance or stand in the way of individual provision or responsibility

Therefore the government response to the Griffiths Report must be read in the light of broader political objectives concerning the desirability of rolling back the state, of reducing welfare dependency, of promoting self-reliance and of creating individual and family responsibilities as a counterbalance to right and entitlements. These themes have informed governmental welfare policies – whether Conservative or Labour – ever since.

Reviewing residential care: The Wagner Report

Before considering the translation of the Griffiths recommendations into policy and legislation, it is helpful to recall that in the same year (1988), the Wagner Report was published. Established three years earlier to review residential services in the light of impending changes in community care arrangements, the Report was subtitled *A Positive Choice*, and sought to portray residential and group care establishments as having a positive and productive role to play as part of a continuum of care provision in the community. Such a view has continued to be supported by writers such as Clough:

'Community Care' – so often taken to mean care at home – should mean care anywhere in the community, including residential homes. If a residential care home is not part of the community, it cannot be playing its role to the full.

(Clough, 1998, p214)

The Wagner Report emphasised the following.

- Given the right information, some service users would make a positive choice to live in a group care setting.

- Residential care settings should see their residents as customers, with consequent rights of appropriate information, choice, opportunities to shape the service and procedures for complaints.

- Service quality should be assured through a set of standards and a framework of inspection and regulation.

- A quality service can be delivered only by a committed, trained and qualified workforce.

Although not formally implemented at the time, it is possible to see, with hindsight, that residential services have developed in accordance with inspection regimes that arose from the Community Care legislation, and shaped by subsequent guidance, such as *Homes Are For Living In* (Department of Health/Social Services Inspectorate, 1989) and *A Better Home Life* (Centre for Policy on Ageing, 1996). Such guidance stressed the importance of residential care homes promoting the values of residents' dignity, fulfilment, choice, self-determination and the desirability of maximising the possibility of living a full and active life.

From Griffiths towards community care

The Griffiths Report led on to the 1989 White Paper *Caring for People* (Department of Health, 1989), which emphasised elements of service design and delivery, including six key objectives.

1. To promote the development of domiciliary, day and respite services to enable people to live in their own homes wherever feasible and sensible.

2. To ensure that service providers make practical support for carers a high priority.

3. To make proper assessment of need and good care management the cornerstone of high-quality care.

4. To promote the development of a flourishing independent sector alongside good-quality public services.

5. To clarify the responsibilities of agencies and so make it easier to hold them to account for their performances.

6. To secure better value for taxpayers' money by introducing a new funding structure for social care.

(Department of Health, 1989, para 1.11)

In summary, the White Paper was grounded in the principles of:

- a move from residential to home-based care;

- a move from *service-led* to *needs-led* provision, on an individual and population level;

- social services changing their role to *enablers*, from being traditionally direct providers of services, which became known a the *purchaser/provider* split;

- the stimulation of independent-sector markets in response to identified need.

The National Health Service and Community Care Act 1990

The NHS and Community Care Act of 1990 did not consolidate other legislation (as had been the case with the Children Act of 1989), but provided a framework for the organisation and delivery of services under existing legislation (the National Assistance Act 1948,

The Health Services and Public Health Act 1968, the Chronically Sick and Disabled Persons Act 1970, the National Health Act 1977 and the Mental Health Act 1983). As has been shown above, it sought to alter the balance of care in four fundamental directions, namely:

- from institutional care to community-based care (note that community-based does not mean residential care in this case);

- from supply-led, provider-dominated services, towards needs-led, purchaser-dominated services;

- from public-sector to independent-sector provision;

- from NHS to local government responsibilities and funding (with the cost implications of this shift).

The Act gave local authorities the responsibility to assess the needs of those seeking care and for making plans to meet the needs identified in partnership with user and carers.

Local authorities were given commissioning powers, including joint commissioning with health, with the stipulation that 85 per cent of the consequent spending should be used to buy services from the independent sector. Thus, central government, whilst transferring funds from the Department of Social Security to local social services departments, was determining that the monies should be used to stimulate the independent and private sector.

The social work role and community care: The rise of the care manager

We're not social workers anymore, we're just care managers.

(cited in Lloyd, 2002, p159)

Even before the implementation of the legislation (in 1993), the trend towards 'Community Care' had been gathering pace, with the dramatic reductions in hospital-based services for a range of service user groups. As Douglas and Philpot noted (1998, p99):

> between 1988 and 1994, the number of National Health Service beds for elderly mentally frail people reduced from 26,500 to 18,200. The number of long-term care beds for elderly people reduced from 55,600 to 37,500 over the same period.

We can thus see that people were leaving hospital, but were they living in the community as such, or in care or nursing homes which were 'in the community' only in as much as they were not hospitals?

The key role in determining the range and location of services offered was to be that of the social worker, employed by the lead agency, the local authority social services department. Significantly, the social work role was redefined as 'Care Management', and was seen as pivotal to achieving the Community Care objectives by aiming to:

- respond flexibly and sensitively to the needs of users and carers;

- allow a range of options;

- intervene no more than is necessary to foster independence;

- prevent deterioration;

- concentrate on those with greatest needs (Department of Health, 1990, para 3.5).

It is unlikely that social workers, informed by their traditions and values, would dissent from these aims. However, the quote from Lloyd at the beginning of this section indicates a profound mistrust and level of dissatisfaction with the change in role from social worker to care manager. Phillips (1992) suggests that the social work role has become purely bureaucratic, aimed at a safekeeping service for the most 'needy'.

The critique of community care policy

1. A primary concern about shifting the focus from a 'medical' to a 'social' model – whilst welcomed in principle by social workers and, most significantly, by users and carers – was the change from a universal, free service (under the NHS) to a selective, means-tested service, run by local authorities. This meant that a number of services carried a price tag.

2. Of an equally problematic nature, and linked to the issue of funding, was the matter of the assessment of need. The definition of need, according to Practice Guidance, is *...the acceptable level of social independence or quality of life, as defined by the particular care agency or authority* (SSI/SWSG, 1991, p12). Thus, the concept of need is a relative one, determined by factors such as the availability of resources. As a consequence, the principle of developing a needs-led service was rapidly enveloped by agencies' anxiety of revealing unmet need, with a consequence that tighter eligibility criteria were established to limit the expression of need.

3. The term 'Community Care' could be interpreted as 'Care *in* the Community' or 'Care *by* the Community'. Pinker's submission to the Barclay Report (1982) (see Chapter 7) – which had been doubtful as to the extent that the community actually 'cared' – came to be seen as prophetic, particularly in relation to the experiences of people with learning disabilities and mental health issues. Nevertheless, Means and Smith (1994, p3) quote the White Paper *Growing Older* (DHSS, 1981), which stated that *care in the community must increasingly mean care by the community*. In reality, this meant care of those in need by relatives, usually women, and not by 'the community' in any sense beyond kinship relationships. Jack (1998, p23) cites the numerous studies that confirmed the degree of mental distress, such as anxiety and depression, experienced by up to 40 per cent of carers (Moriarty et al., 1993) and that 35 per cent felt they would be unable to carry on, given the lack of support (Alzheimer's Disease Society, 1993).

4. The emphasis on the 'mixed economy of care', coupled with the necessary stimulation of private markets to provide the necessary range of services, sat uneasily with the values of many social workers, schooled in the traditions of public service, and suspicious of the profit-based 'caring'.

Contemporary directions

The cornerstone of the current policy for services for older people is the *Putting People First* vision. As its introduction asserts:

> *People want, and have the right to expect, services with dignity and respect at their heart. Older people. disabled people and people with mental health problems demand equality of citizenship in every aspect of their lives, from housing to leisure. The vast majority of people want to live in their own homes for as long as possible.*

> (Department of Health, 2007, p1)

Through the enactment of this vision, services and interventions should ensure that people, irrespective of illness or disability, are supported to:

- live independently;

- stay healthy and recover quickly from illness;

- exercise maximum control over their own life and where appropriate the lives of their family members;

- sustain a family unit which avoids children being required to take on inappropriate caring roles;

- participate as active and equal citizens, both economically and socially;

- have the best possible quality of life irrespective of illness or disability;

- retain maximum dignity and respect.

> (Department of Health, 2007, pp2–3)

Putting People First recognises that services across transport, leisure, education, health, housing, community safety and the criminal justice system and access to information and advice are vital to ensuring people's independence and overall quality of life. In fact, these services may be of greater significance than those more usually associated with responses to older people, such as health and social care.

Although this chapter has focused on services for older people, the community care reforms pertain to the whole range of services users under the umbrella of adult care. In Chapter 8 we will look at some of the current challenges facing social workers in this arena of practice.

Before we leave this section, it is worth revisiting a consistent theme of the book – that the consistent clear messages from service users must transcend and supersede concerns about profesional structures, boundaries and identities.

The following statement from an older person is quoted by David Behan who as Chief Inspector at the Commission for Social Care Inspection (CSCI) stated:

The main point is that you should be able to make your own decisions, depending on what level you feel safe at. You spend your whole life making decisions about things, your work, your relationships, your children, you don't want to suddenly give up that responsibility because you're older.

(Behan, 2005)

In order to realise these aspirations, the government published the Green Paper *Independence, Well Being and Choice* (Department of Health, 2005a) which presaged a major reform of service delivery systems in relation to all vulnerable adult groups.

As we noted at the end of Chapter 4 (*Working with People with Learning Difficulties*). The principle of *Personalisation* is at the heart of the transformation programme for all aspects of adult social care. Systems for self-directed support, the *In Control* approach, and the use of direct payments and individual budgets have all been put in place to create user-led structures. The driving ideological conviction is that real improvements for individuals flow as a consequence of personal control. The implications of these changes are discussed further in Chapter 8. Suffice to say at this stage that the *Putting People First* agenda (Department of Health, 2007) envisages a situation in which people who use services take greater control over their lives, meaning that the role of social workers in adult services may move away from assessment and more towards safeguarding, advocacy, and brokerage.

Listening to people: Human testimony

We will end this chapter by summarising the testimonies of older people who partici-pated in a *New Dynamics of Ageing* study. When recounting their often negative, degrading and humiliating experiences as users of health and social care services, they were able to identify what they found helpful in terms of good or best practice. They appreciated the following.

- *Awareness of others of a need for help.*

- *Being offered help without having to ask.*

- *Awareness of the impact of illness on the person and their sense of who they are.*

- *Acts of kindness and thoughtful gestures.*

- *Respectful attitudes and courteousness.*

- *Being treated as an intelligent person with a part to play in treatment and care.*

- *Being treated as an individual with their own family history, preferences, fears and beliefs.*

- *Being helped at the right pace. Not going too fast.*

- *Having someone help you make difficult decisions – with honesty and respect.*

(from Lloyd et al., 2011, p3)

When considering the notion of Independent Living, the academic and activist Peter Beresford said *What I want to look at isn't rocket science. It is much more complex than that* (Beresford and Hasler, 2009, p52). Working with people is complex because it is subtle, and delicate and unpredictable. It cannot be standardised and routinised, but needs to be negotiated with each unique individual: which is exactly what the older people in the study were saying above.

CHAPTER SUMMARY

In Chapter 6 we have considered contemporary social work through the responses to Hannah, a 70-year-old woman with specific care needs. The 'care' of older people accounts for the largest number of service users within the social care/social work orbit, and current changes in practice thinking have been introduced.

FURTHER READING

Crawford, K and Walker, J (2008) *Social work and older people*. 2nd edition. Exeter: Learning Matters.

A readable source that helps the student and beginning practitioner understand the core issues for practice with older people.

McDonald, A (1999) *Understanding community care*. London: Macmillan.

A clear and accessible guide to working with older people, disabled people, mental health service users and around issues of HIV/Aids and substance abuse.

Means, R and Smith, R (1998) *From poor law to community care*. 2nd edition. Bristol: The Policy Press.

A comprehensive study of welfare services for older people covering the period from 1939 to 1971.

Chapter 7

Formalising and consolidating social work as a profession

Every social worker is almost certain to be an agitator

(Clement Attlee, 1920)

All professions are conspiracies against the laity

(George Bernard Shaw, 1911)

ACHIEVING A SOCIAL WORK DEGREE

This chapter will help you to develop the following capabilities, to the appropriate level, from the **Professional Capabilities Framework**.

- **Professionalism.** Identify and behave as a professional social worker committed to professional development.
- **Values and ethics.** Apply social work ethical principles and values to guide professional practice.
- **Diversity.** Recognise diversity and apply anti-discriminatory and anti-oppressive principles in practice.
- **Justice.** Advance human rights and promote social justice and economic well-being.
- **Knowledge.** Apply knowledge of social sciences, law and social work practice theory.
- **Rights, judgement and economic well-being.** Use judgement and authority to intervene with individuals, families and communities to promote independence, provide support and prevent harm, neglect and abuse.
- **Critical reflection and analysis.** Apply critical reflection and analysis to inform and provide a rationale for professional decision-making.
- **Contexts and organisations.** Engage with, inform and adapt to changing contexts that shape practice. Operate effectively within your own organisational frameworks and contribute to the development of services and organisations. Operate effectively within multi-agency and interprofessional settings.
- **Professional leadership.** Take responsibility for the professional learning and development of others through supervision, mentoring, assessing, research, teaching, leadership and management.

See Appendix 1 for the Professional Capabilities Faremwork diagram.

This chapter will also introduce you to the following standards as set out in the 2008 social work subject benchmark statement.

4.3 Defining principles.
5.1 Subject knowledge and understanding.
5.1.2 The service delivery context.
5.1.3 Values and ethics.

Social work's first formations

Although we have considered social work in relation to a number of specific service user groups, and have offered a brief survey of historical and contemporary practice issues, we need to return to social work as a generic concept, to chart its development from a predominantly charitable, voluntary activity to its current position as a graduate-based profession, operating within a mixed economy of welfare, with its own regulatory body, a process of registration, and a code of practice, although, and paradoxically, such developments now coincide with an era of professional uncertainty in terms of role, purpose and identity.

We have seen from the preceding chapters that the activity we might today recognise as 'social work' emerged in a largely piecemeal fashion, and at different times in relation to different service user groups. By the end of the nineteenth century in Britain the following people were broadly employed in 'social work', although barely any would define themselves as 'social workers': settlement workers, charities officers, superintendents in institutions, school board 'men', police court missioners, NSPCC inspectors, and Children's Visitors, who were employed by the Workhouse Unions, and who supervised the 'boarding out' of children. In modern language, we can thus see the existence of community workers, probation officers, child care workers and NSPCC inspectors, but little else.

Of all these quasi-professional groups, the probation service had been established with the clearest mandate. The Probation Offenders Act 1907, and later the Criminal Justice Act of 1925, permitted and then required the appointment of probation officers to *advise, assist and befriend* probationers, taking up the work initiated on a voluntary basis by the Police Court Missionaries, who had been funded by such organisations as the Church of England Temperance Society. Rooted in a belief that the way to salvation from the evils of criminality was through temperance (a renouncing of alcohol), the Probation Service is a clear example of how legislation in fact led the way to the formalisation of social work, and the transfer of activity from the voluntary to the state sector.

A further group to emerge was hospital almoners – note the use of the title that is rooted in alms-giving – who were originally employed to determine which patients of charity-supported hospitals could afford to pay, but their role eventually expanded into a counselling and social aid service (Clarke, 1993). The first almoner had been appointed at the Royal Free Hospital, London, in 1895. Mary Stewart, who had been schooled in the theory of the Charity Organisation Society (COS), was charged with the task of *checking (controlling) out-patient abuse* (Willmott, 1975, p1), using the conventional COS methods of encouraging thrift and self-help. In 1922 the Institute of Hospital Almoners was formed, and the role increasingly became one of collecting payments for treatment. By 1929, with the founding of the Association of Psychiatric Social Workers, health-related social work established a base in both general and psychiatric medicine. (Eventually, the function of almoners was to change dramatically during the Second World War, when many of them became Regional Welfare Officers, dealing with the social problems arising from the Blitz and from the evacuation of children.)

Most other 'social workers' were employed in voluntary family welfare agencies and as moral welfare workers. We have seen that those so defined as social workers withdrew from the debates about structural poverty (and the possible responses associated with

93

settlements, community development or political agitation for welfare reform), and attempted to develop a professional identity in specific settings, as probation officers, psychiatric/mental health officers and as hospital almoners.

Ending the Poor Law (1929)

In 1929 the Local Government Act abolished Boards of Guardians, and transferred responsibility for Poor Law infirmaries to local authorities. Although a transfer of responsibility indeed took place, and overnight the Poor Law Guardians disappeared, the theoretical ideas that had driven their operation slipped quietly into the workings of the local authorities. Such ideas applied equally to services for adults with mental health needs, with learning disabilities and with offending behaviours. The goal was to reform by enabling the 'client' to be given a fresh start by being dislocated from family, friends and community. Although predicated upon traditional moral precepts of righteousness, these nascent social work bodies – working at the interface between the individual and institutions – were ripe for the professional status that accrues from the acquisition of a more scientifically based theory base.

The emerging theory for practice

The COS was still highly influential in social work's formation and development.

> *With its stern insistence on individualism and self-help, its rejection of state aid except in a minor role and its distinction between deserving and undeserving poor, it might seem to epitomise all that was worst in the Victorian attitude to the poor. Yet despite these attitudes, most historians of social policy agree that the COS had a valuable contribution to make.*

(Rose, 1972, p26)

This 'contribution' (although contested by Steadman-Jones, 1976 and Jones, 1983) lay in the development of family casework and in the training of social workers. In effect, the COS served to position casework – with its belief in individualism as the cause and the solution to problems – as an antithesis to structural reform, critically characterised as 'socialism'.

> *...casework is the outer sign of an inner faith – a faith which rests upon the belief in the individual and with the capacity of the individual to carve out his own life... casework then, becomes the antithesis of mass socialistic measures.*

(Milnes, 1929, cited in Clarke, 1993, p11)

Such a creed, still strongly influenced by religious morality, was buttressed by the importation of psychological theories. In the early part of the twentieth century social work formalised its activities in the wake of developments in other professions. The works of the child psychiatrist Donald Winnicott, and of Clare Winnicott, who was head of the childcare course at the London School of Economics, were highly influential in defining 'casework' as the *modus operandi* for social workers. Psychiatric social workers were as likely to be engaged with children in the Child Guidance Clinics (which emerged in the 1920s and 1930s), as they were to be working in the asylums – probably more so. *The maladjusted child* emerged as a label within the school system, leading not only to a broadening of the scope of 'special education' beyond physical disability and sensory impairment, but also to increased referrals into the Child Guidance arena.

In considering the development of social work theory, Jordan (1984) identifies the transition from the moral absolute of *client self-determination* as upheld by the Victorians, to the 'realisation' from the emerging social sciences that people were not free agents, but were shaped in their thoughts, beliefs and actions by psychological and social forces. Therefore, by the 1920s, *'self-determination' became a* psychological aim *rather than an overriding principle'* (Jordan, 1984, p49). Thus developed the psychological branch of social work, much informed by psychoanalytic, psychotherapeutic and psychosocial theoretical frameworks. Given the fragmented nature of social work practice (as identified above) and the absence of an explicit body of knowledge to define practice, it was inevitable that two branches of work – psychiatric social work, and work with children – would seek intellectual and professional prestige by the adoption of theory from psychiatry and psychology.

> *Most people who became social workers still did so for religious and humanitarian reasons, to help others less fortunate than themselves and to try to repay the debts they owed for happy childhoods or privileged educations. Lacking the previous age's social and moral underpinnings to their altruism, they found in the psychological approach a kind, enabling and uncensorious rationale for their relationships, with seemingly exciting opportunities for liberating latent or crushed human potential.*

(Jordan, 1984, p56)

ACTIVITY 7.1

This exercise invites you to refer back to Activity 1.2. How can we conceive of people's motivations to engage in social work today? How different are they from Jordan's characterisation of those in a previous era?

COMMENT

Social work organisations today offer career structures, promotion prospects, relatively good incomes, relative employment security, pensions and associated benefits, and yet there is a recruitment crisis. Without a theoretical or an ideological commitment to the activity, the financial benefits are clearly not sufficient motivation. Motivation would seem to be driven by a combination of political/ideological, rational/technical or moral/ethical/religious sets of convictions. If the early years of social work philanthropy were rooted in the moral/ethical/religious tradition, then the first period of professionalisation, and social work's interest in psychological theories, indicated a rational/technical adherence. We will see that the challenge to social work came from the political/ideological movements of the 1960s.

The beginnings of qualifications and training

If social work was to gain public respectability, it had to define for itself formal training and accreditation systems. In 1895 the warden of the Women's University Settlement set up a joint lecture series between the Settlement, the COS and the National Union of Women Workers. The subjects of the emerging curriculum included: *the Poor Law, Charity, Almsgiving, the Family and Character, Thoroughness, and Personal Work* (see Smith, 1965, p21). The COS special committee on training in 1898 said *they would like to see in society the nucleus of a future university for the study of social science in which all those who undertake philanthropic work would desire to graduate* (ibid, p27). (Coincidentally, this was the year in which the first US training programme was jointly established by the New York COS and Columbia University.)

Professor Urwick, writing in the Charity Organisation Review of 1903, said of the social work practitioner: *his methods must be made scientific, his practice must be founded on a true knowledge of principle of law: and he, the practitioner, must acquire these methods*, and in the same year the COS developed the school of sociology in London. The curriculum had elements of social theory and administration, including social and economic history, social philosophy and the principles underlying social work. In essence, the focus of study was social administration: the management of the emerging welfare services. Such a perspective accords with the high public esteem in which the leading social workers were held. They had sat on the Royal Commission on the Poor Laws (see Chapter 2), and appeared to herald a role for social work as a profession that would shape the future of Britain's welfare policy. In 1912 the school of sociology was amalgamated with the social science department at the London School of Economics; and the Liverpool School of Social Science was started in 1904 jointly between the university, a settlement and the Liverpool COS.

A troubled relationship emerged between the proponents of training with placements and the purist academics. The schism continued until the establishment of the first mental health course in 1929, based upon an American training model. There were no grants for students, apart from the Home Office decision from 1936 to fund the training of Probation Officers, and the majority of students were – inevitably – drawn from the middle classes and those able to support themselves as students. They were also predominantly women, carrying on the tradition of philanthropic visiting and the COS role. However, this was not exclusively the case. The emerging labour movement also prompted the involvement of those committed to social reform and community development. Seen as *idealistic young people* by Jordan (1984, p45), they included amongst their number such future leading Labour politicians as Hugh Dalton and Clement Atlee.

The emergence of state social work

The search for professionalism needed a theoretical knowledge base to support the claim of expertise. Faced with the choice between three possible directions – social planning and policy; the emerging psychological approaches; and law enforcement in relation to offending behaviours and school attendance – the latter two gained supremacy, one in theory and one in practice. Whilst theoretical training drew heavily upon the various psychological approaches, an increasing number of social workers became employed in state agencies, with associated powers and duties. The expansion of such employment opportunities coincided, according to Foucault (1977), with the recognition by government of social work's capacity to control populations... those troublesome to the social order.

In the next era – after 1945 – social work was to move centre stage as part of the post-war reconstruction and from the creation of the modern welfare state, partly as a result of its work during the war period itself. According to Younghusband (1978), social work *leapt from the margins to the mainstream*. Given today's image of public services, it is somewhat remarkable to note that, in 1965, Richard Titmuss (1965, p85) was able to make the following comment:

> *During the last twenty years, whenever the British people have identified and investigated a social problem, there has been a national call for more social work and more trained social workers.*

After years of slow development – some might even say stagnation – social work had indeed moved to centre stage in the acting out of the new welfare drama.

In 1947 Younghusband's report on the employment and training of social workers offered the following list of *forms of social work*: almoning, child care, church work, colonial social welfare, community centre and settlement work, community organisation, family casework, information and advice services, moral welfare, personnel management, work with the physically and mentally handicapped, probation and other services connected with the penal system, psychiatric social work, youth leadership and social work in the civil service. This is an extensive and wide-ranging purview, and many elements of the list (such as youth work, personnel management, advice services, community work) established their own professional organisations and associated training and qualifications frameworks. Younghusband's description of social workers – mainly women – as *badly paid, overworked and lacking a sense of common professional identity* probably rang true for all working groups in the list, and would prompt little dissent as a comment on the lot of many social workers today.

The core groupings of social workers were located in five specific settings.

- Children's departments (working to the Children Act 1948), providing services to children, young people and families.

- Welfare departments (working to the National Assistance Act 1948), providing services to older people and those with disabilities.

- Health departments (employing mental health officers, working to the Mental Health Act 1959), linked to psychiatric services.

- Health departments, employing lady almoners, and medical social workers from 1965.

- Probation departments, working with offenders in prison, in courts and in the community.

According to Seed (1973), a valid question by the late 1940s could have been *Does the welfare state make social work redundant?* In many respects, this question echoes the beliefs of the Webbs and the Fabians from 50 years earlier. Their 'dream' of a comprehensive welfare system having now been realised, the logical presumption had to follow that the need for individualised, personal welfare would recede and fade away. To many, this question was fundamental. The hopes of many architects of post-war reconstruction was that the personal ills – arising from poverty, destitution, homelessness and desperation so evident in the inter-war Depression years and so palpably not addressed by the old Poor Law – would be significantly reduced, if not eradicated, by the great innovations of the comprehensive welfare state. This question leads us to further consider what is social work in the context of thinking about what kind of social system – if any – could make social work unnecessary. As we have seen in previous chapters, particularly in Chapter 2, social work had been primarily concerned with the personal ills that appear to have arisen from public neglect – from the consequences of mass unemployment, of poverty, of ill health, of inadequate housing or even homelessness, of destitution in old age. Given the deep-rooted nature of these difficulties, it was all too easy for the radical welfare reformers to see the roots of violence, alcohol misuse and child maltreatment as being primarily caused by the absence of welfare, and therefore solvable by the new institutions of the welfare state.

So what was seen as the role of social work in this period of post-war reconstruction? In one literal sense there was no role, as the term 'social work' was absent from the welfare vocabulary, but that is to ignore the clear role defined in the new legislative framework that came on the back of the major welfare reforms.

The meaning of casework

Throughout this post-war period social work – in its fragmented and specialist arenas – continued to espouse a theoretical basis for practice that spanned the disparate arenas of practice. This was the creed of social casework.

> *Social casework is a personal service, provided by qualified workers for those who require skilled help in resolving some personal or family problem. Its aim is to relieve stress, both material and emotional, and to help the client to achieve a realistic adjustment to his social circumstances and mutual satisfaction in his personal relationships. The caseworker seeks to do this by means of a careful study of the client in his family and social setting, and of his problem: by the establishment of a cooperative relationship with him, in which his own capacity for dealing with his problem is increased, and by the mobilisation of such other resources or professional aid as might be appropriate.*

(Davidson, 1965)

Although the term 'casework' has been long abandoned, Davidson's quote reveals a remarkable degree of continuity with present conceptualisations of social work practice.

A significant text, long held as the exposition on the essence of post-war social work practice, is *The Casework Relationship* by Biestek (1961).

It is worth reflecting upon a number of key statements in this defining book by Biestek (1961). These include:

- the relationship is the soul of casework (p134);

- a good relationship is necessary not only for the perfection but also the essence of the casework service in every setting (p19);

- casework (is) a practical living out of a true democracy's philosophy of the dignity and worth of the person (p135).

ACTIVITY **7.2**

Davidson's definition of casework contains a few key terms and phrases (in the left-hand column). Are the same terms used today, or are there different – but equivalent – terms? Note down what they might be in the right hand column

Davidson's model of casework (1965)	Contemporary model of case management
Personal service	
Realistic adjustment	
Careful study	
Client	
Cooperative relationship	
Increased capacity	
Mobilisation of resources	

COMMENT

In a later text Butrym (1976) sets out Biestek's core values as:

- *acceptance and empathy;*

- *non-judgemental attitude;*

- *individualisation and respect for persons;*

- *purposeful expression of feelings or emotion;*

- *controlled emotional involvement;*

- *confidentiality;*

- *client self-determination.*

The reform of social services: Seebohm (1968)

As noted above, children's departments had been established in 1948 under the Children Act of that year and, by 1950, the majority of social workers were employed in local authorities. Mental health officers and hospital-based social workers remained employed by health authorities, whilst those working with adults in the community were employed in welfare departments (taking over from the Poor Law post-1945).

Social work was conducted by a disparate collection of fragmented public, private and charitable agencies, with workers being trained and qualified through the auspices of specialist bodies. The government therefore established a committee under Sir Frederic Seebohm to investigate the situation. The stated terms of reference of the Seebohm Committee were:

> to review the organisation and responsibilities of the local authority personal social services in England and Wales, and to consider what changes are desirable to secure an effective family service.

The report recommended the establishment of a universal and integrated service based on local authority social services departments. The enactment of the report resulted in the following key measures.

- Each local authority to appoint a Director of the social services department, accountable to a Social Services Committee.

- The unification of services in the new departments, breaking down fragmentation of service between children's, health and welfare committees and associated departments.

- The establishment of generic training to be developed through the Central Council for Education and Training of Social Workers (CCETSW).

The task, in a nutshell, was to provide an *effective, family-oriented, community-based service, available and accessible to all*. Consequently, the integration of all departments in Scotland, and all apart from Probation in England and Wales, occurred on 1 April 1971, following the passing of the Local Authority Social Services Act in the previous year. In reality, the Seebohm Report had advocated a whole raft of other measures, including the creation of a service accountable to local communities, and dedicated to promoting the well-being of whole communities, not merely social casualties (Colton et al., 2001, p5). Such a vision was significantly influenced by the commitment to Social Planning as represented by the 1960s trends in Community Development, the establishment of New Town Corporations, in slum clearance and social housing schemes. The appeal of a universal service to respond to universal needs finds echoes in more recent assertions that all members of society require care:

> for a society to be judged as a morally admirable society it must, among other things, adequately provide for care of its members.

> (Tronto, 1993, p126)

The newly amalgamated social services departments, immediately post-Seebohm in 1971, have been seen retrospectively by many authors as the brief period of optimism and 'certainty' within British social work, yet as Clare (2000, p39) recalls, staff struggled to operationalise the generic principles: were practitioners to do everything, or to continue with previous specialisms but to coordinate into an integrated service?

In spite of their reservations – grounded in the voice of experience – the public projection was positive and enthusiastic. The Seebohm Report saw social work, community work and welfare work as equally valid and important. Social work was conceptualised as primarily a local government function, offering an integrated service from *the cradle to the grave*. For the Seebohm authors (1968), residential provision was to be seen as a *community home* rather than as a stigmatising response to individual inadequacy or indigence, and it was therefore anticipated that the new generic, professional departments would spearhead the development of community-based alternatives to the incarceration of thousands of people in Victorian asylums, hospitals, institutions and prisons.

The optimistic spirit envisaged a bright future for social work, in which traditional casework – with its emphasis on the individual helping relationship – would sit alongside groupwork and community work as equal members of a triad of methods and service delivery systems.

The Consumer's Guide to Personal Social Services, originally published in 1967 and updated after the Seebohm reforms, offered the following vision (note the language of the extract):

> ...if you need the help a social worker might give over your mentally subnormal toddler and your difficult teenage daughter, and your frail or senile grandmother, or your own personal problems – whatever they might be – you are rather more likely to see just one local authority social worker instead of the two or three you might have done before.

(Willmott, 1975, p39)

As noted by Parton (2001), the original conception of the new social services departments envisaged a progressive, universal service *available to all and with wide community support*. Bell and Wilson (2003) develop this idea and suggest:

> it depended on a cooperation between local authorities and parents, and reflected the view that the state and family could work together to ensure children had the appropriate conditions in which to develop.

Of course, with hindsight, it can be recognised that the post-1970 commitment to a unified public welfare delivery system is a form of institutionalising of caring in itself – a force with which service user groups have engaged in a struggle for liberation for the past decades. After all, the state was explicitly setting out its stall as the sole provider of care: if you needed residential care as an older person, you went into a council-run 'old people's home'; if you, a person with learning disabilities, lived at home with your family, you attended the local adult training centre, run by social services, and if you could not live at home, for whatever reason, you lived in a special hospital.

From our current position, we can see this provision as service-led – dogmatic in its application, and oppressive in that the service user had to fit the service, not the other way round. Yet, at the time, the commitment to state welfare was seen as a necessary and welcome response to the changes in family, community and social relationships that had emerged in post-war modern British society. As Shakespeare (2000, p54) suggests:

The post-war welfare state led to an institutionalisation of society's caring responsibilities through local authority social service departments, it being recognised that social mobility and the changing family had created the requirement for society as a whole to support people in need.

If the new social services departments were to be successful, they had to be supported by an education and training framework to produce the generic workforce in sufficient numbers and of the required calibre.

Towards social work training and qualifications

Before looking at the new integrated social work qualification that came in post-Seebohm, we need a brief reminder of the situation before 1970. As with the primacy of child care work after 1948, so it was to be expected that the training for child care officers dominated the social work scene.

The first major development in social work recruitment and training occurred in child care after the [Second World] war. The new child care officers were seen in many respects as boarding out officers whose principal task was to find and supervise foster homes and thereby reduce the dependency upon residential homes.

(Parker, 1988, p6)

With regard to training, Younghusband (1947) highlighted a range of concerns.

Training was highly academic, with fieldwork tacked on as a necessary but uninte-grated extra. The prestigious training offered by the Institute of Almoners (hospital social workers) had no examination. Probation training suffered from *the poor educational standards of many applicants* and psychiatric social workers were a *tiny minority in a world of their own*. Returning briefly to the children's departments, it is worth recalling the qualities identified by the Curtis Committee (1946) as making an ideal candidate to become a children's officer in the new children's departments. She or he would be a graduate, with social science qualifications, experience with children and good administra-tive ability. Surprisingly, yet perhaps tellingly, the committee never mentioned the term 'social worker'.

Training remained as fragmented as services until 1954, when the first applied social studies (generic) course was introduced at the London School of Economics (LSE) – equally applicable to medical social workers, probation officers, child care officers and general caseworkers. However, right up to the end of the 1960s, many child care officers possessed the dedicated qualification of Home Office Letter of Recognition in Child Care.

By 1971 the statutory body CCETSW was established to regularise and standardise social work training in Britain, and the generic Certificate of Qualification in Social Work (CQSW) was introduced in 1972. Four years later, CCETSW introduced the Certificate in Social Service (CSS), a qualification designed to enable those in the residential and day care sector, in particular, to gain access to qualification through an employment-based route. The two modes of qualification – CQSW and CSS – were finally merged by the introduction of the Diploma in Social Work (DipSW) in 1989, with the first DipSWs being awarded in 1991.

Certainly, there was a rapid increase in the number of people employed as social workers in personal social services settings.

Number of social workers employed in personal social services

1954	1971	1976	% change per year (1971–76)
3,000	10,346	21,182	20.8%

(*Source: NALGO, 1989, cited in Clarke, 1993, p53*)

Our current debates are about specialism versus genericism, competence versus understanding, training versus education, yet little attention is paid to what might be called the personal qualities of the practitioner. Younghusband (1981) believed that a social worker's chief tool was her or his own personality: that social workers need to develop a *capacity for living* in order to stimulate healing and growth in others.

By the 1970s social work had come to see itself as a 'cradle-to-grave' service, with an increasing interest in social work practice theory, models and methods – systems and unitary theory, family therapy, groupwork, community work – that reflected this concern with the 'social' nature of the work, as distinct from rescuing or treating the individual (which had been the focus of early moral casework and then traditional, psychodynamic casework). The Seebohm Report had charged the fledgling social services departments with the duty to *enable the greatest possible number of individuals to act reciprocally, giving and receiving service for the well-being of the whole community* (Seebohm, 1968, para. 2). Social work was seen essentially as a political activity, with the potential to change and renew individuals, within the context of their families, their social groups and their communities.

The basis of critical practice

The 1960s had witnessed the development of key social perspectives that significantly affected and influenced social work's sense of self.

- The rediscovery of poverty, through various studies which questioned the 'never had it so good' complacency of post-war Britain (e.g. Coates and Silburn, 1970; Townsend, 1979).

- The burgeoning critical literature of institutional dysfunction as noted in previous chapters (Goffman, 1961; Townsend, 1962; Robb, 1967; Miller and Gwynne, 1972).

- A critical analysis of psychiatry (and its corollary of anti-psychiatry) based on the work of Laing and Esterson, 1964; Cooper, 1968; and particularly Thomas Szasz:

  Formerly, when religion was strong and science weak, men mistook magic for medicine; now, when science is strong and religion weak, men mistake medicine for magic.

  (Szasz, 1971, 1973)

- The consciousness of social work as having developed a professionalising imperative that separated it – as with other professions – from its service users (Foucault, 1977; Illich, 1977).

- An honest recognition that it had been the voluntary organisations (Child Poverty Action Group, the Disablement Income Group, Shelter) which had engaged in effective campaigning regarding family poverty, disability rights and homelessness respectively, not the local authority social workers (Seed, 1973, p100).

- A critical self-awareness, wherein social workers began to question their own role as being the 'iron fist in the velvet glove', the acceptable face of state repression and as agents of social control.

Beyond the simplistic position of rejecting social work out of hand, a 'middle way' between the casework traditionalists and the Marxist critics looked for an integration between care for the individual whilst addressing broader issues.

Harriet Bartlett (1970, cited in Baraclough et al., 1996, p63) observed that *in recent years there has been growing recognition of…the need for social work to broaden its efforts in the direction of social policy [and] social planning*, and questioned whether there was a distinction between *people helpers* and *systems changers*. Such a distinction foresaw the potential development of radical social work, and the schism between social work and community work.

Cree (2003, p2) recalls that:

> *during the 1970s and 1980s, radical social workers drew attention to the 'social control' aspects of social work practice, and argued instead for a social work practice which aligned itself more fully with service users and with the trade union movement (Langan, 1993). There was a feeling that the only legitimate social work was community social work or community development; all other kinds of social work were about maintaining the status quo and keeping poor people down.*

The period was characterised by the emerging recognition of the dialectic of the regulation and the emancipation of citizens. The radical critique from within, best exemplified by the establishment of the journal *Case Con* in 1970, and the development of a Marxist perspective on social work (Corrigan and Leonard, 1978), was eventually broadened and enhanced by feminist perspectives (Dominelli, 1989) and anti-racist social perspectives (Dominelli, 1988). In writing about the social worker strike of 1978, Philpot (2003, p34) similarly notes that radical social work's concern with working-class and trade union politics became replaced by a focus on the oppression of women and black people. The emerging awareness of these issues, and the acknowledgement of oppressions beyond the narrow confines of a traditional class-based analysis, was to ultimately contribute to the development of the umbrella term 'anti-oppressive practice', which is discussed later in this chapter. Citing concerns about the control of the individual through the forces of psychiatry as a 'trigger' for action, Douglas and Philpot (1998:15) summarise the radical social work beliefs as follows: *If psychiatry was a 'con', a means of control, so was social work practice as casework*. They note that radical social work's:

primary objection to casework was that casework saw problems rooted in the individual and personal failure rather than the wider social problems of unemployment, poor housing and poverty.

In fact, what radical social work really objected to was the tendency of traditional casework towards a process of *individualisation* – whilst celebrating the uniqueness of the individual, casework stood accused of failing to see the causes of difficulties as residing outside the individual, within the wider social structures.

In contrast radical social work, much informed by critical sociology, emphasised the importance of *deindividualisation*: seeking the connections between people in similar situations of poverty, deprivation, abuse, discrimination and alienation. Solutions were therefore to be found in community-based responses, in community action and in the mobilisation of potent challenges to existing political structures.

Modern social work practice eventually found a resolution between these two polar positions in the theoretical perspective of anti-oppressive practice, which we will discuss at the end of this chapter.

In spite of this debate, the ongoing reality of practice was fated to be shaped and determined by the public responses to the dramatic, to 'the tragic' – the perceived failures of social work to appropriately exercise its publicly charged (and publicly funded) duty to protect the most vulnerable in society, particularly children.

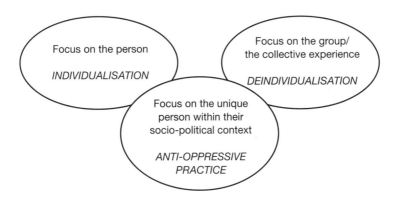

To many critical commentators, the optimistic vision after Seebohm was to be short-lived. Some would say it lasted a mere ten years, until the beginning of Thatcherism as a political philosophy in power. Others would chart the demise of the optimism to earlier factors. The oil crisis and political uncertainty of the early 1970s meant that the will to implement many of the Seebohm reforms was absent, and ultimately the challenge of creating a new, visionary form of social work became overtaken by events, not least being the death of Maria Colwell, as early as 1973, as we have noted in Chapter 3.

The Barclay Report

The catalogue of child abuse tragedies and inquiries had appeared to puncture the enthusiastic and optimistic bubble of generic social services post-Seebohm, and therefore a significant review of social workers and their function was established under the chairmanship of Peter Barclay. Almost anticipating the accelerating crisis that would flow, during the 1980s, from the ensuing high-profile child abuse inquiries, the Barclay Report helpfully recognised that:

Too much is expected of social workers. We load upon them unrealistic expectations and then complain when they do not live up to them. Social work is a relatively young profession. It has grown rapidly as the flow of legislation has greatly increased the range and complexity of its work.

(Barclay Committee, 1982, pvii)

In a less supportive vein, the report criticised social work practice in terms of its failure to engage in partnership arrangements with service users:

Social workers, it is said, frequently fail to explain the reasons for their decisions, fail to give clients essential information about their rights, and fail to make clear to their clients either the reason for their involvement or the extent of the powers which they possess.

(Barclay Committee, 1982, pp188–9)

Such criticisms would be taken forward into the principles for practice when working under the Children Act 1989 and the NHS and Community Care Act 1990. However, the Barclay Report is mostly remembered – and maintains a current and dynamic relevance – for the debate it generated about the ethos, values, purpose and location of services on offer. The debate flourished in the minority reports presented as appendices to the main report.

- Appendix B (by P Brown, R Hadley and K White) was entitled *A Case for Neighbourhood-based Social Work and Social Services* and was based upon evidence that about 80 per cent of social work referrals concern low-key, practical problems, which common sense and good organisation, together with local knowledge, can do much to overcome. The model took the Barclay recommendations further, arguing for local, neighbourhood, decentralised, responsive 'patch' based work, with social workers engaged in local communities, fusing community work, groupwork and social work – in other words, a return to the first principles of Younghusband, and a reaffirmation of the Seebohm vision of providing a much wider range of services.

- Appendix A (by R Pinker) argued that:

social work should be explicitly selective rather than universalist in focus, reactive rather than preventive in approach and modest in it objectives.

(Barclay Committee, 1982, p222)

Pinker saw social work's distinctiveness as residing in traditional specialist casework and counselling, and believed that the consequence of community social work would *prove detrimental to the quality of social work services* (Pinker, 1982, p262). The same author is most scathing about the concept of community:

It is one of the most stubbornly persistent illusions in social policy studies that eventually the concept of community – as a basis of shared values – will resolve our policy dilemmas...the idea that in a complex industrial society the notion of community could provide a basis for shared values (and hence for consistent social policy) is erroneous.

(Pinker, 1982, p224)

Pinker's scepticism about the mythical, almost Arcadian reverence applied by many social theorists to the idea of 'community' echoed Titmuss's view of community care:

Does it not conjure up a sense of warmth and human kindness, essentially personal and comforting, as loving as the wild flowers so enchantingly described by Lawrence in Lady Chatterley's Lover?

(Titmuss, 1968, p104).

Essentially, Pinker's approach accords with the idea that social work in western industrialised societies had arisen to care for those abandoned and rejected by 'the community', so to base professional roles upon the hope of resurrecting community responsibility would be misguided and even dangerous.

In summary, the case for neighbourhood work can be seen as:

- representing broad support for Barclay's community approach;

- advocating that social work should relate to smaller units of the population;

- the view that social work should focus on the neighbourhood and 'patch working';

- recommending that personal social services should devolve their organisation with greater decentralisation of power;

- the view that the goal should be to mobilise community participation in the organisation of personal social services.

Whereas the case against neighbourhood work can be summarised as:

- community social work is based upon unproven assumptions;

- the concept of 'community' is a myth;

- community social work will compromise the quality of social work;

- it will divert attention away from traditional casework, counselling;

- traditional casework is proven to work.

As Clarke (1993, p63) acknowledged, elements of both minority reports influenced social work thinking in the following decade (and to the present day).

ACTIVITY 7.3

On the basis of your understanding of social work so far, was the Barclay Report vision of community social work realistic and empowering, or naïve and unrealistic? Try to connect the above arguments to current notions of the 'Big Society' and Localism.

It is worth noting too that the Barclay Report also recorded the antipathy of most social workers to any form of residential care. The stigma attached to residential care was seen as:

> partly [to do] with the attitudes of those social workers who regard residential care as the [undesirable] last resort...the saying 'a bad home is better than a good institution' still has its adherents.

> (Barclay Committee, 1982, p57)

The consequence was the emergence of a mythical dualism – *Residential Care is Bad, Community Care is Good* – that informed much social work thought at the time. Yet, in spite of these beliefs, social workers willingly or otherwise contributed to a system that perpetuated institutional responses to need – whether in hospitals, nursing or residential homes. Such continued institutionalisation prompted a government-led review of service provision structures.

The business of social work

The advent of the New Right policy under the Conservative government after 1979 ushered in the *introduction of the contract culture in local government service provision* (Adams et al., 2002a, p334). The provision of many goods and services, once the preserve of local government as the automatic provider of welfare, was put out to tender under the ethos of compulsory competitive tendering. Although children's services were largely immune to this change, the community reforms as devised by Sir Roy Griffiths required local authorities to purchase a percentage of units of care from the private and voluntary sector. This became known as the *mixed economy of care*, supported by the Conservative conviction that public sector organisations should be subjected to the rigour of competition with other providers, from the independent and private sectors. The imported business culture required 'clients' to be redefined as 'customers' or 'consumers'. Distinct units within a social services department were to be seen as financial cost centres, working in accordance with business plans. Such developments are described by Adams (1996, p250):

> 'Managerialism' is the term used to refer to the inroads made by management into professional autonomy and power.

'Managerialism' related to the business culture that had arisen from the demands of the New Right for the breaking up of the state monopoly on service delivery, and that has subsequently been carried forward by the third way philosophy of the New Labour government.

In essence, the business culture has taken a lead from the reform of health provision, and has endorsed elements of internal markets, coupled with a business flow sequence:

ACTIVITY 7.4

Can the rigours of the business environment be applied to a public-sector service, such as social work?

COMMENT

Managerialism clearly generates profound emotional responses amongst social workers. At one level, managerialism appears to represent bureaucratic control over professional autonomy, yet at another level management is about accountability, the assurance of service delivery, the appropriate distribution of resources, the avoidance of waste, duplication, and the control of maverick or dangerous practices. As Payne (2002, p223) correctly observes:

> *...good service requires both control and freedom. The presence of both enables control to criticise excessive freedom, and the availability of freedom to criticise excessive control.*

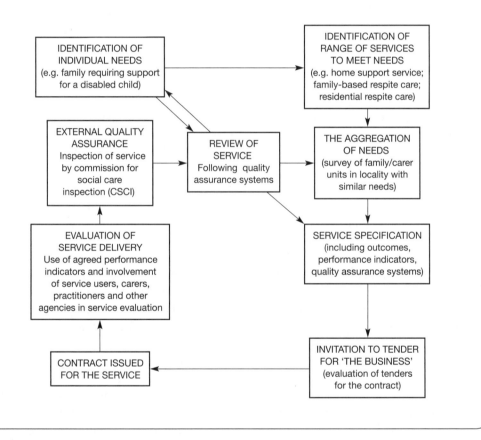

We can link this idea to Chapter 3, concerning the abuse of children in residential care settings. In one important respect, being managed is about being accountable, and accountability rests on the transparency of one's actions, one's service interventions. Institutional abuse has been fostered and incubated in the dark recesses of a social work legacy that celebrated confidentiality, the casework relationship, the notion of a 'private space' between the worker and 'client'. By contrast, the more that interactions are made public, and are open to scrutiny and peer review, the less opportunity there is for abuse or dangerous practice to occur. However, such optimism is to deny the power of group dynamics, and the propensity to cover up dangerous practices and abuses. In this situation, it is precisely because the worker exercises professional freedom outside the domain of being 'managed' that it is possible for poor practices to be challenged and – if no remedy is forthcoming – for 'whistleblowing' to ultimately expose concerns to a wider audience. This essential element of independence, the freedom of action beyond managerial dictat, is predicated upon the social work value base.

Anti-oppressive practice and valuing diversity

Social Work is a moral activity that requires practitioners to make and implement difficult decisions about human situations that involve the potential for benefit or harm...Although social work values have been expressed at different time in a variety of ways, at their core they involve showing respect for persons, honouring the diverse and distinctive organisations and communities that make up contemporary society and combating processes that lead to discrimination, marginalisation and social exclusion.

(Quality Assurance Agency for Higher Education, 2000, p12)

Whilst radical social work was essentially rooted in a white, implicitly male Marxist tradition, with its emphasis on working-class alienation and control (and a belief in the restorative powers of proletarian solidarity as a bulwark against capitalist oppression), the challenge from feminist and black perspectives resulted in the reframing of the meaning of social work values in the 1980s. Formerly, the value base of casework had had its prime origins in the work of Biestek (1961), with an emphasis on the value principles of individualisation, of being non-judgmental, of the purposeful expression of feelings, and of client acceptance. Whilst these values have had an enduring resonance, particularly in the varied fields of person-centred and humanistic counselling, and indeed in various manifestations of practice such as in the hospice movement, in bereavement work and in aspects of mental health practice, the statistically dominant social work agenda – working with children with families, working with people with learning disabilities, with older people – embraced a value base that allowed for client-centred interpersonal values to be fused with a more structural analysis of the service user's social circumstances. The work of Oliver (1990) explored the concept of the 'disabling society' – that people are not disabled by their physical actuality, but by the society that discriminates against them, legally, socially, structurally, financially, physically, emotionally, spiritually and intellectually. Thus, the informed purpose of the social worker, embracing anti-oppressive practice, is to engage with the individual in a manner that values her uniqueness, her experience, her expertise, her self-determination, whilst simultaneously and seamlessly challenging and confronting the features of the 'disabling society' that adversely affect and oppress not only the individual service user, but other people who constitute members of the same devalued group (e.g. people with disabilities, members of the deaf community, older people).

The key understanding needed here is to embrace and identify with the concept that – for example – all disabled people are subjected to oppression, yet each disabled person will have a unique experience of those oppressive processes. Modern social work practice rejects the dichotomy between individualisation and deindividualisation, and perhaps the essence of social work lies in its capacity to see *individuals as both unique in their own right* and *part of a broader web of social and political factors* (Thompson, 2005, pp121–2).

In theoretical terms, anti-oppressive practice enabled the practising social worker to synthesise the critical perspectives arising from the structural critique (deindividualisation), with the long-held values of human uniqueness and individual experience (individualisation).

Anti-oppressive practice, as adopted by CCETSW, came to be seen as an essential element of core social work values and practice, and clearly offered up opportunities for attacks on the profession by the New Right, charging social workers and their employers with an obsession with 'political correctness'. Nevertheless, the establishment of a value base that sought to synthesise the former dichotomy between the personal and the political (Halmos, 1968) and that required social workers to engage holistically with both the person and their circumstances – whilst at the same time recognising the processes of power dynamics at play in the 'helping relationship' – all contributed to an advance in social work practice.

Finally, the establishment of the definition of social work as offered by the International Federation of Social Work has served to legitimise the essentially political nature of practice:

> Social work has grown out of humanitarian and democratic ideals. Its value base is about respect for the dignity and equality and worth of all people. The main aim of social work is to alleviate poverty, to liberate vulnerable and oppressed people with the ultimate aim to promote social inclusion.

(International Federation of Social Work, 2001 cited in QAA, 2000, 2008, p1)

ACTIVITY 7.5

The politics of social work values

To what extent can you agree with the definition above?

Do you think the definition sits easily with the government's current expectations of social workers?

CHAPTER SUMMARY

In this chapter we have charted the development of social work over the past three decades, and paid particular attention to the formalisation of social work through training and qualifications, and influential reports, such as Seebohm and Barclay. The past decade has seen enormous change in terms of the experience of social work practitioners – what they do, what others expect of them, where they work, how they are trained, how they are monitored, evaluated, regulated. It is these elements of the 'What is social work?' question that will be examined in the next chapter.

Douglas, A and Philpot, T (1998) *Caring and coping: A guide to social services*. London: Routledge.

Although more than ten years old, this text is still readable and relevant. A helpful summary of major themes and issues still facing the development of professional social work and social care.

Lymbery, M and Butler, S (eds) (2004) *Social work ideals and practice realities*. Basingstoke: Palgrave Macmillan.

This edited text introduces the reader to a range of contemporary challenges and themes, such as organisational structures, managerialism, the mixed economy of provision and professional identity issues.

Somerville, P (2011) *Understanding community*. Bristol: Policy Press.

A detailed yet readable exploration of the concept of community, a critical analysis of the 'Big Society' and the relationship between social work and community development.

Chapter 8
Current services, practices and issues

Surveying the territory

As a new social work student, or perhaps as someone contemplating entering the profession, or even as a generally interested reader, it is essential to have a familiarity with the range and breadth of current social work practice across the service sectors. By way of summarising much of what has been discussed in this book so far, social work can be considered in a number of ways.

- Firstly, in relation to itself, by considering its sense of historical legacy, its values, identity and purpose.

- Secondly, by reference to the current policy, legal and procedural frameworks that define its role and function.

- Thirdly, through a consideration of what social workers actually do – their activities, their methods, their practices, using a social construction model (Parton and O'Byrne, 2000).

- Fourthly, by examining what others, particularly those defined as service users and their carers, want from social workers.

- Fifthly, by reviewing the research literature about social work's effectiveness, its achievements, the evidence of outcomes (Newman et al., 1996, cited in Frost, 2002).

An holistic approach towards understanding social work requires a reflection and analysis of all these 'ways of seeing' the practice of being a social worker. It is easy to see the particular picture – to look at a specific service, such as working in the arena of visual impairment, or with care leavers – but we need to be able to see the whole picture, whilst we still have a generic concept of 'social work' as a coherent set of activities undertaken by a distinct group of commonly trained and registered practitioners.

In the following section, you are invited to consider some of the broader themes confronting social work practice in most settings.

Being a social worker: General practitioner or service specialist?

Although social services departments (since the implementation of Seebohm reforms in 1971) until recently retained a generic function overall (in that they provided services to a full range of service users), in practical terms departments were increasingly divided by functions and user groups. As we have seen in the preceding chapters, the key factors leading to the demise of the generic principle were:

- the increasing complexity of generic social work practice, in terms of ever more sophisticated procedures and legal contexts;

- the series of child abuse inquiries into the deaths of children known to social services departments, leading to the perceived necessity of establishing child care as a specialism;

- the recognition that users of general 'adult services' were getting the 'thin end of the wedge' in comparison with the rampant and voracious appetite for child protection and child welfare concerns;

- the advent of mental health as a specialism, arising from the Approved Social Worker role as defined by the 1983 Mental Health Act, that served to further remove attention from services for older people and those with various disabilities;

- the recognition that various key functions – such as the recruitment of foster carers of sufficient quantity and quality, or undertaking social work with members of the deaf community – would occur only if defined as the responsibility of dedicated and specially trained workers;

- the advent of new roles accruing to personal social services – such as working with young offenders – which were located in specialist teams, such as the Youth Offending Service;

- the introduction of the care manager function, arising from the community care reforms, which served to separate adult from child and family services, and heralded roles for which various professional qualifications were deemed suitable (such as occupational therapy, physiotherapy and community nursing, as well as social work);

- a desire by many practitioners to attain a higher professional status through the development of specialisms and assumed expertise.

Within most social services departments only two areas of generic practice survived to the 1990s – hospital-based social work and out-of-hours/emergency duty teams – and currently, even most hospital social work departments are divided into specialist teams, or at least are split between children and adult care. It is true to say, at the time of writing, that a small number of generic posts are re-emerging, an example being those practitioners working in front line access settings, such as for care lines, or based in GP surgeries. Certainly, feedback from service users (see Chapter 9) and from other agencies indicates the desirability of 'one stop shops' – single access points to services, requiring generic, broad skills from front line, access point staff.

That said, the advent of children's services in response to the 2004 Children Act, as outlined in Chapter 3, meant an end to the generic dream of Seebohm. Not only have departments changed from generic to specialist structures, but they have also changed rapidly in terms of their relationships with other welfare organisations, such as health, housing and education.

Changing the topography of social work and social care

Today, social work – and its broader context of social care – is undertaken within 150 top-tier local authorities in England, together with some 25,000 private and voluntary-sector bodies. Those people doing social work – even if they are not called social workers, but instead are labelled care managers, youth offending workers, personal advisers – are working in an increasingly diverse range of settings, with often complex employment arrangements.

At the heart of the modernising agenda (Department of Health, 1998b) is the conviction held by government that *'what matters'* is the quality of practice and the service outcomes, not the structures within which the service is delivered. Thus, a driving imperative is the perceived necessity for 'joined up' working between social work services and other organisations, such as health, education and housing.

To this end, the Health and Social Care Act of 2001 facilitated the development of combined, collaborative health and social service ventures, with the advent of joint trusts and integrated departments. The legislation allows for one party in the partnership to take a lead role as commissioner, managing pooled budgets.

In the light of these significant organisational changes, we will briefly consider the key current challenges facing various service sectors.

Working with children, young people and their families: New challenges

The advent of the Department for Children, Schools and Families (DCSF) in 2007 was based upon the vision of creating integrated children's services, as recommended by *Every Child Matters* – bringing together schools and education services, social work and the full range of children's social care services, *Connexions* and youth services, youth justice, leisure and recreation and housing, and even child health services, ideally. Whether professionals are literally co-located, or operationally 'joined', the objective has been to break down historic barriers to integrated services:

> *The creation of an organisation defined by the client group rather than professional functions offers an important opportunity to involve children and young people in decision-making.*

> (DfES, 2003, p78)

The blueprint for integrated service delivery was set out in The *Children's Plan: Building Brighter Futures* (DCSF, 2007).

Beyond the establishment of children's services directors, the changed agenda sees the introduction of a national children's database, and integrated services, based upon single assessment and identification, referral and tracking systems. The consistent theme has been the search for coordination, cooperation, partnership and strategic planning of services, an example being government guidance on coordinated services for young disabled children *Together from the Start* (DfES/Department of Health, 2003).

CASE STUDY

Anne and Jack

It is 2014, and we now find that Anne is living in a local authority flat in London, with her one-year-old son, Jack. She has minimal contact with her family, who are over 100 miles away. She feels isolated, lonely and struggles to cope with her emotional and financial pressures. Her GP has treated her for depression.

- *The Children's Services Trust employs both Anne's health visitor and her social worker.*

- *They undertake a joint visit, using a single assessment framework, the Common Assessment Framework, known as CAF, and record any information on an integrated data system (ICS), which was introduced in January 2007.*

Continued

> CASE STUDY *continued*
>
> - *They recommend a package of support and guidance, offered by a Family and Children's Centre, including a facilitated support group, parent skills training, and ongoing monitoring of Anne's parenting capacity.*
>
> - *A central plank of service delivery is the use of family group conferences (currently used by 38 per cent of local authorities in England and Wales, according to Brown, 2002), as a means of transferring the decision-making into the hands of the child and the family.*
>
> - *The social worker and health visitor have retained their professional identity in terms of registration, clinical supervision, continuing professional development (training), and specialist areas of responsibility, yet they operate in an integrated team and are developing an allegiance to the Trust rather than their 'parent' authority.*

With regard to child protection, the campaign to outlaw smacking and thereby remove the defence of 'reasonable chastisement' is set to gain political and theoretical momentum. Such a proposal, if it ever were to gain fruition, would materially change the nature of child protection, but more importantly the role of family support services, in that families and carers would need substantial assistance to develop child management regimes that were not reliant upon traditional and culturally legitimated violence.

Indeed, family support is an essential plank of the Children Act 2004 agenda, achieved in part through the establishment of 3,500 children's centres by 2010, servicing children in every community. Many children's services have adopted the model of 'Strengthening Families' teams, trying to build upon the strengths of parents and carers whilst developing effective and proven intervention strategies to address parenting capacity difficulties to safeguard children and young people. The main role of the children's centres is to ensure that services are delivered and that targets – on such things as children's health and development, access to services, and parental involvement – are all met by communicating with the community and liaising with different professionals. The concept of the extended school – offering 'wrap around' care and a range of activities and services – is also a crucial part of the *Every Child Matters* strategy, and all of these initiatives are connected to the broad objectives of the social inclusion strategy – reducing teenage pregnancies, improving children's health, addressing issues of parental responsibility and promoting the involvement of fathers in the upbringing of their children.

The publication of the latest version of *Working Together to Safeguard Children* (DfES, 2006) was linked to three key policy developments.

1. The creation of integrated children's services under the duty to cooperate.

2. The setting up of Local Safeguarding Children Boards.

3. The duty on all agencies to make arrangements to safeguard and promote the welfare of children.

Working with families with multiple problems (FMP)

It has become the belief of successive governments, at least in the twenty-first century, that a disproportionate amount of community disruption, local crime, anti-social behaviour, and resulting expenditure is generated by a core of 'problem families'. The coalition government has suggested that such 'troubled families' are costing the state an estimated £9 billion a year in terms of spending on the NHS, the police and social services.

The government has therefore pledged to 'turn around' the lives of 120,000 'problem families' by 2015. So how are these families identified and so categorised? Families with multiple problems (FMPs) are defined as those family units who have five or more of the following disadvantages (Department for Work and Pensions, 2006).

- No parent in the family is in work.
- Family lives in poor quality or overcrowded housing.
- No parent has any qualifications.
- Mother has mental health problems.
- At least one parent has a longstanding limiting illness, disability or infirmity.
- The family has low income (below 60% of the median).
- The family cannot afford a number of food and clothing items.

A further dimension includes having at least one child with special educational needs (SEN) or behaviour problems (including being excluded from school, having involvement with the police or having run away from home).

Outcomes for family interventions

According to government data, the impact and outcomes of the intervention programmes (April 2010 to March 2011) has been as follows.

- 85% (2,569 families) left the intervention for a successful reason (e.g. formal sanctions had been lifted).
- 10% (316 families) left for a reason that cannot be counted as a success or a failure (e.g. family moved away, child taken in care).
- 5% (142 families) left for an unsuccessful reason (i.e. the family refused to engage).
- There was significant improvement in outcomes for 3,675 families who had exited an intervention, compared to their circumstances at the start. There was, on average, a reduction in the proportion of families experiencing the following issues:
  - 53% reduction in truancy, exclusion or poor behaviour in school (down from 58% of families with the issue at the start of the intervention to 28% of families with the issue at exit);
  - 58% reduction in anti-social behaviour (from 81% to 34%);
  - 34% reduction in child protection issues (from 27% to 18%);

- 57% reduction in domestic violence issues (from 28% to 12%);
- 23% reduction in mental health problems (from 36% to 28%);
- 40% reduction in drug problems (from 32% to 20%).

It is important to note that the 120,000 figure has been systematically questioned, as have Government outcome levels, but the concept of targetting particular families remains a core plank in the prevention strategy.

That said, and beyond the prevention agenda, social work with children and families has, in the past few years, been overshadowed by the death of Peter Connolly in 2007 in the London Borough of Haringey and subsequently by the allegations against the then director of children's services, Sharon Shoesmith, subsequently found, in 2011, to have been wrongfully dismissed by her employers at the behest of the government.

In the summer of 2010, the new Education Secretary, Michael Gove, asked Professor Eileen Munro to produce a review of child protection policy, procedures and practices.

The Munro Review

The Review set out to address the question: 'what helps professionals make the best judgments they can to protect a vulnerable child?'.

The first report in October 2010 (Munro, 2010) described the child protection system in recent times as one that has been shaped by four key driving forces:

1. *the importance of the safety and welfare of children and young people and the under-standable strong reaction when a child is killed or seriously harmed;*

2. *a commonly held belief that the complexity and associated uncertainty of child protection work can be eradicated;*

3. *a readiness, in high profile public inquiries into the death of a child, to focus on professional error without looking deeply enough into its causes; and*

4. *the undue importance given to performance indicators and targets which provide only part of the picture of practice, and which have skewed attention to process over the quality and effectiveness of help given.*

It was suggested that these forces have come together to create a defensive system that puts so much emphasis on procedures and recording, and that insufficient attention is given to developing and supporting the expertise to work effectively with children, young people and families.

The review's second report (in February 2011) (Munro, 2011, p6), considered the child's journey through the child protection system – from needing to receiving help – to show how the system could be improved. It concluded that instead of 'doing things right' (i.e. following procedures) the system needed to be focused on doing the right thing (i.e. checking whether children and young people are being helped).

To many commentators, academics and practitioners, this was the most explicit call for the resurrection of professional practice – in the face of the tide of managerialism – probably since the Seebohm Report of 1968, and certainly since the Barclay Report of 1982.

In effect, Munro was saying: If you want social work practitioners to be able to effectively protect children and young people, you have to employ them in a system that liberates their capacity for judgement and allows their practice wisdom to flourish.

Because of its significance and its potential to fundamentally shift the nature of social work with children young people and their families for a generation of practitioners the 15 Recommendations of the Report are reproduced in Appendix 6.

Before turning our attention to developments in adult care and adult services, it is salutary to reflect upon the eight principles for practice set out by Munro.

1. The system should be child-centred.

2. The family is usually the best place for bringing up children and young people, but difficult judgements are sometimes needed in balancing the right of a child to be with their birth family with their right to protection from abuse and neglect.

3. Helping children and families involves working with them and therefore the quality of the relationship between the child and family and professionals directly impacts on the effectiveness of help given.

4. Early help is better for children: it minimises the period of adverse experiences and improves outcomes for children.

5. Children's needs and circumstances are varied so the system needs to offer equal variety in its response.

6. Good professional practice is informed by knowledge of the latest theory and research.

7. Uncertainty and risk are features of child protection work: risk management can only reduce risks, not eliminate them.

8. The measure of the success of child protection systems, both local and national, is whether children are receiving effective help

(Munro, 2011, p24)

Working within adult services: New challenges

Before considering current issues in relation to specific service arenas, it is worthwhile commenting briefly upon the broader policy initiatives that impinge upon all adult care work. The White Paper *Modernising Social Services* (Department of Health, 1998b) extended direct payments schemes to people over the age of 65. The *Fair Access to Care* initiative (Department of Health, 2001a) produced consultation documents on consistency in eligibility criteria, risk assessment and charging for services, as well as emphasising regular reviews of services.

The Royal Commission on Long term Care (1999), chaired by Sir Stuart Sutherland, recommended that nursing and personal care should both be supplied free in care homes. This recommendation sought to address the anomaly between the health and social care arenas that was identified soon after the implementation of the Community Care reforms. Importantly, the Scottish Executive has accepted the Sutherland recommendations, and funds both nursing and personal care cost in residential settings. Meanwhile, in England and Wales, the perverse incentive remains for the individual to be allowed to deteriorate towards the need for (free) nursing or health care, rather than being supported and sustained by (fee-attracting) personal care.

Across services in the adult arena, different commissioning strategies have emerged, to secure appropriate services. These include the following.

- In-house or external provision?

- Strategic or tactical purchasing? (Long- or short-term goals?)

- Open tendering or preferred providers?

- Purchasing for cost or quality?

- Contract type? (Block or spot?)

- Competition or collaboration with providers?

These commissioning strategies need to be considered elsewhere, but their operation has become, in only a short number of years, exemplary of the third way model of social work and social care as advocated by the New Labour government (for a discussion see Jordan and Jordan, 2000).

The number of residential care homes for adults in England, which had increased progressively to 1998, has since fallen to 24,100 in March 2001 and then to 21,000 in March 2004 and by a further 10 per cent up to 2010. Of this number, 71 per cent are privately owned and 17 per cent are under the control of voluntary organisations. The number of people resident in independent care sector establishments continues to fall at a rate of about 4 per cent per annum and in 2005 was down to 206,000 with a further 38,000 in local authority residental care homes (National Statistics, 2005). That said, the progressive ageing of the population means that the Department of Health predicts a rise in the number of older people in residential care of around 23 per cent between 2000 and 2020 based upon current patterns of need and service provision – unless alternative models can be found to support people in their own homes. By this date, it is estimated that 25 per cent of the population will be around 65 years and over, and as Crawford and Walker note (2008, p22) in 2006 there were 4.7 million people aged 75 and over. The number is projected to increase to 5.5 million by 2016 and to 8.2 million by 2031.

How will services to this burgeoning group be coordinated?

We have already noted that the social worker in the realm of working with older people faces profound structural and organisational changes in the coming years. These include working in Care Trusts, developing practice in multi-disciplinary teams, offering 'seamless' services, and using the single assessment process (SAP) as outlined in the *National Service Framework for Older People* (Department of Health, 2001c) – all things wanted by government and service users (see Chapter 9).

As has always been the case, social workers and care managers are engaged with older people at times of crisis, change and transition (Ray and Phillips, 2002), but what has changed is the response to these issues. Beyond the confines of the care management role, the same authors are keen to explore the range of distinctive social work interventions with older people, such as empowerment, biography and life course work.

If the period up to the 1980s can be summarised as the 'medical mode', with long-term hospitalisation the almost inevitable response, then the 1980s and early 1990s can be seen as the 'institutional care' mode, with the funding system favouring admission to care or nursing homes. A more recent trend has been the 'intermediate care' mode, as defined by a Health Service Circular/Local Authority Circular (2001, p6):

> *…Intermediate Care should be regarded as describing services that meet all the following criteria, in that they:*
>
> *(a) are targeted at people who would otherwise face unnecessarily prolonged hospital stays or inappropriate admission to acute in-patient care, long-term residential care, or continuing NHS in-patient care;*
>
> *(b) are provided on the basis of a comprehensive assessment, resulting in a structured individual care plan that involves active therapy, treatment or opportunity for recovery;*
>
> *(c) have a planned outcome of maximising independence and enabling patient/users to resume home living;*
>
> *(d) are time-limited, normally no longer than six weeks and frequently as little as 1–2 weeks; and*
>
> *(e) involve cross-professional working, with a single assessment framework, single professional records and shared protocols.*

The key message from the circular is that

> *intermediate care should form an integrated part of a seamless continuum of services linking health promotion, preventative services, primary care, community health services, social care, support for carers and acute hospital care.*

CASE STUDY

Hannah

So, in the second decade of the twenty-first century, where would we find Hannah?

Hannah is a 75-year-old woman, born in St Kitts and resident in Nottingham since 1961. Hannah came to England with her husband, who died two years ago. She lives alone – she has three children, two of whom live within the same city and one who lives in Birmingham. Hannah has had two strokes in the past three years; she has a diabetic condition and has been hospitalised due to a recent fall, resulting in fractures in one arm and one leg.

Continued

CASE STUDY *continued*

The modern plan is that after a period of intermediate care, Hannah should be offered a negotiated individual care plan that would include:

- *strategies for reablement;*

- *intensive home care (more than ten hours contact per week);*

- *support services drawing upon culturally appropriate, community-based resources.*

As we noted in Chapter 6, the key direction of modern services to older people is based upon the *Personalisation* agenda (see Chapter 6).

For many older people, home care is seen as the essential support system that allows them to maintain their stated goal of residing in their own home.

According to the Department of Health (2002c):

> home care is defined as services that assist the service user to function as independently as possible and/or continue to live in their own home. Services may involve routine household tasks within or outside the home, personal care of the service user or a short term break in support of the individual's regular carers.

In 2004–05, an estimated 583,000 clients received home care, 478,000 clients received equipment and adaptations, 420,000 received professional support (such as occupational therapy) and 242,000 received day care as a service following an assessment of need (National Statistics, 2005). There has also been a significant shift in provider patterns: in 1992, local authorities provided 98 per cent of contact hours in home care; in 2000, this had fallen to 44 per cent (Department of Health, 2002c).

The challenges facing social workers in working with older people are made more complicated by new organisational structures and consequential processes, but the social model of promoting capacity, independence, dignity, worth, rights and consultation reflect social work's historic commitment to ethical, critical practice.

Wistow (2000), in recalling that Seebohm had advocated that social work should retain a separate base from medicine, asserts that whatever the new structures pertaining to the new health/social care formation, certain social care functions and tasks will remain to be fulfilled. These include:

- empowering vulnerable people: supporting autonomous decision-making;

- mobilising community resources: developing care networks;

- promoting well-being and primary prevention;

- advocating integrated services and integrated accountability;

- promoting holistic governance to meet the holistic needs of individuals in their communities.

In an era when practitioners are being asked to 'think the unthinkable', recent proposals (by Kent County Council, for example) have suggested local authorities could take over hospital care for older people, and that caring for people within their own homes could halve the costs of hospital care. A key issue will be the development of appropriate and affordable social housing – lifetime homes, with built-in capacity to meet the needs of older or disabled people, and communities that reflect Wistow's assertion that *independence comes through interdependence*.

Is personalisation the new social work?

We have referred often to personalisation in the preceding pages, and it is therefore timely at this juncture to reflect on whether personalisation as a concept has fundamentally changed the roles, tasks and functions of social work. Arising out of a number of political strands, such as the Darzi review of the NHS (Department of Health, 2008), and the *'Our Health, Our Care, Our Say* White Paper (Department of Health, 2006b), it is influenced by moves towards a more service-user focused, socially inclusive way of understanding social care needs in general. Whether applying it to working with older people, those with disabilities or intellectual impairments or with mental health problems, the same challenges for social work apply. If service users are to be more 'in control' then necessarily social workers, along with all other professionals, are going to be less in control. As Goemans (2012, p71) notes, *the ethos of personalisation is a shift in the power balance between service provider and service user, with 'individually tailored' care packages being based on what the service user needs rather than what the service is set up to provide (DH, 2010). Goemans goes on to suggest (2012: 71) that the development of personalisation has the potential to be a defining moment in the history of social work. Despite a very slow process of gradually increasing influence on the way mental health services are actually delivered (five years in and still only a minority of service users receiving a personal budget), personalisation forces services to ask what service users want. It is a big step away from the paternalistic 'doctor knows best' culture, towards the self-determinism of service users dictating which services work best for them.*

Working with vulnerable groups: New challenges

Supporting People (2003) is the government programme for funding, planning and monitoring housing-related support services, essentially to provide housing-related support services to vulnerable groups to enable them to live independently within the community. The programme acknowledges and develops the essential link between the social inclusion of vulnerable people and the crucial issue of availability of suitable, accessible and affordable social housing of sufficient quality and quantity. The stated objectives of the programme are as follows.

- *Help older people remain in their own home as long as they wish to by funding visiting support services.*

- *Continue to provide services (e.g. wardens) in sheltered schemes.*

- *Help young people leaving care prepare for greater independence through training in basic skills such as cooking and hygiene.*

- *Help people leaving institutions (e.g. prison) or who have been homeless set up home.*

- *Provide ongoing support for people adjusting to more independent living, if moving into their own home after living in a special housing and support scheme.*

From the Office of the Deputy Prime Minister (2003)

In pursuance of these goals, a number of unitary top-tier authorities (such as London and various Metropolitan Boroughs) have established departments for Adult Care and Housing. The future for social care in relation to all vulnerable groups will depend in large measure upon social policy directives in relation to housing, if Britain is to avoid the ghettoisation of service users into socially excluded environments. The links between social care, housing and health are also at the forefront of government thinking and practice developments. More than 15 million people have long-term health needs and, all PCTs have established a joint health and social care team to help those with long-term needs.

Working in adult care: New challenges

In parallel with the establishment of the aspirational outcomes of the Children Act 2004 (see Chapter 3), the Green Paper *Independence, Well Being and Choice* (Department of Health, 2005a) and the White Paper, *Our Health, Our Care, Our Say* (Department of Health, 2006b) set out seven outcomes against which services in adult social care are to be tested.

- *Improved health and well being.*

- *Improved quality of life.*

- *Making a positive contribution.*

- *Exercising choice and control.*

- *Freedom from discrimination or harassment.*

- *Economic well being.*

- *Personal dignity.*

Furthermore, the Green Paper contained a number of core proposals, namely:

- the right to request not to enter residential care;

- the proposed integration of the Single Assessment Process (for older people), the Care Programme Approach (in relation to mental health) and Person Centred Planning (for people with learning disabilities) in order to streamline assessment systems;

- the extension of direct payments (to agents acting on behalf of service users);

- the extension of individual budgets;

- the modernisation of regulation, by merging the Healthcare Commission and CSCI by 2008, which became the Care Quality Commission from April 2009;

- the introduction of the Care Broker role, with the social work role reserved for more complex cases (this proposal matches and mirrors the lead professional role for children's services, and further serves to destabilise social work's sense of identity and purpose, in spite of the affirmation of status via registration with the GSCC).

Working with disabled people: New challenges

Some people with physical disabilities have been long-term service users, having been identified as children in need by virtue of their disability during infancy or later. Many other service users have acquired such a status by virtue of significant events, crises, accidents or physical developments. The role of social work, as with any other service user group, is complex and contested. As Sapey notes (2002, p185):

> ...social work can contribute to the disablement of people with impairments, but it is also true that many people, both with and without impairments, need and benefit from the help social work can provide.

As we have seen in relation to all marginalised and oppressed groups, the common history of people with physical disabilities has been one of institutionalisation and depersonalisation. Nevertheless, arguments continue to rage about the relevance and contribution group care settings have to offer. The following definition appears to be relatively neutral:

> A residential home is: a place whose purpose includes the provision of residential accommodation, care and services for people who choose to live in a group or whose needs are best met through group care.

(Residential Forum, 1996)

However, according to Jack (1998, p24):

> the anti-residential care movement, in its narrowness of focus, tunnel vision and over-reliance on rhetoric at the expense of scientific rigour, has the characteristics of zealotry and ideology.

To support his case, Jack cites Oliver (1993, p13) who stated:

> *...if we are serious about supporting disabled people to live independently, we must acknowledge residential care has no significant role to play in a modern welfare system and is incompatible with the entitlements of citizenship that disabled people are demanding.*

We can thus see that social work in this arena – whilst embracing and endorsing the general thrust of the anti-institutional ethos – has to sometimes recognise that a broader view of disability (one that encompasses those with mental health problems or learning disabilities) might see some form of group care as a means towards maximising independence, autonomy and personal development, rather than diminishing it.

The government drive towards direct payments presents, paradoxically, one of the greatest threats for social work status and role. Without doubt, disabled people will use their financial resources to engage personal assistants, but will they buy social work services?

With regard to people with learning disabilities, the Mental Incapacity Act 2005 has generated heated debates. By proposing a single test of capacity, the Act allows the granting of Lasting Powers of Attorney to relatives and carers, in relation to decisions concerning welfare, health care and financial matters. The government, when introducing the legislation, saw it as assisting *millions of people, including those who lack capacity, the estimated 6 million people who care for them and professionals who have contact with them* (Department of Constitutional Affairs, 2005). However, some organisations, such as People First, feel that it further oppresses disabled people, by vesting too much power in the hands of parents and carers, whereas other bodies, like the Making Decisions Alliance, welcome the proposals, as long as they are supported by effective advocacy systems.

The reality of social work as dealing with complex, moral dilemmas – about power, dignity, rights, and responsibilities – can be well illustrated by the Sexual Offences Act, which outlaws sex for people with learning disabilities if they lack the capacity to consent. The charity Mencap supports a statutory test of capacity to consent to sex, based upon its 2001 research *Behind Closed Doors*, highlighting the incidence of sexual abuse perpetrated on people with learning disabilities. However, members of the National Forum of People with Learning Difficulties see such a proposed test as an affront to dignity and privacy.

Given the government's commitment to establishing an integrated, coherent and comprehensive response to the complex needs of a range of vulnerable adults, it is instructive to look at one local authority's strategic approach to putting users and carers at the heart of service review and development.

Lincolnshire is Listening: Report on the development of a vision for Adult Social Care 2008–11

From six consultation events held with people currently being supported by Mental Health Services, Learning Disability Services, Physical Disability Services and Older Persons Services, seven key personal outcomes were identified.

Continued

---

1. *Being in control of their lives*

2. *Maintaining their personal dignity*

3. *Keeping and feeling healthy and safe*

4. *Respected as a citizen*

5. *Improved quality of life*

6. *Feeling included*

7. *Confident in the future.*

Furthermore, participants identified eight key areas of service and support as key priorities for development.

1. *Transport and accessibility*

2. *Support services to reduce isolation*

3. *Supported housing*

4. *Respite services*

5. *Flexible support*

6. *Carers' support*

7. *Access to information*

8. *Access to daytime opportunities.*

In summary: ... individuals want to have more choice and control over the social care services they will be able to purchase in the future. People's aspirations identified that they wished to be supported by personal assistants. People want to live in their own homes for as long as possible and make their own decisions about the right support that they need.

(Lincolnshire County Council, 2008, p8)

Reforming adult services

As the social activist Simon Duffy recently suggested at a University of Lincoln conference on personalisation (20 April 2012) welfare reform is necessary because *the Welfare State is a good thing: it is just designed wrong.* He went on to allege that when decarceration occurred for the most vulnerable citizens – with the closure of workhouses, psycho-geriatric wards, long-stay hospitals and asylums – *we did not leave the institution behind: we took it with us.* The evidence for this assertion is that the social care system still spends 92 per cent of its total available resources on segregated services (specialist care homes, group homes, care homes, nursing homes) and thus only 8 per cent on community services (supporting people to live their lives, in the way they want, with the individual being in control of budgets, services, processes and outcomes).

In summary, Beresford and Hasler (2009, p8) have identified five key policies for improving social care. These are:

- personalisation;

- early intervention, to prevent problems getting worse;

- improving services for dementia, which is a large and growing problem;

- ensuring people are treated with dignity in services;

- improving help and support for unpaid carers.

We will return to these themes when considering the future of social work in the final chapter.

Social work and criminal justice

It has not been the remit of this book to look at the criminal justice system, largely because the last Conservative government explicitly decoupled the Probation Service from social work, in terms of training, registration, identity and ethos. Although noting the origins of Court Missioners in the early part of the twentieth century, the preservation of the Probation Service at the time of Seebohm – and in contrast to its absorption in the new social work departments in Scotland – presaged its total detachment in the 1990s, by adopting a different training and qualifications regime. It is therefore fair to say that the relationship between social work and the criminal justice system is one of tension and flux and general detachment. According to Harris (1996) the Probation Service has resolved the tension by compromising its social work roots. The arena of youth justice stands as an anomaly, being still linked to social services as much as to the Probation Service. Papers such as *No More Excuses* (Home Office, 1997) and *Misspent Youth* (Audit Commission, 1996) have led to the establishment of the Youth Offending Service under the auspices of the Youth Justice Board. The emerging refined youth criminal justice system is replete with the language of accountability – for the system, the practitioner, and the offender. Everyone is to be called to account for their behaviour and the responses to that behaviour, primarily through the concept of *restorative justice*, together with the objectives of *responsibility, reparation and reintegration*.

Youth Offending Teams represent a model for future development, in that they are collaborative, jigsaw organisations, drawing in workers from various disciplinary and employment bases, who work together in terms of a mission, a strategy, a set of precepts and operational procedures.

The Modernising Social Services agenda

Social Services are for all of us (Department of Health, 1998b, para 1.1)

Much of the story that has preceded this point gives the impression of social work as a profession in crisis, lacking in certainty, conviction and self-worth, unclear of its role, purpose and function, running scared, or losing its way. The following two passages reinforce that analysis, and offer some explanations of the sorry state.

If the late 1960s and early 1970s could be seen as a period of optimism amongst social workers both about their capabilities and occupational futures, the years since have witnessed considerable changes. From the mid 1970s onwards social work has been subject to a series of child abuse inquiries and media opprobrium, which has had the effect of both undermining morale and undermining public confidence in its abilities.

(Parton, 2000, pv)

In a similar vein, Terry Bamford lamented the failure of social work to establish its identity, its credibility.

Twenty years after the Seebohm Report, social work has failed to establish its independent professional status, has a basic training shorter than that of other occupational groups involved in community care, and has dropped precipitately in public esteem.

(Bamford, 1990, pix)

But, as Jennifer Barnard (formerly Chief Executive of CCETSW) enthused in a 2003 conference speech: *It's time for us [social workers] to admit who we are, what we do, and not to say 'I work for the council'.*

It is within the context of the climate as identified by the above authors that the incoming Labour government in 1997 set about the task of reforming the strategic direction for social work, together with the structures of social work regulation, with the stated aims of modernising the social services and improving the status of, and confidence in, the social work profession. As a consequence, according to Munro (2000, p1):

Social workers are coming more and more under the control of politicians and social services management. Increasingly, our work is subject to scrutiny and measurement.

A year after being elected, the last Labour government published the *Modernising Social Services* White Paper (Department of Health, 1998b), to lay out plans for the sector's future. In the Paper, the value of social services was encouragingly stated:

We all need good social services to be there at such time of crisis, to help in making the right decisions and working out what needs to be done.

(Department of Health, 1998b)

However, social services stood accused of:

failing to provide the support that people should expect.

(Department of Health, 1998b, p5)

ACTIVITY **8.1**

On the basis of your learning to date, what do you think were the six key concerns of the government about the performance of the then social services? In what way had social services failed to provide the support the people should expect?

Continued

ACTIVITY *8.1* *continued*

1.

2.

3.

4.

5.

6.

COMMENT

The main concerns were:

- *poor standards in care homes;*

- *children leaving care being ill-equipped to deal with independent living;*

- *failures in community care for some mentally ill people and associated risks to the public;*

- *bed-blocking, particularly in relation to older people, due to a lack of appropriate services;*

- *poor accessibility to social services;*

- *inconsistent availability and standard of services across the country (the so-called 'postcode lottery'); and*

- *most importantly, a perceived failure for different organisations to get beyond their own interests, to reach out beyond their professional silos and to pursue a vision of shared outcomes for service users.*

To improve this gap between expectations and actual standards, the government outlined six areas to be addressed. These were:

- *protection* of vulnerable children and adults;

- *coordination* between agencies and authorities;

- *flexibility* to ensure the delivery of person-centred services;

- *clarity of role* with greater understanding of the role social services should undertake;

- *consistency* of service delivery across the country;

- *efficiency* of service delivery, to ensure best use of public money.

In addition, the government announced four main principles that underpin public service reform. These were:

- high national standards and full accountability;

- devolution to the front line to encourage diversity and local creativity;

- flexibility around the needs of users in how staff are employed and how services are organised;

- the promotion of alternative providers and greater choice.

As Cree (2002, p23) summarises:

> *The recommendation is for a 'third way for social care': one which would promote independence, improve consistency, ensure quality of opportunity to children (especially in relation to education), protect adults and children from abuse or neglect in the care system, improve standards in the workforce, and improve delivery and efficiency.*

Such laudable objectives stand as givens, in that nobody engaged in the care sector would argue for inefficiency, for a lack of protection, for inequality. The debate lies in the means to achieve these agreed ends.

Central to the government's strategy towards achieving these goals has been a number of key policy initiatives and structural developments, a number of which comprise *a new national infrastructure for quality* (Department of Health, 1998b, p1).

Fourteen years on from this policy direction, it is salutary to note that the last report produced by CSCI (the Commission for Social Care Inspection) in 2009 suggested that *personalisation* was not a reality for many with complex needs, with services impeded by poor strategic commissioning, a lack of person-centred care and 'marginalisation' of human rights. Furthermore, some commentators (such as Blewett et al., 2007) have questioned the theoretical and philosophical basis of the Personalisation agenda, being based as it is upon an assumption that everyone is able to make rational choices once offered appropriate information and advice. This may indeed be true for some people with complex physical needs and sensory impairments, who have long demanded, quite correctly, control over their own resources. Whether such a model applies equally to people experiencing mental distress, to people in a state of trauma or crisis, or profound loss and grief, remains to be seen.

Elements of agenda: 'The big four'

Consistent with other elements of regulatory government, a range of new organisations was established in the years after 1997 to promote, develop, regulate and quality assure social work, within the broader umbrella of social care. These were the General Social Care Council (GSCC), the Social Care Institute for Excellence (SCIE); two sector skills bodies – Skills for Care (for adult social care) and CWDC (the Children's Workforce Development Council for children, young people and families); and the Commission for Social Care Inspection (CSCI), which was then replaced by the current regulatory body, the Care Quality Commission (CQC), with effect from April 2009. Children's services are all now inspected by Ofsted (the Office for Standards in Education). These bodies represent an integrated objective of raising quality standards through the regulation of three inter-connected systems: the service system, the staff system and the training system.

The joined-up quality and regulation framework

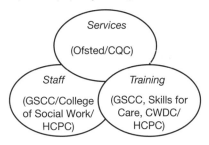

We will examine the mission and strategic objectives of these organisational elements of the Modernising Agenda.

Regulating the social care workforce: The General Social Care Council in England (GSCC), the Health and Care Professions Council (HCPC) and the College of Social Work

The GSCC mission statement says:

> The General Social Care Council exists to promote the highest standards of social care in England for the benefit and protection of people who use services and the wider public...

Furthermore, the GSCC defines itself as a:

> guardian of standards...champion of the profession.

> (General Social Care Council, 2002, p1)

The GSCC was established to regulate social care staff, including social workers, by establishing a register of staff. Entry to the register depends upon a candidate attaining the required qualification that demonstrates that s/he has met the occupational standards for the particular role and under the legislation it is a *criminal offence for anyone else to use the title 'social worker'* (Brayne and Martin, 2001, p4).

The GSCC also issued codes of practice for employees and employers. The code states that social care workers must:

- protect the rights and promote the interests of service users and carers;

- strive to establish and maintain the trust and confidence of service users and carers;

- promote the independence of service users while protecting them as far as possible from danger or harm;

- respect the rights of service users whilst seeking to ensure that their behaviour does not harm themselves or other people;

- uphold public trust and confidence in social care services; and

- be accountable for the quality of their work and take responsibility for maintaining and improving their knowledge and skills.

(General Social Care Council, 2002)

Similar organisations have been set up in Scotland (the Scottish Social Services Council), in Wales (the Cyngor Gofal Cymru/Care Council for Wales) and in Northern Ireland (the Northern Ireland Social Care Council). The GSCC has been charged, under Section 63 of the Care Standards Act 2000, with the task of accrediting universities and other higher education institutions who provide social work degrees based upon the Department of Health's *Requirements for Social Work Training*. The Requirements state:

> *the new degree level qualification must prepare social workers for the complex and demanding role that will be required of them.*

(Department of Health, 2002b, p1)

As part of the coalition government's 'bonfire of the quangos', the GSCC was disestablished from July 2012, with its regulatory and registration functions transferring to the Health and Care Professions Council (HCPC).

The HCPC is an independent, UK-wide health and care regulator set up by the Health Professions Order (2001). The HPC keeps a register for 15 different health professions and only registers people who meet the standards it sets for their training, professional skills, behaviour and health. The HPC will take action against people who do not meet these standards or who use a protected title illegally. Social workers and social care workers have joined the 15 health-related profession groupings, which includes occupational therapists, physiotherapists, dieticians, radiographers, speech and language therapists and psychologists.

Sector Skills Council bodies: Skills for Care, the Teaching Agency and the Department of Education

Initially, Training Organisation for Personal Social Services (TOPSS) was established as the lead body for care sector training, with the goal of providing a coherent education and training strategy to underpin the delivery and the development of social work, social care and related activities.

From April 2005, TOPSS was replaced by two parallel bodies – Skills for Care and the Children's Workforce Development Council – which together formed England's part of 'Skills for Care and Development', the UK-wide sector skills council for social care, children and young people, alongside the already-existing Scottish Social Services Council, Care Council for Wales, and Northern Ireland Social Care Council. Skills for Care has responsibility for the whole workforce engaged in adult care and has assumed a lead role in addressing the practice learning needs of those undertaking qualifying degree training.

The Children's Workforce did likewise for all those engaged in child care work, youth work, and practice within children's services structures. One of the *Every Child Matters* recommendations was that there should be:

A common core of training for those who work solely with children and families and those who have wider roles (such as GPs and the police) to help secure a consistent response to children's and families' needs and a better understanding of professional roles (DfES, 2003, para 20). Future goals will be to develop mechanisms for multi-professional education (learning alongside but to perform parallel tasks) and inter-professional education (learning alongside towards integrated, 'seamless' practice), and this applies equally to the adult and children's workforces.

As part of the same reorganisation that has seen the end of the GSCC, the CWDC closed on 31 March 2012 with its key work transferring to either the Teaching Agency (for Early Years, Educational Psychology and Standards and Qualifications) or the Department for Education (Sector Leadership and Social Work).

The responsibility for promoting and developing Integrated Working has transferred to the Children's Improvement Board (CIB) and visitors to this work area are being redirected to **https://knowledgehub.local.gov.uk/**

The Children's Improvement Board (CIB) is leading an important new initiative to help councils improve their performance of children's services. A partnership between the Local Government Association (LGA), the Association of Directors of Children's Services (ADCS) and the Society of Local Authority Chief Executives (SOLACE), the CIB supports local government to take charge of its own performance and improvement in the interests of children and young people.

From April 2012 the CWDC social work support programme was transferred to the Department for Education (DfE) and formed part of the Safeguarding Group.

Assuring the quality of social care provision: The Care Quality Commission (CQC)

In April 2002 inspection and regulation functions transferred from local authorities to the National Care Standards Commission (NCSC), which then rapidly became the Commission for Social Care Inspection. The current regulatory body, the Care Quality Commissions (CQC), is charged with overseeing all health and social care services in England, be they provided by the NHS, local authorities, private companies or by voluntary organisations. The Commission manages registrations, monitoring and inspection functions, using enforcement powers to assure quality and to protect patients or service users, conduct reviews and generate reports on outcomes.

Improving the quality of social care practice: The Social Care Institute for Excellence (SCIE)

Established to mirror and complement the Health Service's NICE (the National Institute for Health and Clinical Excellence), SCIE has been established to *develop and promote knowledge about what works best in social care* (Department of Health, 2002a, p3), and to then disseminate knowledge through best practice guidance. The initiative is driven by a form of scientific thinking, and influenced by the *What Works* agenda from the Probation Service. SCIE disseminates guidance to inform practice, regulation, inspection, review, and associated human resource issues of staff recruitment, selection, management and training.

SCIE's main functions are:

- reviewing knowledge about social care;

- developing practice guides based on that knowledge;

- promoting the use of practice guides in policy and practice.

The College of Social Work

Arising from the Social Work Reform Board, the new College of Social Work takes over some of the functions of the GSCC, alongside a responsibility to advance the standing of Social Work in the eyes of the public, of other professionals and of society as a whole. The College defines its Vision and Mission as follows.

Vision

The College of Social Work exists to ensure that social workers are able to work to the highest possible standards, engage as effectively as possible with people who use social work services and their carers, and allow children and adults to achieve their full potential.

Mission

The mission of The College is to develop a strong profession, confident about the unique contributions it makes to the individuals, families and communities it serves, with a clear sense of its identity, values, ethics and purpose.

The College will have responsibility for endorsing higher education institutions wishing to offer qualifying degrees in social work under the new arrangements. *The College is leading a number of areas of reform, from helping universities select the right people at interview, to advising on the curriculum, to ensuring that social workers in practice receive the support they need to operate effectively* (College of Social Work, 2011).

New guidance on the content of social work degree programmes has been produced by the College of Social Work in collaboration with social work educators. The curriculum guides produced thus far, funded by the Higher Education Academy, focus on a range of topics, including those stipulated by the Social Work Reform Board. Written by leading social work educators, the first guides cover:

- substance use;

- mental health and distress;

- communication skills;

- behavioural/parenting problems for children and families;

- neglect, violence and abuse of children and adults;

- human growth and development.

SCIE	CQC	HCPC	College of Social Work	Skills for Care
Determining 'what works'	Registration, inspection and regulation	Regulates 15 health professions, and now social work	Representative membership body	Sector Skills Council
Disseminating best practice guidance	Defining care standards	Holds Register of Qualified Social Workers	Endorsement of HEI providers of qualifying social work degrees	Setting occupational standards
Consultation with users, carers, representative organisations	Publications and service reports	Disciplinary and deregistration powers	Public relations for the profession	Focus on adult social care

Auditing the quality of social services departments

The Audit Commission (concerned with the efficient and effective use of public funds) and the Social Services Inspectorate (SSI) have conducted Joint Reviews, resulting in an assessment of the authority's performance and this work is now undertaken by CQC in relation to the Adult and Community Care Services Departments. Similarly, Ofsted has assumed responsibility for inspecting all children's services' activity, thus creating a comprehensive system of inspection and regulation covering child care, schools, colleges, children's services, teacher training and youth work. Within each local authority, all services have been measured against the Five Outcomes of the Children Act 2004 (see Chapter 3) via a Joint Area Review (JAR) and as defined by Section 23 of the Children Act 2004. According to Ofsted (2005):

Joint area reviews will report on the well-being of all children and young people who are vulnerable to poor outcomes. Two such groups will be covered in detail in every review: children and young people who are looked after by the council; and, children and young people with learning difficulties and/or disabilities.

On a broader canvas, all local authorities have been subject to a Performance Assessment Framework, with identified indicators of the department's capacity to meet particular targets, and finally resulting in a league table of star ratings. It is expected that, where necessary, local authorities will dispense with traditional but outmoded practices, and accept the need to embrace the *What Works* philosophy of doing what is proven to be effective.

CASE STUDY

A Joint Review conducted in Nottinghamshire County Council identified particular noteworthy features of service delivery. Overall, the report was highly complimentary, and identified the authority as having 'good prospects'. It also set an agenda for future development by identifying key areas of improvement as follows.

- Concentrating on meeting the needs of users and carers, irrespective of the provider.

- Achieving a better balance of top-down and bottom-up commissioning of services, with increased capacity at both levels, in order to accelerate the trend towards more diverse community-based services.

- Investing in joint commissioning of services with health and streamlining the decision-making arrangements.

- Continuing to sharpen service quality by focusing on measurable outcomes for users and carers.

- Targeting resources still more effectively, especially in-house services – reducing overhead costs, investing in competitive salaries and funding services across all sectors at appropriate levels.

Assuring social work and social care: Best Value and commissioning

The *Best Value* government framework, which was introduced in 2000, requires the commissioning and delivery of services to be based not just on economy and efficiency, but also on effectiveness and quality. Replacing, in part, the previous government's doctrine of compulsory competitive tendering, Best Value can be understood, according to Thompson (2002a, p101), in terms of the *Four Cs of Best Value*:

- challenging why and how the service is best provided;

- comparing performance with others (including non-local government providers);

- competing – the authority must show that it has embraced the principles of fair competition in deciding who should deliver the service;

- consulting local service users and residents on their expectation about the service.

It is therefore not possible to practise within the social care arena – whether as a commissioner or as a provider of services – without being involved in Best Value processes. The consequence of Best Value reviews is an ever-broadening array of service providers in the social work and social care landscape. The vision of successive governments is that the landscape will become even more diverse.

Under recent government guidance, modifying previous directives, Best Value authorities are under a general Duty of Best Value to *make arrangements to secure continuous improvement in the way in which its functions are exercised, having regard to a combination of economy, efficiency and effectiveness* (Department for Communities and Local Government, 2011).

The modernising agenda: Fourteen years on

Improving public protection, raising professional standards.

When addressing the Community Care Live conference in 2002, the then Health Minister Jacqui Smith revealed government thinking about the technocratic nature of modern social work:

Social work is a very practical job. It is about protecting people and changing their lives, not about being able to give a fluent and theoretical explanation of why they got into difficulties in the first place.

Such pragmatic, even anti-intellectual thinking reveals a presumed position for modern social work practice – that it should be efficient, that it should be amenable and answerable to inspection, regulation, audit and evaluation, that it should be well-managed, and that it must 'prove its worth' in the face of potential competitors.

It is instructive to examine key passages from the speech by the then Secretary of State for Health, Alan Milburn, to the Annual Social Services Conference in 2002:

We live in a consumer age. People demand services tailor-made to their individual needs...People expect choice and demand quality.

(Milburn, 2002, p2).

Later in the same address the Secretary of State clearly identified the focus of government attention:

It is the means of delivery – not the values of social services – that need to change.

He concluded by emphasising the centrality of social work values and principles:

...and social services are nothing if they are not about empowering the powerless: giving older people the power to stay in their own home; giving young people in care the chance of a stable family life; protecting the most vulnerable children from abuse and neglect; promoting independence and self-reliance; bringing hope to families where hope has almost gone.

As expected, the changes heralded by the minister have come to pass. Those *monolithic, single social services departmental structures*, as described by Alan Milburn, have indeed disappeared, and now every local authority area has two locations for social work and social care activity: children's services and adult care services. Significantly, the cradle-to-grave vision of generic social work practice has been finally abandoned, and social work with children, young people and families resides within the larger home of education, and social work with a range of vulnerable adults sits alongside, if not always within, the broader health structures.

Yet his affirmation of the centrality of social work values and principle is what matters, as we will discuss in the final chapter.

Social work resilience?

Much of the information described above has been just that – information. It is essential that you, as a beginning practitioner entering the profession, are aware of the political context shaping social work and its practice arenas.

The book began with the question 'What is social work?' and you may still feel it has not been answered, although you hopefully have a clearer understanding of what social workers do in relation to particular service user groups, and you have a beginning awareness of the factors influencing the fast-moving structures within which social work takes place. Nearly a quarter of a century ago, the threatening question 'Can social work survive?' was asked by Brewer and Lait (1980). Today, the answer would appear to be Yes, if only because this book is being written and yet another new social work degree is about to be introduced. Certainly it is very different, but it is still here, and is undergoing a 'make-over' in the image of social and public policy initiatives. The role for social work that is envisaged by government has attracted critical commentary. Many see this as an increasingly narrow, restrictive and authoritarian role. Referring to the impact of New Labour on social work, Drakeford (2002, p35) states that:

> when the government acted in generous mode – in the Sure Start scheme for disadvantaged children to take just one example – the term 'social work' almost never appeared in official discourse, even when the tasks to be undertaken – advice, guidance, practical help and so on – appeared very close indeed to social work itself. Only when the government turned to authoritarian mode – in its treatment of 'anti-social' children, the regulation of the family, or the compulsory treatment of the mentally ill – did the place of social work seem secure.

Such a view alleges a worryingly narrow role for social work, one that is reliant upon its statutory control function, without the counterbalance of the enabling, empowering and caring function.

And yet, a new degree structure for social work was instituted from September 2003, and yet another new programme will be introduced from September 2013. The knowledge base has been challenged and renewed, the locations of work are changing, the identification with the traditions of local government are being weakened, yet social work's sense of coherence and self-identity continues to be buttressed by recourse to its value base. As Neil Thompson observes, in the face of new structures:

> Social work has an important part to play in helping to 'humanise' a society in which the human dimension is so easily lost beneath the pressures of a fast moving world riven by conflicts, discrimination, oppression and driven by the pursuit of power and wealth – often at the expense of other important aspects of life, such as compassion, a shared sense of humanity and spiritual fulfilment.

(Thompson, 2005, p185)

Similar sentiments are expressed in the definition of social work adopted by the International Federation of Social Workers, that we cited in the introduction to the book:

> *The social work profession promotes social change, problem solving in human relationships and the empowerment and liberation of people to enhance well being. Utilising theories of human behaviour and social systems, social work intervenes at the point where people interact with their environments. Principles of human rights and social justice are fundamental to social work.* (**www.ifsw.org***)*

These definitions serve to provide social work with a sense of identity and purpose that may be more long-lasting than the ever-changing economics of service delivery systems.

According to Clare (2000, p40) some particular challenges still face social workers, namely:

- that social workers must be equipped to work in a complex and rapidly-changing environment where the requirements of technology and demands for visibility and accountability challenge the traditional view of the 'autonomous professional' (see Hugman, 1991);

- that practitioners need to be equipped to operate in an 'anxious' socio-political context of rapid change and uncertainty, and of ambivalence about the contribution of or need for social work (see Morrison, 1990);

- that in order to withstand these pressures and maintain integrity, hope and direction, the preparation and training received by social workers prior to qualification needs to equip them to become resilient self-managers able to respond to and actively participate in fluid and uncertain situations.

As the social work profession prepares itself for the implementation of the Social Work Reform Board requirements it is instructive to remind ourselves of the views expressed by the outgoing profession's Regulatory Body, the GSCC. In a summary statement, it affirmed that:

- *Social Work is an established professional discipline with a distinctive part to play in promoting and securing the well-being of children, adults, families and communities;*

- *Social Work makes a particular contribution where there are high levels of complexity, uncertainty, stress, conflicts of interest, and risk, particularly to children and vulnerable adults;*

- *Employers need to identify the situations where a registered, experienced social worker should always be involved.*

(General Social Care Council, 2008a, p4)

As we noted in Chapter 7, the Barclay Report of 30 years ago, when examining the Roles and Tasks of Social Workers opined that: *'Too much is generally expected of social workers. We load upon them unrealistic expectations and we then complain when they do not live up to them'* (Barclay Committee, 1982, pvii). Such difficulty inherent in the role was acknowledged by Ed Balls, former Secretary of State for Children, Schools and Families. In his ministerial statement heralding the Social Work Taskforce (see Chapter 9), he stated that:

Social workers carry out highly challenging work, often in extremely difficult circumstances. They have a vital role in protecting children and young people from harm and in supporting adults. Enabling social workers to deliver consistent high quality practice and services is a key priority for this Government. Our ambition is for social work to be a high quality, self-confident profession, with the support and esteem of the public.

(Ministerial statement at the launch of the Social Work Taskforce, January, 2009)

In the final chapter we will return to fundamentals, to basics. If social work is not to be driven by the moralising cant of its originating formations, nor to be narrowly wedded to an ideological, 'top-down' *modus operandi*, nor to be passively tossed about upon the seas of government whim, fashion and panic, then it needs to reassert its historic commitment to listening to and responding to the voice of dispossessed, marginalised and excluded individuals, groups and communities.

CHAPTER SUMMARY

In Chapter 8 we have outlined aspects of the *Modernising Social Services* agenda, and seen how the New Award in Social Work has been determined, together with the new structures, such as the General Social Care Council, which have been established to regulate and shape social work as a profession.

FURTHER READING

Jordan, B and Jordan, C (2000) Social work and the third way. London: Sage.

A book that combines critical policy analysis with practice issues. Social work is discussed in terms of government agendas, initiatives and control.

Pierson, J (2002) *Tackling social exclusion.* London: Routledge.

A text for students wishing to locate thinking about social work within a broader social context.

Social Work Reform Board (2011) *Building a safe and confident future: One year on – detailed proposals.*

A really important document for all social work students and practitioners, setting out the agenda for social work over the coming years, from the establishment of the College of Social Work, to the new degree and with the outcome being the new Professional Capabilities Framework.

Chapter 9
Summarising remarks and signposts

The emphasis of social work varies depending on the society that it serves.

(Payne, 2005, p2)

Whither modern social work?

The absence of the history of English charity, philanthropy and social work from the mandatory curriculum of professional education and training has been noted with concern (Forsythe and Jordan, 2002) and a significant proportion of this book has unapologetically attempted to explore the historical antecedents of current social work practice – largely because we believe that those entering a new profession, or equally those wishing to update their thinking about their current practice, need to start from an informed position about our collective identity as social workers. As Jordan and Jordan note (2000, p16):

> to understand the evolution of the social work profession within social policy, one needs to analyse its emergence both historically and comparatively

and this we have done, albeit as a whistle-stop tour through the centuries. However, Adams et al. (2002a, p331) rightly warn the reader to be sceptical about the 'history' that is offered as an explanation of the profession's past, and to ask 'whose history' has come to dominate. Essentially liberal views will see social work as a contributor to stability, largely based upon the efforts of philanthropists and reformers. Latterly, such a perspective tends to celebrate the small yet significant contribution made by social work towards the empowerment of oppression and marginalised groups within society. However, on the other hand, more critical and radical theorists will draw attention to social work's collusive part in the oppression of the 'underclass' and those seen by the dominant society as 'different' or a threat – gay and lesbian people, people with physical and learning disabilities, those with mental health issues, or people with different lifestyles. Most readings of social work's history – whatever the theoretical perspective – will attest to the complexity of practice, and acknowledge that:

> social work practice has always worked in the space between law and policy on the one hand, and family, neighbourhood and community on the other.

> (Jordan and Jordan, 2000, p77)

143

By offering a synopsis of social work's history, and introducing the reader to a range of literature and research, we hope to have stimulated interest in exploring the plurality of social work's histories, within the context of recognising social work as a social construction. Almost by definition, social work, as a subject for study, is slippery and elusive. It is complex and contested, ambiguous and fluid – and yet this uncertainty is, in many ways, its strength. Furthermore, the magnitude and breadth of the current changes facing the activity known as 'social work' – and probably daunting for any new entrant to professional qualifying training – can be seen as a threat or a challenge. As Adams et al. (2002a, p335) note in their concluding remarks:

> *change can offer both opportunities and risks...there may be advantages in being more closely associated with a more universal and less stigmatised service [health care and education services] than social care has become. On the other hand, social explanations and needs may lose ground to more powerful medical models or educational priorities.*

This uncertainty is not unique to social work, but cuts across all of the public-sector activities. The difference lies in the degree of uncertainty and change. For example, it is reasonable to suggest that someone entering a teaching qualification programme can expect, upon qualification, to teach a given social group (children), an agreed subject (English) in an institutional structure (a school). Similar logic could be applied to general nursing training. A student undertaking a nursing degree can assume that their interest in paediatrics will result in obtaining a job in this field, working on a children's ward in a general hospital. By contrast, such certainties are not afforded the new entrant to social work training. The focus of work (the client/service user), the mode of work (the method) and the location (organisational structures) are all up for grabs. Nothing is sacrosanct.

The irony for social work is that many of the challenges to its role, status and function have – by virtue of their origins in the user empowerment movements – been reluctantly welcomed and celebrated by practitioners. Tom Shakespeare recounts the views of disabled people and other service users about the frustrations of engaging with local authority services:

> *Local authorities can deliver schemes. But social services is based on the model of dependency and care. They're not going to change... ideally, local authorities would deliver services but people have become so disillusioned with the lack of control they have had to go outside local authorities.*

(Shakespeare, 2000, p56)

Most social workers would accept this criticism. In their practice as employees, they both represent the authorities and challenge the constraints of bureaucratic systems.

In a very real sense, social work with some 'user groups' can be seen to be running on borrowed time. The user movements amongst various groups, who have traditionally occupied dependency roles in relation to social services, have begun to systematically challenge the role and functions of local authority departments and their employees (social workers). Their experiences of services over the recent decade, since the advent of the Community Care reforms, have often served to reinforce a sense of powerlessness and frustration. A team leader interviewed by Hadley and Clough (1998, p291) suggested that, from the point of view of users and carers, services are:

...complicated, fragmented and delayed by the split between case assessment, care management and social work. They are left confused and irritated.

Whilst more conventional attempted solutions to these problems are presumed to reside in procedural reorganisations, there are alternative and critical perspectives (as noted in Chapter 8) which seek to obviate the need for social work by addressing the surrounding 'disabling' forces:

Were disabled people to command incomes and resource through paid work, and were the social and physical environment suitably adapted so as to remove the obstacles that currently deny disabled people their citizenship, what kinds of duties would then remain for the statutory and voluntary agencies to perform?

(Drake, 1996, p163)

Thus while social work seems to be increasingly preoccupied with the boundaries between itself and other professional groups (such as professions allied to medicine), it sometimes does not seem to notice that aspects of its historic mandate – to act as a financial and service broker between service users and resource holders – are potentially becoming redundant through a combination of empowerment, changes in legal structures (such as direct payments and personal budgets), and the consequences of broader social inclusion initiatives (such as Welfare to Work schemes). Cree (2002, p26) is of the view that:

Social Work clients have become 'customers' and the introduction of direct payments has given service users much more power over the nature of the service they receive, transforming the role of social worker to that of adviser and facilitator.

The centrality of user perspectives

The panoply of new structures claims to have *service users at the heart* of the modernising reforms.

ACTIVITY 9.1

Based upon your current experience and practice, and your acquired knowledge and understanding, how would you define 'service users'?

COMMENT

You might find it useful to look at various definitions, such as – service users: People who voluntarily or non-voluntarily need support from the public, voluntary and private sectors, to carry out ordinary daily activities *(see NISW and Rowntree Foundation, 2001;* **www. shapingourlives.org.uk***). The Shaping Our Lives organisation expresses a vision:*

of an equal and fair society where people have opportunities, choices, rights and responsibilities; a society where people have choice and control over the way they live and the support service they need.

Service users from the margins to the heart: a model of inclusive development (Adapted from Christine Barton, 2003)	
From	To
Service providers in control	Service users in control
Fragmented services, separated by rigid boundaries	Services working together in a person-centred, joint approach
Service providers having separate budgets and services	Service providers having pooled budgets and seamless services
Fragmented information, jargon-laden and in one format	Single access points, plain English, other languages and different formats
Service provider determines support needs and solutions	Service user determines support needs and solutions
Single disciplines and specialist skills in rigid services	Multi-disciplinary teams, with multi-skilled flexible workers
Welfare or individual rights approach	Social approach to dismantle barriers

Service users at the heart: a holistic approach

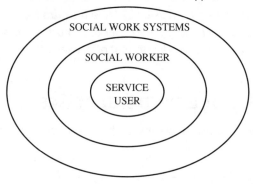

SCIE (2002) has contributed to *Setting the Agenda for Change* by undertaking a 'listening exercise', that involved front line staff, managers, researchers/trainers, service users and carers.

Summary of findings from the listening exercise report (SCIE)

There was strong feeling that services were not designed around the needs of users and carers, and that these groups should be more involved in design and delivery.

There was concern that services were not of uniform quality – either geographically or across various user groups.

Specifically priority concern was identified for:

- users and carers: access to and participation in services, as well as involvement in planning and delivery;

- practitioners and front line staff: need to make services needs-led rather than service-led and it was felt there is insufficient scope for practitioners to treat users as individuals;

- managers: concerned about management issues, such as planning, human resources, standards and quality, service coordination and communication;

- researchers, trainers and planners: concerned with the cultural and organisational framework, and systems for providing information and knowledge.

Consultations by NISW and Rowntree Foundation (1998) had shown that service users generally accept:

- the social model of mental health and disability;

- the need for users to identify their own preferred outcomes in assessment, support, care and control;

- users' wishes to manage their own resources through direct payment arrangements and growth of user-led services;

- their expertise as a major resource of knowledge for developing policy, services and practice;

- services and practice addressing issues of gender, race or disability discrimination.

In a relatively recent speech entitled *Impact of Regulation and the Future of Inspection*, the then Chief Inspector of CSCI David Behan (2005) affirmed that people want:

- choice;

- flexibility;

- information;

- being like other people and taking risks;

- respect and being heard;

- fairness and non-discrimination;

- cost and value;

- safety.

So, if the above gives us a sense of what matters to service users – and this list has been remarkably consistent over decades, even if the language has changed – then what do users want social workers to be like?

147

Finding out what users want social workers to be like

When the GSCC announced the then reform of social work education in 2002, with the institution of a new qualifying award, it set up a series of focus groups to ask key stakeholders – service users, carers, students, academics, employers – to identify the desired personal characteristics of social workers, thereby helping to shape the curriculum for the New Award in Social Work Qualification.

ACTIVITY 9.2

What do you think service users identified as what matters to them? What do service users want social workers to be like?

COMMENT

What matters to service users is summarised in two short statements in their report. They identified:

1. *the need for social workers to understand what a person's life is really like, and not to make assumptions and judgements about what they think the person wants or needs;*

2. *the importance of the quality of the relationships that the social worker has with the service user.*

More specifically, service users want social worker to be:

- physically and emotionally available;

- supportive, encouraging and reassuring;

- respectful;

- patient and attentive to the service users' problems;

- committed to the independence of the individual;

- punctual;

- trustworthy;

- reliable;

- friendly but not frightened to tell people how they see things;

- empathic and warm.

In addition, service users want social workers to have practical knowledge and information about law, benefits and diverse cultures; to possess skills in listening, counselling, assessing, case managing and finding practical ways to help service users; and service users want to keep the same social worker or have a good handover if they must change (Reform Focus Groups, 2002).

The coherence of user perspectives

There would appear to be a remarkable consistency amongst service users as to the qualities of social workers that are valued and valuable to them. Note the following statement from the learning disability advocacy group, Shaping our Lives, suggesting that service users:

> ... value a social work approach based on challenging the broader barriers they face. They place a particular value on social work's social approach, the social work relationship, and the positive personal qualities they associated with social workers. These include warmth, respect, being non-judgemental, listening, treating people with equality, being trustworthy, open, honest and reliable, and communicating well. People value the support social workers offer as well as their ability to help them access and deal with other services and agencies.

(Shaping Our Lives/P Beresford, 2007, pp6–7)

In short, service users value social workers who:

- enable them to work out their own agendas with them;

- give them time to sort things out;

- are available and accessible;

- provide continuity of support;

- are reliable and deliver;

- are responsive;

- have a good level of knowledge and expertise;

- value the expertise of the service user.

(Shaping Our Lives/P Beresford, 2007, p6)

Similarly, in children's services, it is plainly apparent that children and young people value quality relationships with professionals. Consider these three statements from young people themselves:

> The qualities my ideal social worker would have are: to be friendly and compassionate, to listen to what I want and what ways I can go around things to get it, to always be there for me, not to nag at me when I don't know what to do for my future.

> I thought you were meant to get a working relationship with social workers, but it's like I do not even know her.

(DCSF, 2009a, pp9–10)

> My ideal social worker would be a good listener, caring, reliable, punctual, understanding and would help me have a say in reviews.

(General Social Care Council, 2008a, p18)

The view of the service user

The following narrative recounts a conversation with a service user of a drug and alcohol centre.

Q: What qualities do you feel a social worker should have?

A: They should start by seeing everyone as individual. You need to get to know a person's uniqueness...show you are interested in a person...be able to show friendship... it's about connecting. (About the relationship) It's a gradual process, with building blocks. You need to take time to see service users in different settings – at home, at the (office), other places.

Q: What knowledge and training do social workers need?

A: Some drug awareness, about what drugs do to people's minds, their bodies. You need to know signs and symptoms when you can talk to people and when you can't. But don't rely on checklists. You put yourself at risk if you don't see the signs and symptoms.

Mostly, social workers need to know about communication – how to control and lead a conversation, how to get service users interested. You need to learn about body language.

Q: What has been your experience of social workers?

A: I've had bad social workers, and good ones who leave. Why am I always being passed on? You're always having to let someone else in.

Clients need to be assertive: to get everything they need and deserve from the service, and then say goodbye.

I want a free choice of who I work with, who I associate with. You can't have that as a service user – the service determines who you talk to.

The testimony above highlights a number of key learning points.

1. *The importance of relationships with workers that make a difference to people's lives. These can be called* resourceful friendships *(Holman, 2003).*

2. *The importance of stability and consistency of contacts. Research by Godfrey (2000) reveals that older people in residential care homes most valued 'naturally' kind, caring and understanding staff and were more likely to perceive these qualities in staff who had spent a long time in post.*

3. We all, social workers and service users alike, have unmet wants, and if these are ever to be met we must make our story visible and look at the stories of others, to see our situations not as 'no exit' places but as places capable of reform *(Milner and O'Byrne, 2002, p36).*

As we have noted elsewhere, these human testimonies are crucial to an ethically informed understanding of the lives of those people who use social work services.

What do carers want social workers to be like?

It is instructive to begin with some facts about carers, to offer a context.

- According to Bill Kilgallon (Chief Executive of SCIE), *one in three of us will have a caring responsibility at some point in our lives.*

- Carers look after family members, partners or friends in need of help because they are ill, frail or have a disability.

- Carers are unpaid – care workers are paid.

- There are over 6.1 million carers in the UK, including 50,000 young carers.

- The value of carers' contribution to the UK economy is the equivalent of £57.4 billion.

- *Carers are often in difficult situations – they are not being difficult carers.* For example, being a carer evokes complex and difficult feelings: *I always feel guilty when she goes. Then when she's gone, I feel free* (Levin et al., 1994, p110).

(Information from Alex Aebescher: Action for Carers, Surrey. Speech to *Social Work Steps Forward Conference*, 12 May 2003, London.)

When asked about their preferred qualities in social workers...*carers across the groups generally felt that social workers lacked autonomy and the ability to make creative decisions or even day to day decisions that would impact upon carers and those cared for* (Carers UK and City and Guilds Affinity, 2002). In addition, they felt that social workers needed to:

- consider changing their name to 'advocate' (suggestion from minority ethnic carers focus group);

- be better equipped with practical and communication skills;

- be able to listen to what they are being told and to unspoken messages from carers;

- possess counselling skills in order to work with people in difficult circumstances;

- develop cultural awareness;

- receive a practical training in information and legal skills;

- be adept at knowing how to access information (rather than knowing everything themselves);

- be able to manage the tension on the 'front line' of balancing needs and resources due to tight eligibility criteria.

What do employers want social workers to be like?

Bill McKitterick (formerly Chair of ADSS Human Resources and Training Committee) identified the prime responsibilities for social workers.

1. Achieving personal change and an increase in capacity.

2. Undertaking holistic assessments.

3. Arranging and reviewing high-risk cases.

4. Making judgements on the quality of services being provided.

5. Helping and empowering people and their carers.

6. Providing advice, information, personal support, counselling and therapy.

7. Working within a range of agency and multi-disciplinary settings.

The above must be delivered in accordance with a values and skills base, that means:

- acting as joint guardians of the GSCC Code of practice;

- promoting independence and self-determination;

- celebrating diversity;

- tackling inequality;

- working from a strong research base;

- rigorous graduate level analytical and problem-solving capacity.

Social work's objectives should include:

- promoting independence for older and disabled people;

- increasing life chances for children, young people and their families;

- reducing health inequalities and social exclusion.

In addition, service users need:

- workers who understand disability, mental health issues, the needs of older people, the development issues of children and young people;

- workers who can communicate effectively;

- workers who can undertake appropriate assessments within the context of legal frameworks;

- workers who can operate from a clear value base, that celebrates diversity, and that promotes participation, partnership and empowerment;

- workers who can ensure the effective delivery of appropriate services by working through inter-professional collaboration or by operating within multi-professional teams;

- workers who can engage in reflective practice, who seek out feedback from service users, and who can recognise areas for improvement, development and change.

In December 2008, the GSCC conducted a regional meeting with employers, to find out if they were getting the graduate from the new degree, fit for purpose, for the demands of being a newly qualified social worker. Within the context of general satisfaction, a number of key pointers to improvement emerged, including:

- employers need students (and future employees) to possess core communication skills, face-to-face and via the phone: the ability to take accurate messages and write coherent records;

- employers need students (and future employees) to have a good standard of literacy, developed IT skills and financial ability.

Which direction now?

The above lists – from service users, carers, and employers – offer a vision for social work's future, but the question remains about where social work is positioned within society, its angle, its pitch. Jordan and Jordan (2000, p37) ask:

> whether professional social work any longer seeks to be credible at street level, with service user and carers, or whether it is developing into an arm's length, office bound, report-writing, official kind of practice, which leaves face-to-face work to others.

In a similar vein, Stevenson and Parsloe, (1993, p59) wondered whether the ideological life-blood of social work was being squeezed out by the sheer weight of the bureaucratic task:

> [In social services departments] there is a genuine warmth towards ideas of empowerment. Yet there is also a mechanistic, controlling trend which arises from the specification of assessment procedures, eligibility criteria, budgetary control, and the contract culture.

Indeed, such is the level of concern about the degree of bureaucratisation confronting the job that *Community Care* magazine conducted a survey of 2,200 professionals in 2005 and found that more than half spend at least 60 per cent and over a fifth spent at least 80 per cent of their working week on paperwork. The Munro Report (DfE, 2011) has similarly highlighted the bureaucratisation of current practice.

The limits of information as the source of making the right decisions

Such a high level of administrative activity is hardly surprising, as all employing agencies become necessarily 'risk averse' when faced with the possibility of being the next authority 'named and shamed' by the tabloids or by government. Therefore, the inevitable tendency is to manage uncertainty by gathering more and more information. The assumption is that the ultimate correctness of decisions is in direct proportion to the quantity of information available. Thus, in relation to vulnerable children and young people, the model is as follows: as long as all professionals in all agencies are working in an integrated way, sharing the maximum amount of information about children and young people, they will be safeguarded. We can, of course, recognise this as spurious logic.

In relation to every case, practitioners – along with their colleagues and managers – have to travel a complex path from data (hard facts), to information (softer 'facts') to knowledge (understanding of a situation), to wisdom (making 'wise' decisions about intervention and risk). This is a challenging journey, and no amount of information-gathering and sharing will ultimately provide the answer to the question: *What are we going to do?* The contemporary desire for standardised information, via the latest data processing systems, exemplifies Modernity, which as Fook (2002, p11) asserts:

> the characteristic feature of the modernist world is the belief that conditions can
> be progressively bettered through the establishment of reliable, universal and
> generalisable knowledge, developed through the use of reason and scientific methods.

However, there is undoubtedly a feeling that information technology, and the demand for recording data, has taken over the social work task in relation to all service user groups. A number of commentators have begun to question the value of rule-based regulation, and instead advocate the value of judgement-based regulation. In other words, we need to develop ways to evaluate the quality of decision-making as distinct from monitoring the adherence to rules. As things stand, the quest for performance management denies the reality that social work is essentially about uncertainty. Indeed, it might be the case that as with many professional spheres, the best social work can flourish and grow only in a working environment in which the worst social work can also occur. To eradicate risk means to micro-manage practice to the point where all relationships of meaning and value – with strong elements of dynamic creativity and reciprocity – are essentially prohibited. As organisations become more complex and matrix management systems become ever more the norm, the establishment of effective supervision processes – that address the needs of the professional as well as the management of the case – become all the more essential (Peach and Homer, 2007).

So, it is important to allow the reforming zeal of new entrants to the profession to flower. Social work is not only a bureaucratic endeavour, but also one in which creativity is constantly required to think out new solutions to old problems:

> The skills and commitment of social workers as they take up new roles in new settings
> offer the chance for every worker to have an impact, to make a difference not only to
> the lives of the people with whom they work, but also to the impact that social work
> might have on the societies in which we live.

(Adams et al., 2002a, p335)

As an agent for change, social work needs to constantly imagine what could be improved, what needs to change. Social work has an enduring mission, to hark back to its earliest identity. It is destined to be difficult, to stand alongside individuals and groups who are constantly demanding a 'rethink' about their rights and responsibilities from the dominant social groupings. In fact, it could be said that if social work ended up getting a 'good press' – given the nature, indeed, of the majority British press – the mission might indeed be lost.

It is this tradition of being difficult and awkward, of challenging assumptions and 'givens' in the social order, that most represent social work's distinctiveness. Dominelli (1997, p248) exhorts practitioners to be:

proud of embarking on a journey to remove the shackles of oppression, which distort and destroy the lives, the humanity that is the right of every individual to experience. Social work has a critical role in enabling each person to develop their full potential in social setting.

Significantly, in spite of the fears about social work being 'swallowed up' by the leviathan of the Health Service, the Department of Health affirms a commitment to social work itself:

We want to create a different environment, which reinforces core social work values of supporting individuals to create control of their lives, and to make choices that matter to them. We therefore emphasise the role that skilled social work will continue to play in assessing the needs of people with complex problems and in developing constructive relationships with people who need long term support.

(Department of Health, 2005b, p10)

To this end, we need to reflect upon the current situation of those defined as service users, and try to imagine the critical discourse of future hindsight.

ACTIVITY **9.3**

The year is 2025, and a review is being conducted of social work practice over the first quarter of the twenty-first century. Inevitably, critical commentators are shocked and perturbed at some of the accepted practices of only a few years earlier. What aspect of our current practices would the future reflective practitioner be most concerned about?

COMMENT

It is very difficult to anticipate the sensibilities of hindsight, but we can be sure of only one thing: there will be much to be concerned about. Such is the nature of change and evolving practice. When current students have been asked the same question, they have made the following predictions.

- *The apparent incapacity of child welfare systems to offer any kind of stability to the most troubled and damaged children and young people.*

- *The absence of continuing care and responsibility for children and young people brought up in public care.*

- *The persistence of poverty as the key determinant in the social construction of 'clienthood'. This is particularly pertinent given the apparent inability – or unwillingness – of government to introduce measures to reduce the number of children, families, disabled people or older people living in poverty.*

- *The massive expansion of the 'managerial' class in public welfare systems which, given a relatively static resource base, has meant a shift from front line services towards management and regulatory strata.*

Continued

COMMENT *continued*

- *The apparent reticence to relinquish power – in the form of money – through direct payments and similar schemes which have been slow to expand, particularly in relation to older people.*

- *The shift in balance towards 'public protection' at the expense of the rights of the most damaged and vulnerable people (particularly people with enduring mental health problems and those with learning disabilities).*

Future visions

The edited text *From Welfare to Wellbeing* (Kendall and Harker, 2002) sets out a vision for social care in 2020. Significantly, the authors envisage an end to social work, as we currently know it, and the demise of social services departments, which would be replaced by age-related organisations. Today's practitioners would endorse many aspects of the thesis – a shift of focus from crisis reaction towards preventative services, configured around community involvement and an enhanced role for the voluntary sector. As the authors state in the book briefing:

> *By 2020, social care's focus should be on empowering individuals to maximize their abilities and opportunities, to lead lives that are as independent and autonomous as possible, and to participate in lifestyles that are valued by wider society. This vision can only be achieved within and through strong communities.*

(Kendall and Harker, 2002)

Greater dissension would stem from the authors' belief in the elimination of genericism, to be replaced by specialist training for specialist workers, for example those engaged in a dedicated child protection service.

Much of what was predicted in 2002 has already come to pass. Social services departments have fragmented and specialist services have emerged.

Concluding remarks

> *Social work is about a group of people who constantly talk about what social work is.*

The essence of this book has been to explore the nature of social work and social care by offering a brief account of its history, its evolution, its development and its sense of self. Whilst the question might have appeared easy, the answer could never have been anything other than complex and perhaps confusing. We have shown that there are many 'social works', each with contested histories. Cree (2003, p4) concludes

> *that there is no essential social work task. Rather, social work is best understood as a collection of competing and contradictory discourses that come together at a particular moment in time to frame the task of social work, defining not just its capabilities, but also its potential.*

Yet, in spite of this accepted degree of ambivalence, the concepts of 'social work' and 'social care' persist, given new life by the establishment of an array of regulatory, educational and 'professionalising' bodies, as discussed in Chapter 8.

Given the diversity of 'social works', and the plurality of histories, one might be tempted to concur with the suggestion from Thompson (2000, p13) that *at one level, we could simply say that social work is what social workers do*. Indeed, such a position has merit, although we need to consider the public's perception of the dominant image of social work, and the location of this activity. After all, in the public imagination, 'nurses' work in hospitals, even though many work 'in the community'. Similarly, 'teachers' are seen to work in schools, although some do not (such as home tutors). So, if *social work is what social workers do*, we have to be mindful that, given the predominance of the discourse concerning child protection and child welfare, then social workers are bound to be seen as either effective (by taking children away from their homes – but not too many), or they are ineffective (by failing to take them away, thereby exposing them to unacceptable risk of harm or even death). Such is the dimension of measurement in the public arena. Yet social work, as a profession, stands or falls by the judgements made on a daily basis by its lowest ranks.

The gathering storm or a new dawn?

Not for the first time, social work is facing intense public and political scrutiny as to its role, function and effectiveness. The almost predictably periodic outcry that follows the death of a child who was known to a statutory agency that employs social workers at the point of the tragedy leads to a reopening of the debate about social work: how does it fail to protect children when it is suggested in relation to each such case that 'common sense' would have lead to statutory action to remove and 'save' the child?

It is instructive to note that social work, as a profession, is uniquely vulnerable to the alleged deficiencies of one of its number being extrapolated to call into question the efficacy of all. Dominelli (2009; pp21–2) addresses this point in a most pointed fashion:

> When Harold Shipman, GP, murdered 250 patients between 1971 and 1998 before getting caught, the medical profession was not brought into disrepute ... (I)n sharp contrast, the social workers' entire profession is castigated when not they, but other carers, e.g., a mother's boyfriend, murder a child. For them, demands for wholesale changes to practice become unstoppable after an inquiry report.

A tragedy in the child protection/safeguarding system leads, inexorably, to the discrediting, by association, of social workers engaged in providing services to other groups, such as those working with older people, with people experiencing mental distress, or with people with learning difficulties. Such a repeated dynamic has led to calls, from some quarters, to split the profession – into adult care workers and children's services workers – with separate training routes, separate registrations and separate career pathways.

So far, the government and the GSCC have consistently endorsed the qualifying degree as being 'generic'. This keeps social work on a shared footing with other professions that offer a generic training, such as for nurses and doctors with specialisation being located at the post-qualifying level.

As we have already noted, in January, 2009 the Departments of Health and for Children, Schools and Families launched a joint Social Work Taskforce. Its remit was to 'undertake a comprehensive review of frontline social work practice' which would include recommendations to reform social work education. The Taskforce was required to identify barriers social workers face in doing their job effectively.

The remit of the Taskforce (2009) was to consider the following.

- *How professional social workers are deploying their time now.*
- *Why they prioritise their time in the way they do.*
- *What support and supervision they receive and whether it is effective and fit for purpose.*
- *What actions and behaviours by professional social workers make the most difference to vulnerable children and adults.*
- *How to ensure there are the right number of social workers on the front line to secure high-quality services and support.*
- *What changes are needed to drive improvements in frontline practice.*

According to the former DCSF Minister, Ed Balls: *The role of the taskforce will be to support and develop their [social workers'] work, training, recruitment and day-to-day practice so that social work is, and is seen to be, a high quality and self confident profession with the confidence and esteem of the public.* The Statement stated that:

> *The Taskforce's work will inform how we take forward our long-term priorities for change in social work, which are:*
>
> - *improving initial social worker training – to give more focus on practical skills and specific knowledge needed to work with children and families and high quality induction once they enter employment;*
>
> - *driving quality in professional practice to improve continuing professional development for frontline social workers as well as tightening requirements for social workers to keep skills and knowledge up to date;*
>
> - *attracting and retaining the brightest and best in social work by developing more pathways into social work and giving better incentives for excellent social workers to work in tough frontline roles;*
>
> - *strengthening the leadership, management and supervision of frontline social workers; and making inspection and quality assurance arrangements better able to challenge poor practice where it exists.*
>
> Ministerial statement at the launch of the Social Work Taskforce, January, 2009

The ambition for the Taskforce was that by 2010 *social work would be better understood, better supported and challenged; that this opportunity would have been seized and that the rewards would be protected children and professional confidence and enhancement.*

It was expected that the Taskforce would include the role and functions of managers within its purview.

In December 2009 the Social Work Task Force made 15 recommendations for the comprehensive reform of the social work profession. As a result, the Social Work Reform Board brought together key partners from across the sector to develop the recommendations for implementation, monitor and report on progress, and to advise and influence the sector and government.

The Reform Board's reports (Social Work Reform Board, 2010, 2011) set out plans for five key areas of reform.

- A Professional Capabilities Framework – which has established expectations of social workers at every point of their career – from entry onto the social work degree to advanced social work roles.

- Standards for Employers and a Supervision Framework – which set out the responsibilities of employers in respect of their social work workforce.

- Principles that should underpin a Continuing Professional Development Framework aligned to the Professional Capabilities Framework, to help social workers develop specialist knowledge, improve their practice and progress in their careers.

- Proposed requirements for social work education – so that student social workers receive high-quality preparation for joining the profession.

- Proposals for effective partnership working – between employers and higher education institutions in providing practice placements for degree students and continuing professional development (CPD) for social workers.

Perceived gaps in knowledge, understanding and skills

Evidence to the Social Work Taskforce had suggested that some social work students were passing when they should not be doing so, that some newly qualified social workers (NQSWs) were deficient in key areas such as assessment, mental health and substance misuse, and that students were not being taught the essential knowledge, skills, methods and values to become a social worker in some courses. In a similar vein, the former Select Committee on Children, Schools and Families (2009, para 65) commented in its report on the education of social workers working with children and families that: *It is unacceptable that social work courses, or any element of them, should have a reputation for being 'difficult to fail'.*

In the light of these concerns, the Social Work Reform Board recommendations will make student selection, progression, assessment (both academically and in practice) and accreditation as suitable for professional registration much more rigorous and closely scrutinised.

It is instructive to note that hitherto the term 'social worker' has applied only to 'front line' practitioners. Whilst schoolteachers are managed by senior teachers and head teachers, social workers are managed by – managers. A survey of contemporary social services departments indicates a remarkable desire by workers to divest themselves of the term 'social worker' at the earliest opportunity. The point is made powerfully by Sapey (2002, p188):

> *Social workers work in organisational structures which devalue direct work with clients,*

and

> *In order to have a career in social work in the conventional sense of moving up the hierarchy and salary scale, social workers have to actively seek posts with reduced or no contact with their clients.*

This development can in large measure be attributable to the systematic importation of a culture of managerialism into all aspects of public life, especially public services. It might, however, also be a consequence of the disdain in which the term 'social worker' is held. Thus, the senior officer of say an adult social services department, when chatting at a social gathering, does not have to introduce herself or himself as a social worker – however senior – but can proclaim that the surrounding audience is graced by the presence of a service manager, an operations manager, a commissioning manager. It would be akin to meeting a senior teacher from a secondary school, who introduced herself as a strategic educational manager (academic performance and review).

This linguistic change has been most marked over the past decade, coinciding with the era of managerialism in the public sector. Compare the charts below, taken from the City of Sheffield Children's Department Report (1967), from job adverts in *Community Care*, the first in 1989 and the second in 2003, and from the Children's Services Directorate and adult care services in 2006.

The changing identity of social work organisations

Children's department (1967)	Social services department (1989)	Social services directorate (2003)	Children's services directorate (2006)	Adult care services (2006)
Children's officer	Director of social services	Director of social services	Director of children's services	Director of adult care services
Deputy children's officer	Assistant director of social services	Assistant director/head of service	Director of delivery/of planning performance and partnership	Assistant director of operations/of performance and commissioning
Principal assistant children's officer	Divisional director	Group manager/head of strategic planning and commissioning/joint commissioning manager	Commissioning manager	Commissioning manager
Area children's officer	Principal social worker	Operation manager/sector manager/performance review and information manager/ locality manager/ strategic development manager/service improvement manager	Service manager	Service manager
Senior child care officer	Senior social worker	Team manager/service manager	Team/practice manager	Team/practice manager

Child care officer	Social worker/ trainee social worker	Social worker/senior practitioner/care manager	Senior practitioner	Care manager
Child care assistant	Social work assistant	Community care assistants or social work assistants	Child and family social worker	Individual budgets support brokers
	Domiciliary care organiser	Home care organiser	Family support workers	Community care workers

The impact of managerialism has been more than a matter of a linguistic makeover, more than a cultural shift. Whilst the number of social services staff fell by 7 per cent between 1995 and 2000, the number of directors and senior staff rose by nearly 50 per cent over the same period (Department of Health, 2001a). The situation has yet to turn around, in spite of government proclamations of their determination to reduce bureaucracy. There were approximately 20,200 WTE central/strategic and HQ staff in 2010. Significant increases across the past ten-year period have been seen in senior professional support, senior directing staff, planning staff and training staff. The largest increase was shown by senior professional staff, an increase of 35 per cent (1,500 WTE staff) over the ten-year period to 5,700 in 2010. Critical observers might, perhaps cynically, discern a self-serving triangular synergy between those who generate an ever-increasing raft of requirements for outcome measurements, performance indicators, returns and reports; those who, in management positions, process and return the data; and those who inspect they have done it satisfactorily. Such managers, performance reviewers, and inspectors – invariably former social workers – are now engaged in the burgeoning Quality Assurance industry.

Powell (2001, p67) suggests that in spite of the language of managerialism and the importation of quality control mechanisms:

> *ultimately, social work's value system is located in the classical humanist notion of a virtuous society, based upon a commitment to humanity, equality and social justice, rather than the vagaries of fortune that define market capitalism*

and perhaps it is these enduring, if not immutable values, that might prove more resilient than the transient fashions of organisational delivery structures. As Cree sumarises (2002, p28):

> *Social work has a long tradition of working alongside people, valuing difference and having concern for social justice and inequality. These are the aspects of social work that we must build on in the future, wherever social working is located.*

After all, critical theory and analysis would lead us to recognise that a social worker cannot sit on the fence. Once we allow ourselves to become engaged with a whole host of people – who have fewer opportunities, fewer choices and less power than us as individuals and the systems we represent – our actions, or inactions, matter and are significant. Vernon (2002, p67) quotes Read (1988), who points out that in a society that is riddled with oppression there is no neutral ground. In a very real sense, social work operates at the border post between the socially included and the socially excluded.

161

End comment

So, what is social work? Many readers of this book will be undertaking government-funded, government-approved qualifying training courses, so it is useful to remind ourselves of 'official' definitions of social work before we move towards concluding remarks.

> *Social workers work with people in difficulty, sometimes in crisis, helping them make crucial decisions, and regain control of their lives.*
>
> *Social workers form partnerships with people: helping them to assess and interpret the problems they face, and supporting them in finding solutions.*

(Department of Health, 2002f)

Some authors, such as Thompson (2000, p173), have acknowledged the need for introductory texts about social work to be *realistic about the challenges, demands and dilemmas of social work*, which hopefully will enable those entering the profession to engage in the ongoing debates about social work's current and future goals and purpose. It is an activity that requires its practitioners to embrace and thrive upon uncertainty, upon 'not knowing'. Social work does not exist as an entity apart from what social workers do; practice shapes its identity. Yet its practice is determined by the interaction between those in need of a service, and society's delegation of a response to the practitioner – the social worker. Butrym (1976, pix), over a quarter of a century ago, encapsulated this dilemma:

> *Social work derives from the society of which it is part. The preoccupation of social work with people and their social circumstances creates its main occupational risk – a lack of specificity, an inherent ambiguity.*

It is this very ambiguity of social work that is its strength, and we hope you, the student, feel better equipped to engage in such a practice context, at least armed with the knowledge of social work's histories, traditions and legacies, and better equipped to engage in the ongoing debates about social work's future.

At the recent House of Commons Awards, Hilton Dawson, chief executive of BASW, summed up the ambiguity and dilemmas facing us all when asked where he saw the social work profession in five years time. He said, *Where social work is in five years, is down to us. We can make it or break it* (cited in Beresford, 2011).

According to Peter Beresford (2011):

> *waiting for the politicians and policymakers to get it right, will have us waiting for a very long time indeed. Social workers, in alliance with service users and their organisations, must see themselves as holding social work's future in their hands. It is a massive responsibility, in very difficult times. But it is undeniably the way to go... having confidence must be at the heart of our resolutions for the future.*

The very last word: Key messages for beginning social workers

We end this introductory text by going back to users and carers and reflecting upon their ideas about how social work students should be trained:

It is important to have training from the carer's perspective. They need to 'walk a mile in my shoes'

and

social workers don't speak the same language as carers.

(Carers' submissions to the focus groups)

and:

Without exception, participants in the focus groups wanted trainee social workers to have a placement that gave them the opportunity to step into carers' shoes. Suggestions ranged from shadowing a carer, a placement with a carer organisation to living with a carer for a week…there was a consensus that students should have one placement during education and training that gave them direct, or at very least, indirect experience of carers.

(Carers UK and City and Guilds Affinity, 2002)

So, in summary, what do service users and carers want from you?

Regular contact, a pro-active approach, better understanding, empathy, better communication. A contract would be good. A named contact. Social workers to stop using the excuse – 'lack of money' – for not being able to provide services. Even when resources aren't available, alternatives can be provided.

The fear of social work losing its identity is, in one sense, a fear of engaging in *Les Liaisons Dangereuses* with the much larger organisations of education and health. To the service user, it is the quality of service towards the quality of outcome that matters, not who delivers it. When we begin to look at people's complex needs – often sitting at the interface between health, housing, income support, education and personal care systems then we can see the essential need for a service navigator (Rankin and Regan, 2004) to make a real difference.

Much of what we achieve is driven and shaped by our aspirations for others and ourselves. According to the Department for Children, Schools and Families (DCSF, 2008, p6), everyone who works with children and young people should be:

* **ambitious** for every child and young person;
* **excellent** in their practice;
* **committed** to partnership and integrated working;
* **respected** and valued as professionals.

The outcome of learning, training, qualification and practice might be to deserve the following testimony:

I would like to hang onto my social worker: she is experienced and sensitive as well as consistent.

Good luck in your quest.

FURTHER READING

Blewett, J and Tunstill, J (2007) *Fit for purpose? The social work degree in 2007*. London: Synergy Research & Consulting Ltd.

An examination of *Children's Plan* (Secretary of State for Children, Schools and Families, 2007) and the reforms in adult care services will affect social work practice – and therefore what kind of qualifying award is most appropriate for the future.

GSCC (2008) *Social work at its best: A statement of social work roles and tasks for the 21st century*. London: GSCC.

An important statement of social work's purpose from its regulatory body, the GSCC. The Statement identifies a range of situations in which social workers may have a lead role, and the functions requiring social work skill and expertise.

Harris, J and White, V (eds) (2009) *Modernising social work*. Bristol: Policy Press.

A very informative, challenging exploration of the impact of the *Modernising Social Services* agenda on social work practice and management.

Martyn, H (ed.) (2000) *Developing reflective practice*. Bristol: The Policy Press.

A fascinating book that explores how social workers learn, reflect upon and develop their practice.

Pitkeathley, J (1989) *It's my duty, isn't it? The plight of carers in our society*. London: Souvenir Press.

An early text that acknowledges the contribution of carers to the welfare system.

Scottish Executive (2006) *Changing lives: report of the 21st century Social Work Review*. Edinburgh: The Scottish Executive **www.scotland.gov.uk/publications**

This document, although referring to Scotland, is an inspiring affirmation as to the role and purpose of social work in the twenty-first century.

Social Care Institute for Excellence (2002) *Listening exercise: Summary of findings*. London: SCIE.

A key document that finds out what constituent stakeholders – service users, carers, practitioners – think about social work and social care.

Appendix 1 Professional Capabilities Framework

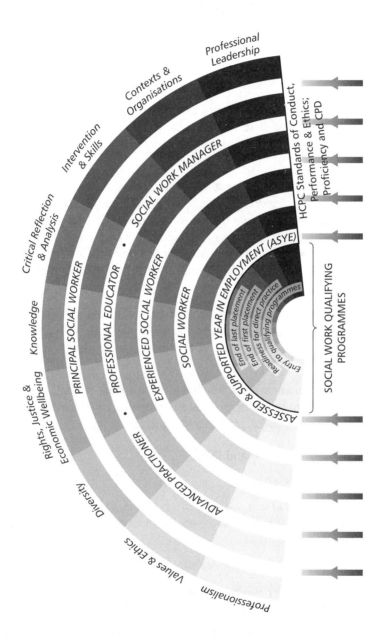

Professional Capabilities Framework diagram reproduced with permission of The College of Social Work.

Appendix 2 Subject Benchmark for Social Work

Defining principles

4.3 Contemporary definitions of social work as a degree subject reflect its origins in a range of different academic and practice traditions. The precise nature and scope of the subject is itself a matter for legitimate study and critical debate. Three main issues are relevant to this.

- Social work is located within different social welfare contexts. Within the UK there are different traditions of social welfare (influenced by legislation, historical development and social attitudes) and these have shaped both social work education and practice in community-based settings including residential, day care and substitute care. In an international context, distinctive national approaches to social welfare policy, provision and practice have greatly influenced the focus and content of social work degree programmes.

- There are competing views in society at large on the nature of social work and on its place and purpose. Social work practice and education inevitably reflect these differing perspectives on the role of social work in relation to social justice, social care and social order.

- Social work, both as occupational practice and as an academic subject, evolves, adapts and changes in response to the social, political and economic challenges and demands of contemporary social welfare policy, practice and legislation.

Subject knowledge, understanding and skills

Subject knowledge and understanding

5.1 During their degree studies in social work, honours graduates should acquire, critically evaluate, apply and integrate knowledge and understanding in the following core areas of study.

5.1.2 The service delivery context, which include:

- the location of contemporary social work within historical, comparative and global perspectives, including European and international contexts;

- the complex relationships between public, social and political philosophies, policies and priorities and the organisation and practice of social work, including the contested nature of these.

5.1.3 Values and ethics, which include:

- the nature, historical evolution and application of social work values.

Appendix 3 A code of ethics for social work (BASW) values and principles

Social work is committed to five basic values:

- human dignity and worth;
- social justice;
- service to humanity;
- integrity;
- competence.

Social work practice should both promote respect for *human dignity* and pursue *social justice*, through *service to humanity*, *integrity* and *competence*.

The statements concerning the five values are as follows.

1 Human dignity and worth

Every human being has intrinsic value. All persons have a right to well-being, to self-fulfilment and to as much control over their own lives as is consistent with the rights of others.

2 Social justice

Social justice includes:

- the fair and equitable distribution of resources to meet basic human needs;
- fair access to public services and benefits, to achieve human potential;
- recognition of the rights and duties of individuals, families, groups and communities;
- equal treatment and protection under the law;
- social development and environmental management in the interests of present and future human welfare.

The pursuit of social justice involves identifying, seeking to alleviate and advocating strategies for overcoming structural disadvantage.

3 Service to humanity

Service in the interests of human well-being and social justice is a primary objective of social work. Its fundamental goals are:

- to meet personal and social needs;
- to enable people to develop their potential;
- to contribute to the creation of a fairer society.

4 Integrity

Integrity comprises honesty, reliability, openness and impartiality, and is an essential value in the practice of social work.

5 Competence

Proficiency in social work practice is an essential value.

(Source: **www.basw.co.uk**)

Appendix 4 Mapping services in modern social work and social care settings

People with a physical disability	People with a learning disability	Older people	People with a mental illness	Children, young people and families
Social workers	Integrated community support – learning disability practitioners	Social workers; occupational therapists and community care officers	Locality mental health teams – health and social services staff	Social workers; child protection; family support; looked after children; children with disabilities
Equipment and adaptations	Social inclusion skills training	Equipment and adaptations	Assertive outreach	Equipment and adaptations for children with disabilities
Housing adaptations; direct payments	Direct payments	Housing adaptations; direct payments	Hospital treatment	Youth offending teams
Employment opportunities	Finding work	Lunch clubs and activities	Substance misuse teams	Children's centres
Home care and personal assistants	Personal care	Home care	Crisis teams	Family care
Community meals	Personal care	Community meals		
Day services	Day services	Day services	Day services and community support	Family centres and day care
Independent living schemes	Community supported living	Independent living schemes	Supported living	Foster families
Residential or nursing home care	Residential or nursing home care	Residential or nursing home care/intermediate care	Residential or nursing home care	Children's homes
Supported housing	Drop-in centres	Supported housing	Social housing after care	Housing for care leavers
Disabled badge scheme	Advice on welfare benefits	Disabled badge scheme	Employment support	Children's disability register
Help for carers	Help for carers	Help for carers	Help for carers	Help for carers

Appendix 5 Timeline of the development of social work

1598 1601	Poor Laws	– compulsory poor rate – 'overseers' of relief – 'setting the poor to work'
1722	Parliamentary Act	Parishes empowered to build workhouses
1762	Private Members Act	Duty on parish clerks to keep accurate records of the children in parish care
1766	Hanway's Act	All parish children under 6 were to be sent out of London, to be brought up by paid nurses in the country
1805	Lunacy Select Committee	Reported 1807. Identified appalling conditions of pauper and criminal lunatics in private madhouses. Advocated building large asylums
1808	Lunacy Act	Allowed magistrates to erect publicly funded asylums in each county
1828	County Asylums Act and Act for the Regulation of Mad-Houses	Compelled each county asylum to provide information to the Home Office
1834	Poor Law (Amendment) Act	Restricted outdoor relief, and forced more into workhouses
1845	Lunatics Act	Building of County Asylums made compulsory. Created the Lunacy Commission – inspections. Asylums to be run by medical practitioners
1853	Establishment of Charity Commissioners	
1858	General Medical Act	Medical practitioners given a monopoly over treatment of illness
1867	Metropolitan Poor Law Act	Separation of lunatics and those with infectious diseases out of workhouses
1869	Founding of the Charity Organisation Society	
1872	Infant Life Protection Act	Sought to address the problem of 'baby farming' – paying women to look after the infants – the result of campaigning by Infant Life Protection Society.
1874	Registration of Births and Deaths Act	Significant milestone: the state could now enumerate births and deaths
1883	Formation of the Fabian Society	Influential group advocating social welfare reforms
1884	London Society for the Prevention of Cruelty to Children founded	Changed named to National Society for the Prevention of Cruelty to Children (NSPCC) in 1889
1886	Idiots Act	Powers to detain people with learning disabilities in institutions
1886	Guardianship of Infants Act	Child's welfare was to be considered by the court in custody disputes

1889	Prevention of Cruelty to and Protection of Children Act	The 'Children's Charter'. Police powers to arrest anyone ill-treating a child, and warrant to enter a home
1890	Lunacy Act	Rule of certification and detention
1896	Founding of National Association for Promoting the Welfare of the Feeble Minded	Body that preceded MENCAP and other voluntary organisations
1891	Custody of Children Act	Courts empowered to determine custody of children based upon welfare principles
1893	Elementary Education (Blind and Deaf Children) Act	Duty on local authorities to ensure children with sensory impairments received 'efficient and suitable' education
1894	Amendments to 1889 Act	Recognition of mental cruelty; offence to deny a sick child medical attention
1895	Royal Commission on the Aged Poor	Including proposals to build almshouses to protect the aged poor from having to mix with 'undeserving' workhouse inmates
1903	First training course for social workers	
1904–08	Royal (Radnor) Commission	Examination of services for the 'feeble minded'
1905	Royal Commission on the Poor Laws (reported 1909)	Minority and Majority Reports
1907	The Probation of Offenders Act	Permitted the appointment of Probation Officers to 'advise, assist and befriend' probationers
1908	Children's Act	Establishment of juvenile courts; registration of foster carers
1908	Punishment of Incest Act	Sexual abuse in families a matter of state jurisdiction
1908	Royal Commission on the Care and Control of the Feeble Minded	Radnor Report. Advocated total segregation of 'feeble minded' children and adults
1909	Poor Law Royal Commission Reports	Majority (COS) and Minority (Fabian) Reports
1913	Mental Deficiency Act	Powers to detain those labelled as 'idiots', 'imbeciles' and 'moral defectives'. Duty of local authorities to exercise care and control for all 'mental defectives' in their area. Left education and care of children with LEAs
1924	Royal Commission on Lunacy and Mental Disorder	Reported in 1926
1925	Criminal Justice Act	Required the appointment of Probation Officers to 'advise, assist and befriend' probationers
1925	Guardianship of Infants Act	Child's welfare was to be 'first and paramount' consideration in custody disputes (compare with Act of 1886)
1926	Adoption Act	First adoption legislation, to clarify and safeguard position of children brought up by adults other than their birth parents
1927	Mental Deficiency Act	Duty of local authorities to provide training for 'defectives', leading to Occupational or Industrial Centres
1929	Local Government Act	Poor Law responsibilities given to counties and county boroughs, through public assistance committees. Transfer of Poor Law infirmaries to local authorities

1930	Mental Treatment Act	Focus on treatment rather than detention. Medical emphasis – away from use of courts towards medical control (weakening of legal protection)
1930	Poor Law Act	Restated duty of family members to support those in need
1933	Children and Young Persons Act	Duty on local authorities regarding child protection; powers to remove children in emergency situations
1942	Beveridge Report	Blueprint for the British Welfare State
1944	Education Act	Included special provision for the education of disabled children; defined duty of parent to ensure their child is properly educated, either at school, or 'otherwise'
1944	Disabled Persons (Employment) Act	Obligation placed on employers to employ a quota of people with disabilities
1945	Death of Dennis O'Neill	Monckton Report (August 1945)
1947	*Report on the Employment and Training of Social Workers* (1st Younghusband Report)	Trained Council in Child Care established
1946	Curtis Committee	Report of the Care of Children Committee
1948	National Assistance Act	Local authorities required to provide suitable accommodation for older people, those with disabilities
1948	Children Act	Establishment of children's departments
1951	*Social Work in Britain* (2nd Younghusband Report)	Led to foundation of National Institute for Social Work (NISW)
1954–57	Royal Commission on the Law Relating to Mental Illness and Mental Deficiency	Major review resulting in the 1959 Mental Health Act
1958	Adoption Act	Consolidation of provisions for adoption
1959	Mental Health Act	Emphasis on medical treatment; weakened legal checks on medical discretion; heralded demise of the Victorian asylum
1962	Ministry of Health Hospital Plan	Enoch Powell's vision of psychiatric services in the community and in general hospitals
1962	National Assistance (Amendment) Act	Local authorities allowed to offer home meals services
1963	Children and Young Persons Act	First legislation to allow local authorities to engage in preventative family work
1968	Seebohm Report	Report of the Committee on Local Authority and Allied Personal Social Services. Recommended 'generic' social working unified departments
1968	Health Services and Public Health Act	
1969	Children and Young Persons Act	'Welfare-led' reform: young offenders to be seen in need of care rather than punishment
1970	Local Authority Social Services Act	Implemented 1971 – realisation of Seebohm

1970	Chronically Sick and Disabled Persons Act	Local authorities required to find out the number of people with disabilities in their area, to inform them of relevant services, and to provide a range of practical services
1971	Establishment of CCETSW	Unified six predecessor bodies. Creation of CQSW (1972) and CSS (1976) qualifying courses
1971	Formation of British Association of Social Workers	Unified seven separate professional bodies
1971	*Better Services for the Mentally Handicapped*	DHSS report – first major strategy for this service user group
1973	Death of Maria Colwell	Inquiry held in 1974, leading to development of Area Child Protection Committees (ACPCs)
1974	Wolfenden Report	Report into the future of voluntary organisations
1975	Children Act	SSDs given greater powers over children in public care – easier to sever parental/family links and move towards adoption. Introduction of *Guardians ad litem*
1976	Adoption Act	
1977	National Health Service Act	Mandatory home care service
1979	Jay Report on Mental Handicap nursing and care	Recommended closures of long-stay hospitals and development of housing services in community
1980	Child Care Act	Voluntary care arrangements
1981	Education Act	Stated that disabled children have a right to be educated in mainstream school where it is 'compatible with the efficient use of resources'
1982	Barclay Committee Report	*Social Workers: Their Roles and Tasks*
1983	Mental Health Act	Established role of Approved Social Worker (ASW); CCETSW required to provide ASW training
1984	Registered Homes Act	Duty of local authority to register and inspect residential homes provided by the independent sector
1985–87	Inquiries into the deaths of Jasmine Beckford, Tyra Henry, Kimberley Carlile	Three reports with a significant impact on the 1989 Children Act
1986	Creation of Department of Health	Dismantling of Department of Health and Social Security
1986	Audit Commission	*Making a Reality of Community Care*
1986	Disabled Persons (Services, Consultation and Representation) Act	Local authorities required to publish relevant services and to involve people with disabilities in decisions
1987	Cleveland 'crisis'	Cleveland Report (Butler-Sloss), and *Working Together* guidance
1988	Griffiths Report	*Community Care: Agenda for Action.* Overview of Community Care policy: recommending purchaser/provider split
1988	Wagner Report	*Residential Care: A Positive Choice. Report of the Independent Review of Residential Care.* Aimed to raise status of residential work
1989	White Paper on Community Care	*Caring for People*

1989	Children Act	Implemented in 1991. Reform of all public and private law relating to family support, child protection, care proceedings, children looked after, day care etc.
1989	Revision of social work qualifying awards	Diploma in Social Work (DipSW) introduced, to replace CQSW and CSS
1990	National Health Service and Community Care Act	Implemented in 1993. Transfer of funding from DSS to SSDs. Duty of local authority to inspect local authority residential homes
1990	Introduction of the Diploma in Social Work (DipSW)	Replaced CQSW (for field workers) and CSS (for residential and day care workers)
1991	Registered Homes (Amendment) Act	Registration and inspection of broader range of services, including daycare, home care and adult placement schemes
1991	Criminal Justice Act	Establishment of Youth Courts for 10–17 year olds
1992	Warner Report	*Choosing with Care.* Recruitment, selection, development and management of staff in children's homes
1993	Education Act	Assessments of educational needs of children with disabilities
1995	Mental Health (Patients in the Community) Act	Community Care plans for mental health services
1995	Carers (Recognition and Services) Act	Local authorities required to assess – on request – needs of carers when determining services
1995	Disability Discrimination Act	Protection of people with disabilities from discrimination in areas of employment, access to buildings, access to goods and services
1996	Community Care (Direct Payments) Act	Allowed local authorities to give money to those in need to purchase their own services directly
1996	Mental Health (Patients in the Community) Act	Established the Care Programme Approach and supervision registers
1998	Modernising Social Services	White Paper setting out New Labour vision for personal social services
1998	Establishment of National Training Organisation	Training Organisation for Personal Social Services (TOPSS) set up
1998	Crime and Disorder Act	Established Youth Offending Teams, under the Criminal Justice Board
1998	Human Rights Act	Incorporated European Convention on Human Rights into British Law
1999	Public Interest Disclosure Act	Requirement for public bodies to institute 'whistleblowing' procedures
1999	Protection of Children Act	Screening and scrutiny of people working with children
1999	*National Service Framework for Mental Health*	Established targets for mental health services
1999	Disability Rights Commission Act	Established a Disability Rights Commission
2000	Carers and Disabled Children Act	Involvement in assessment and choice in provision of services
2000	Children (Leaving Care) Act	Amended the Children Act to ensure coordinated and sustained support for care leavers
2000	Care Standards Act	Establishment of the General Social Care Council (GSCC); the National Care Standards Commission (NCSC); the Social Care Institute for Excellence (SCIE)

2001	General Social Care Council established (October)	CCETSW closed; GSCC established as qualifications regulator and registration body for social workers
2001	Health and Social Care Act	Local authorities and Health Authorities and Trusts required to develop joint plans for services. Enabled establishment of Care Trusts
2001	Special Educational Needs and Disability Act	SENDA amended previous legislation (Education Act 1996) and integrated disability discrimination law into education arenas
2001	Carers and Disabled Children Act	Extension of direct payments to young people and carers
2001	Public Inquiry into death of Victoria Climbié	The Laming Report, including recommendations for Children's Trusts
2001	*National Service Framework for Older People*	
2001	*Valuing People*	A strategy for Learning Disability for the 21st century
2002	Adoption and Children Act	Broadening criteria as to eligibility to adopt
2002	Nationality, Immigration and Asylum Act	Permitted asylum seekers and their children to be held in detention centres; restricted support for asylum seekers
2003	Health and Social Care (Community Health and Standards) Act	Established the Commission for Social Care Inspection (CSCI), to amalgamate the Social Services Inspectorate (SSI) and the National Care Standards Commission (NCSC)
2003	Community Care (Delayed Discharges) Act	SSDs charged for cost of extended hospital care for older people
2003	Draft Mental Incapacity Bill	Single definition of capacity; Lasting Powers of Attorney (LPA); criminal offence for ill-treatment of a person who lacks capacity
2003	Community Care, Services for Carers and Children's Services (Direct Payments) (England) Regulations	Disabled people may use direct payments to employ close relatives, including spouses. Councils obliged to offer direct payments as alternative to existing services for adults
2003	Sexual Offences Act	Defining issues of informed consent for people with mental disorders/ learning disabilities
2003	Health and Social Care (Community	Establishment of Commission for Social Care Inspection
2003	*Supporting People* programme	A housing related programme to support vulnerable people to maintain independent living
2003	*Every Child Matters*	Determines the framework for children's services after the Laming Report
2003	The Victoria Climbié Inquiry	Report of an Inquiry by Lord Laming
2004	*National Service Framework for Children, Young People and Maternity Services*	Standards for health and social services and the interface with education
2004	Children Act	Implementation of *Every Child Matters*, bringing together education and child and family social work into a children's services structure
2004	Bichard Inquiry	Inquiry into vetting failures resulting in the Soham murders
2004	Carers (Equal Opportunities) Act	Affirmed carers' rights of access to education, training, employment and leisure

175

2004	*Wanless Report: Securing good health for the whole population*	Statement of targets to improve health and address health inequalities
2004	Draft Mental Health Bill	Sought to introduce new powers for compulsory detention and treatment (now abandoned)
2005	Green Paper: *Independence, Well Being and Choice*	Consultation document on new structure for adult services
2005	ChildCare Bill	Setting out government plans for quality child care available for all children under five years old
2005	Mental Capacity Act	Defining capacity to consent – to treatment, services, relationships; established the Court of Protection and the Public Guardianship Office
2005	Education Act	Introduction of Trust Schools
2005	Green Paper: *Youth Matters*	A review of services to young people
2006	White Paper: *Our Health, Our Care, Our*	Following the Green Paper, setting out refined targets *Say: A New Direction for Community Services*
2006	*Working Together to Safeguard Children: A Guide to inter-agency working to safeguard and promote the welfare of children*	New guidance for all agencies – Area Child Protection Committees replaced by Children's Safeguarding Boards, post-Bichard (see 2004, above)
2006	Safeguarding Vulnerable Groups Bill	Establishment of a vetting and barring scheme
2006	Wanless Report	Review of funding for social care for older people
2006	*Options for Excellence – Building the Social Care Workforce of the Future*	Review of social care workforce, published by DoH and DfES
2007	*Care Matters: Time for Change*	White Paper: statement of plans to improve outcomes for children and young people in public care
2007	Equality and Human Rights Commission formed	Merged from Equal Opportunities Commission, Commission for Racial Equality and Disability Rights Commission
2007	*Children's Plan: Building Brighter Futures*	Strategic plan for integrated children's services
2007	Common Assessment Framework for Children and Young People: Practitioners' Guide	Published by the Children's Workforce Development Council
2007	*Putting People First: A Shared Vision and Commitment to the Transformation of Adult Social Care*	Policy statement enabling those who use services to take greater control over their lives, to give people more independence, choice and control through high-quality and personalised services
2007	The Sustainable Communities Act (SCA)	A statutory framework for councils to put forward proposals on sustainable improvements to economic, environmental and social wellbeing
2008	*Social Work At Its Best*	Statement of roles and tasks by GSCC
2008	Evaluation of the New Social Work Degree	Published by GSCC

2008	*Care Matters: Time to Deliver for Children in Care*	White Paper policy document for improving the lives of children in public care
2008	2020 Children and Young People's Workforce Strategy	Consultation on qualifications frameworks for the whole children's services workforce
2008	*Transforming Adult Social Care*	Local authority circular setting the *Personalisation agenda*
2008	*Children and Young Persons Act*	Legislation to enact *Care Matters*, and included provision regarding the well-being of children, private fostering, child death notifications and research.
2009	*Valuing People Now: A New Three Year Strategy for People with Learning Disabilities*	The delivery plan: governance structure and the actions, with timescales and responsibilities
2009	*Health Bill*	Plans to increase patient choice and control over the care they receive
2009	*Welfare Reform Bill*	Major reform of the post-1945 benefits system
2009	*Adult Social Care Workforce Strategy*	Consultation on qualifications frameworks for the whole adult social care workforce
2009	*National Skills Academy for Social Care established*	
2009	*The Protection of Children in England: A Progress Report*	Lord Laming's follow-up report
2009	Establishment of Social Work Taskforce	Interim Report (July) *Final Report: Building a Safe, Confident Future* (December) with 15 Recommendations
2009	*Vision and Progress: Social Inclusion and Mental Health (National Social Inclusion Programme, 2009)*	Review of progress since 2004 Report *Mental Health and Social Inclusion*
2010	Establishment of Social Work Reform Board	*Building a Safe and Confident Future: One year on. Detailed proposals from the Social Work Reform Board*
2010	*A Vision for Adult Social Care: Capable Communities and Active Citizens*	Department of Health publication identifies personalisation as the core principle of service delivery
2010	*Government announce transfer of Regulation of Social Work from GSCC to Health Professions Council (HPC)*	July 2012
2010	*Establishment of Munro Review*	Review set up following the inquiry into the death of Peter Connolly
2010	Equity and Excellence: Liberating the NHS *and* Healthy Lives, Healthy People	First iteration of the Health and Social Care Act
2010	*Working Together to Safeguard Children*	Defines how organisations and individuals should work together to safeguard and promote the welfare of children and young people in accordance with the Children Act 1989 and the Children Act 2004
2011	The Munro Review of Child Protection: Final Report. A child-centred system	15 key recommendations for a whole new system of Child Protection

2011	*No Health without Mental Health: a cross-government mental health outcomes strategy for people of all ages*	Establishes six shared objectives to improve the mental health and well-being of the nation, and to improve outcomes for people with mental health problems through high-quality services
2011	*Adult Social Care Outcomes Framework (ASCOF)*	An outcome-focused approach to assessing adult social care
2011	*The Dilnot Commission on Funding of Care and Support*	Review into how *the future system of funding social care could be made to be sustainable and resilient, fairer for individuals, families and society, value for money and as clear and simple as possible*
2012	*Dementia 2012: A National Challenge*	Government policy statement on Dementia: needs and costs
2012	Health and Social Care Act	Reform of NHS systems and the establishment of Health and Wellbeing Boards

Appendix 6 Summary of recommendations from the Munro Report

Recommendation 1: The Government should revise both the statutory guidance, *Working Together to Safeguard Children* and *The Framework for the Assessment of Children in Need and their Families* and their associated policies to:

- distinguish the rules that are essential for effective working together, from guidance that informs professional judgment;

- set out the key principles underpinning the guidance;

- remove the distinction between initial and core assessments and the associated timescales in respect of these assessments, replacing them with the decisions that are required to be made by qualified social workers when developing an understanding of children's needs and making and implementing a plan to safeguard and promote their welfare;

- require local attention is given to:

  - timeliness in the identification of children's needs and provision of help;

  - the quality of the assessment to inform next steps to safeguard and promote children's welfare; and

  - the effectiveness of the help provided;

- give local areas the responsibility to draw on research and theoretical models to inform local practice; and

- remove constraints to local innovation and professional judgment that are created by prescribing or endorsing particular approaches, for example, nationally designed assessment forms, national performance indicators associated with assessment or nationally prescribed approaches to IT systems.

Recommendation 2: The inspection framework should examine the effectiveness of the contributions of all local services, including health, education, police, probation and the justice system to the protection of children.

Recommendation 3: The new inspection framework should examine the child's journey from needing to receiving help, explore how the rights, wishes, feelings and experiences of children and young people inform and shape the provision of services, and look at the effectiveness of the help provided to children, young people and their families.

Recommendation 4: Local authorities and their partners should use a combination of nationally collected and locally published performance information to help benchmark performance, facilitate improvement and promote accountability. It is crucial that performance information is not treated as an unambiguous measure of good or bad performance as performance indicators tend to be.

Chapter 4: Clarifying accountabilities and improving learning

Recommendation 5: The existing statutory requirements for each Local Safeguarding Children Board (LSCB) to produce and publish an annual report for the Children's Trust Board should be amended, to require its submission instead to the Chief Executive and Leader of the Council, and, subject to the passage of legislation, to the local Police and Crime Commissioner and the Chair of the health and wellbeing board.

Recommendation 6: The statutory guidance, *Working Together to Safeguard Children*, should be amended to state that when monitoring and evaluating local arrangements, LSCBs should, taking account of local need, include an assessment of the effectiveness of the help being provided to children and families (including the effectiveness and value for money of early help services, including early years provision), and the effec-tiveness of multi-agency training to safeguard and promote the welfare of children and young people.

Recommendation 7: Local authorities should give due consideration to protecting the discrete roles and responsibilities of a Director of Children's Services and Lead Member for Children's Services before allocating any additional functions to individuals occupying such roles. The importance, as envisaged in the Children Act 2004, of appointing individuals to positions where they have specific responsibilities for children's services should not be undermined. The Government should amend the statutory guidance issued in relation to such roles and establish the principle that, given the importance of individuals in senior positions being responsible for children's services, it should not be considered appropriate to give additional functions (that do not relate to children's services) to Directors of Children's Services and Lead Members for Children's Services unless exceptional circumstances arise.

Recommendation 8: The Government should work collaboratively with the Royal College of Paediatrics and Child Health, the Royal College of General Practitioners, local authorities and others to research the impact of health reorganisation on effective partnership arrangements and the ability to provide effective help for children who are suffering, or likely to suffer, significant harm.

Recommendation 9: The Government should require LSCBs to use systems methodology when undertaking Serious Case Reviews (SCRs) and, over the coming year, work with the sector to develop national resources to:

• provide accredited, skilled and independent reviewers to jointly work with LSCBs on each SCR;

• promote the development of a variety of systems-based methodologies to learn from practice;

- initiate the development of a typology of the problems that contribute to adverse outcomes to facilitate national learning; and

- disseminate learning nationally to improve practice and inform the work of the Chief Social Worker (see chapter 7).

In the meantime, Ofsted's evalution of SCRs should end.

Chapter 5: Sharing responsibility for the provision of early help

Recommendation 10: The Government should place a duty on local authorities and statutory partners to secure the sufficient provision of local early help services for children, young people and families. The arrangements setting out how they will do this should:

- specify the range of professional help available to local children, young people and families, through statutory, voluntary and community services, against the local profile of need set out in the local Joint Strategic Needs Analysis (JSNA);

- specify how they will identify children who are suffering or who are likely to suffer significant harm, including the availability of social work expertise to all professionals working with children, young people and families who are not being supported by children's social care services and specify the training available locally to support professionals working at the frontline of universal services;

- set out the local resourcing of the early help services for children, young people and families; and, most importantly

- lead to the identification of the early help that is needed by a particular child and their family, and to the provision of an 'early help offer' where their needs do not meet the criteria for receiving children's social care services.

Chapter 6: Developing social work expertise

Recommendation 11: The Social Work Reform Board's Professional Capabilities Framework should incorporate capabilities necessary for child and family social work. This framework should explicitly inform social work qualification training, postgraduate professional development and performance appraisal.

Recommendation 12: Employers and higher education institutions (HEIs) should work together so that social work students are prepared for the challenges of child protection work. In particular, the review considers that HEIs and employing agencies should work together so that:

- practice placements are of the highest quality and – in time – only in designated Approved Practice Settings;

- employers are able to apply for special 'teaching organisation' status, awarded by the College of Social Work;

- the merits of 'student units', which are headed up by a senior social worker are considered; and

- placements are of sufficiently high quality, and both employers and HEIs consider if their relationship is working well.

Chapter 7: The organisational context: supporting effective social work practice

Recommendation 13: Local authorities and their partners should start an ongoing process to review and redesign the ways in which child and family social work is delivered, drawing on evidence of effectiveness of helping methods where appropriate and supporting practice that can implement evidence based ways of working with children and families.

Recommendation 14: Local authorities should designate a Principal Child and Family Social Worker, who is a senior manager with lead responsibility for practice in the local authority and who is still actively involved in frontline practice and who can report the views and experiences of the front line to all levels of management.

Recommendation 15: A Chief Social Worker should be created in Government, whose duties should include advising the Government on social work practice and informing the Secretary of State's annual report to Parliament on the working of the Children Act 1989.

Appendix 7 The standards of proficiency for social workers in England and the Professional Capabilities Framework

This is a joint statement issued by the Health Professions Council and the Social Work Reform Board.

In July 2010 the government announced that the regulation of social workers in England will transfer from the General Social Care Council (GSCC) to the Health Professions Council (HPC). This is expected to take place in July 2012, subject to legislation. The HPC recognise that whilst it is preparing for this transfer, the Social Work Reform Board (SWRB) is taking forward its plans to reform social work in England. The HPC is a member of the SWRB and is supportive of its vision to create a safe confident future for social work.

As part of its provisions for the transfer, the HPC is required by its legislation to develop standards of proficiency for social workers in England. Part of the SWRB's work includes developing a Professional Capabilities Framework (PCF) which supports social workers throughout their career. As both pieces of work are being developed at the same time, the HPC and SWRB are keen to set out how the standards of proficiency and the PCF work in conjunction.

- The HPC's standards of proficiency are the threshold standards necessary for safe and effective practice within a profession. They set out what a social worker in England must know, understand and be able to do following the completion of their social work degree.

- Alongside the standards of proficiency, the HPC also sets separate standards for conduct, performance and ethics and continuing professional development.

- All of the HPC's standards must be adhered to in order to remain on the Register. These standards are how a registrants' (individual on the HPC Register) 'fitness to practise' is determined.

- By contrast, the PCF is designed to support social workers throughout each stage of their career, beyond the threshold standards set by the HPC.

- The PCF acts as an overarching framework by setting out key capabilities expected of a social worker as they develop in their career. These include professionalism, values and ethics, knowledge, intervention and skills and professional leadership.

The HPC will continue to work with the SWRB to ensure consistency and understanding about the standards of proficiency and the PCF wherever possible and to support developments in social work practice.

Appendix 8 Building a safe and confident future (July 2009)

The *Public Description of Social Work* below was first published as part of The Social Work Taskforce Final Report.

Social work helps adults and children to be safe so they can cope and take control of their lives again

Social workers [can] make life better for people in crisis who are struggling to cope, feel alone and cannot sort out their problems unaided

How social workers do this depends on the circumstances. Usually they work in partnership with the people they are supporting – check out what they need, find what will help them, build their confidence, and open doors to other services.

Sometimes, in extreme situations such as where people are at risk of harm or in danger of hurting others, social workers have to take stronger action to protect them – they have the legal powers and duties to do this.

You may think you already do this for your friends and family but social workers have specialist training in fully analysing problems and unmet needs, in how people develop and relate to each other, in understanding the challenging circumstances some people face, and in how best to help them cope and make progress. They are qualified to tell when people are in danger of being harmed or harming others and know when and how to use their legal powers and responsibilities in these situations.

You may think that you'll never need a social worker but there is a wide range of situations where you or your family might need one, such as:

1. caring for family members;

2. having problems with family relationships and conflict;

3. struggling with the challenges of growing old;

4. suffering serious personal troubles and mental distress;

5. having drug and alcohol problems;

6. facing difficulties as a result of disability;

7. being isolated within the community; or

8. having practical problems with money or housing.

Resources and useful websites

Acts of Parliament since 1988: **www.legislation.gov.uk**

Age UK: **www.ageuk.org.uk**

Alzheimer's Society: **www.alzheimers.org.uk**

Audit Commission: **www.audit-commission.gov.uk**

British Agencies for Adoption and Fostering: **www.baaf.org.uk**

British Association of Social Workers: **www.basw.co.uk**

British Institute of Learning Disability: **www.bild.org.uk**

CACHE (Council for Awards in Care, Health and Education) **www.cache.org.uk**

Centre for Policy on Ageing: **www.cpa.org.uk**

Centre for Welfare Reform: **www.centreforwelfarereform.org.uk**

Children's Improvement Board (CIB): **www.local.gov.uk**

Community Care magazine: **www.communitycare.co.uk**

College of Social Work: **www.collegeofsocialwork.org**

Department for Education: **www.education.gov.uk**

Department of Health: **www.dh.gov.uk**

Electronic Library for Social Care: SCIE: **www.sciesocialcareonline.org.uk**

Foundation for People with Learning Disabilities: **www.learningdisabilities.org.uk**

General government information: **www.direct.gov.uk**

General Social Care Council: **www.gscc.org.uk**

Health Professions Council: **www.hpc-uk.org**

Home Office: **www.homeoffice.gov.uk/**

Independent Living Fund: **www.dwp.gov.uk/ilf/**

International Federation of Social Workers: **http://ifsw.org**

Joseph Rowntree Foundation: **www.jrf.org.uk**

Learning Disability Coalition: **www.learningdisabilitycoalition.org.uk**

Local Government Association: **www.local.gov.uk**

Mental Health Foundation: **www.mentalhealth.org.uk**

MIND: **www.mind.org.uk**

National Autistic Society: **www.autism.org.uk**

National Care Forum: **www.nationalcareforum.org.uk**

National Children's Bureau: **www.ncb.org.uk**

National Development Team for Inclusion: **www.ndti.org.uk**

National Statistics: **www.statistics.gov.uk**

Parliament and legislation (HMSO): **www.legislation.gov.uk**

People First: **www.peoplefirst.org.uk**

Shaping Our Lives: **www.shapingourlives.org.uk**

Share the Care: **www.sharethecare.org.uk**

Skills Academy for Social Care: **www.nsasocialcare.co.uk**

Skills for Care: **www.skillsforcare.org.uk**

Social Care Association: **www.socialcareassociation.co.uk**

Social Care Institute for Excellence (SCIE): **www.scie.org.uk**

Social Services Research Group: **www.ssrg.org.uk**

Social Work Reform Board: **www.education.gov.uk/swrb**

Supporting People: **www.communities.org.uk**

Think Local, Act Personal: **www.thinklocalactpersonal.org.uk**

UK Centre for the Advancement of Inter Professional Education: **www.caipe.org.uk**

Values into Action: **www.viascotland.org**

Young Minds: **www.youngminds.org.uk**

References

Adams, R (1996) *The personal social services: Clients, consumers or citizens?* Harlow: Longman.

Adams, R, Dominelli, L and Payne, M (eds) (2002a) *Social work: Themes, issues and critical debates.* Basingstoke: Palgrave.

Alzheimer's Disease Society (1993) *Deprivation and dementia.* London: Alzheimer's Disease Society.

American Psychiatric Association (1994) *Diagnostic and statistical manual of mental disorders.* 4th edition. Washington, DC: American Psychiatric Association.

Anfilogoft, S with Starr, M and Mathias, P (2002) Carer and carer trainers focus groups report to DH from Carers UK and City and Guilds Affinity.

Archambeault, J (2009) *Social work and mental health.* Exeter: Learning Matters.

Association of Child Care Officers (1963) *The duties and functions of child care officers.*

Atkinson, D (1997) *An auto/biographical approach to learning disability research.* Aldershot: Ashgate.

Atlee, C (1920) *The social worker.* London: Bell.

Audit Commission (1986) *Making a reality of Community Care.* London: HMSO.

Audit Commission (1996) *Misspent youth.* London: The Audit Commision.

Bailey, D (2002) Mental health, in R Adams, L Dominelli and M Payne (eds) *Critical practice in social work.* Basingstoke: Palgrave Macmillan.

Bamford, T (1990) *The future of social work.* London: Macmillan Education.

Bamford, T (2006) Social work identity. *Community Care,* July.

Banks, S (1995) *Ethics and values in social work.* London: Macmillan.

Baraclough, J, Dedman, G, Osborn, H and Willmott, P (1996) *100 years of health related social work.* Birmingham: BASW.

Barclay Committee (1982) *Social workers: their roles and tasks.* London: National Institute for Social Work/Bedford Square Press.

Barker, R (2009) *Making sense of Every Child Matters.* Bristol: Policy Press.

Barnett, H (1918) *Canon Barnett, his life, work and friends.* London: John Murray.

Barret-Ducrocq, M (1989) *Love in the time of Victoria.* Harmondsworth: Penguin.

Barton, C (2003) Conference presentation: *Developing the new world of practice learning.* 8 April 2003.

Barton, R (1959) *Institutional neurosis.* Bristol: John Wright.

Beckett, C (2006) *Essential theory for social work practice.* London: Sage.

Behan, D (2005) *Impact of regulation and the future of inspection. CSCI Speech 10 May.*

Bell, M and Wilson, K (eds) (2003) *The practitioner's guide to working with families.* Basingstoke: Palgrave.

Beresford, P (2007) *Shaping our lives: The changing roles and tasks of social work from service users' perspectives.* London: GSCC.

Beresford, P (2011) *'The big picture'.* December. www.communitycare.co.uk/blogs

Bereford, P and Hasdler, F (2009) *Transforming social care: Changing the future together.* Brunel University Press: Shaping Our Lives / Centre for Citizen Participation.

Beresford, P and Shaping our lives (2008) *What future for care?* York: Joseph Rowntree Foundation.

Biestek, F (1961) *The casework relationship.* London: Allen and Unwin.

Blewett, J, Lewis, J and Tunstill, J (2007) *The changing roles and tasks of social work.* London: GSCC.

Blewett, J and Tunstill, J (2007) *Fit for purpose? The social work degree in 2007.* London: Synergy Research & Consulting Ltd.

Bornatt, J (1998) Anthology: voices from the institution, in M Allott and M Robb (eds) (1998) *Understanding health and social care.* London: Sage.

Boyd, W (1996) *Confidential inquiry into homicides and suicides by mentally ill people* ('Boyd report'). London: Royal College of Psychiatrists.

Brandon, D (1998) The monastic tradition and community care, in R Jack (ed.) *Residential versus community care.* London: Macmillan.

Brayne, H and Martin, G (2001) *Law for social workers.* 7th edition. Oxford: Oxford University Press.

Brewer, C and Lait, J (1980) *Can social work survive?* London: Temple Smith.

Bridge Child Care Consultancy (1996) *The Rikki Neave report.* Cambridge: Cambridgeshire County Council.

British Association of Social Workers (BASW) (2002) *A code of ethics for social workers.* Birmingham: BASW.

Brown, L (2002) *A survey of family group conference use across England and Wales.* Bath: University of Bath.

Busfield, J (1986) *Managing madness.* London: Hutchinson.

Butler-Sloss, E (1988) *Report of the inquiry into child abuse in Cleveland, 1987.* London: HMSO.

Butrym, Z (1976) *The nature of social work.* London: Macmillan.

Bytheway, B, Bacigalupo, V, Bornat, J, Johnson, J and Spur, S (eds) (2002) *Understanding care, welfare and community.* London: Routledge.

CCETSW (2001) *History and achievements.* London: CCETSW.

Cambell, J and Oliver, M (1996) *Disability politics.* London: Routledge.

Cameron, C (2003) An historical perspective on changing child care policy, in J Brannen and P Moss (eds) *Rethinking child care.* Buckingham: Open University Press.

Care Quality Commission (CQC) (2011) *The state of care report 2010/11.* London: Care Quality Commission.

Centre for Policy on Ageing (1996) *A better home life: A code of practice for residential and nursing home care.* London: Centre for Policy on Ageing.

Chase, E, Simon, A and Jackson, S (eds) (2006) *In care and after: A positive perspective.* London: Routledge.

Children and Young People's Unit (CYPU) (2001) *Building a strategy for children and young people.* London: Stationery Office.

Children, Schools and Families Committee (2009) *Seventh report. Training of children and families social workers.* House of Commons.

City of Sheffield (1967) *Annual report of the children's department.* Sheffield: City of Sheffield Council.

Clare, B (2000) Becoming a social worker: learning, doing and being, in J Harris, I Paylor and L Froggett (eds) *Reclaiming social work: The Southport papers.* Birmingham: Venture Press.

Clarke, J (1993) *A crisis in care? Challenges in social work.* London: Sage.

Clough, R (1998) The future of residential care, in R Jack (ed.) *Residential versus community care.* Basingstoke: Macmillan.

Coates, K and Silburn, R (1970) *Poverty: The forgotten Englishman.* Harmondsworth: Penguin.

College of Social Work (2011) *The contribution of social work.* London: SCIE.

Colton, M, Sanders, R and Williams, M (2001) *Working with children.* Basingstoke: Palgrave.

Cooper, D (1968) *Psychiatry and anti-psychiatry.* London: Tavistock.

Corby, B, Doig, A and Roberts, V (2001) *Public inquiries into abuse of children in residential care.* London: Jessica Kingsley.

Corrigan, P and Leonard, P (1978) *Social work practice under capitalism: A Marxist approach.* London: Macmillan.

Crawford, K and Walker, J (2008) *Social work with older people.* Exeter: Learning Matters.

Cree, V (2002) The changing nature of social work, in R Adams, L Dominelli and M Payne (eds) *Social work: Themes, issues and critical debates.* Basingstoke: Palgrave.

Cree, V (ed.) (2003) *Becoming a social worker.* London: Routledge.

Cree, V and Myers, S (2008) *Social work making a difference.* Bristol: Policy Press.

Curtis Committee (1946) *Report of the care of children committee.* Cmnd 6922. London: HMSO.

Davidson, E (1965) *Social casework.* London: Bailliere, Tindall and Cox.

De Largy, J (1957) Six weeks in – six weeks out: A geriatric hospital service for rehabilitating the aged and relieving their carers. *Lancet* 23 February, 418–19.

Department for Children, Schools and Families (2007) *Children's plan: Building brighter futures.* London: Stationery Office.

Department for Children, Schools and Families (2008) *2020 Children and young people's workforce strategy.* London: Stationery Office.

Department for Children, Schools and Families (2009a) *Piloting the social care practice model: A prospectus.* London: Stationery Office.

Department for Communities and Local Government (2011) *Best value statutory guidance.* London: Department for Communities and Local Government.

Department for Constitutional Affairs (2005) Mental Capacity Act: frequently asked questions (avaliable at: http://webarchive.nationalarchives.gov.uk/+/http://www.dca.gov.uk/menincap/faq.htm)

Department for Education (2011) *Munro Report on child protection.* London: DfE.

Department for Education and Skills (2003) *Every child matters.* London: DfES.

Department for Education and Skills (2006) *Working together to safeguard children.* London: Stationery Office.

Department for Work and Pensions (2006) *Families with children in Britain: Findings from the 2004 Families and Children Study (FACS).* London: Department for Work and Pensions.

Department of Health (1989) *Caring for people: Community care in the next decade and beyond.* London: HMSO.

Department of Health (1990) *Community care in the next decade and beyond: Policy guidance.* London: HMSO.

Department of Health (1991) *Patterns and outcomes in child placement: Messages from current research and their implications.* London: HMSO.

Department of Health (1995) *Child protection: Messages from research.* London: HMSO.

Department of Health (1998a) *Quality protects: Framework for action.* London: HMSO.

Department of Health (1998b) *Modernising social services: Promoting independence, improving protection, raising standards.* Cm. 4169. London: Stationery Office.

Department of Health (1999a) *Modernising mental health services: Safe, sound and supportive.* London: HMSO.

Department of Health (1999b) *National service framework for mental health.* London: HMSO.

Department of Health (2000a) *Working together to safeguard and promote the welfare of children.* London: HMSO.

Department of Health (2000b) *Framework for the assessment of children in need and their families.* London: The Stationery Office.

Department of Health (2000c) *Reforming the Mental Health Act: Part I the new legal framework.* London: The Stationery Office.

Department of Health (2000d) *Lost in care (the Waterhouse report).* London: The Stationery Office.

Department of Health (2001a) *Fair access to care services.* London: The Stationery Office.

Department of Health (2001b) *Valuing people: A new strategy for learning disability for the 21st century. A White Paper.* London: The Stationery Office.

Department of Health (2001c) *National service framework for older people.* London: The Stationery Office.

Department of Health (2002a) *Quality in social care: The National Institutional Framework.* London: The Stationery Office.

Department of Health (2002b) *Requirements for social work training.* London: Department of Health.

Department of Health (2002c) *The residential care and nursing home sector for older people: An analysis of past trends, current and future demand.* London: Department of Health.

Department of Health (2002f) *Carers in social work.* London: Department of Health.

Department of Health (2003a) *The Victoria Climbié inquiry: Report of an inquiry by Lord Laming.* London: The Stationery Office.

Department of Health (2003b) *Our inheritance, our future: Realising the potential of genetics in the NHS.* London: The Stationery Office.

Department of Health (2004) *Mental Health Bill.* London: Stationery Office.

Department of Health (2005a) *Independence, well-being and choice.* London: DoH.

Department of Health (2005b) *Choose health: making healthier choices easier.* London: Stationery Office.

Department of Health (2006a) *Options for excellence – Building the social care workforce of the future.* London: Stationery Office.

Department of Health (2006b) *Our health, our care, our say: A new direction for community services.* London: The Stationery Office.

Department of Health (2007) *Putting people first: A shared vision and commitment to the transformation of adult social care.* London: Stationery Office.

Department of Health (2008) *High quality care for all* (The Darzi report). London: Department of Health.

Department of Health (2008a) *Transforming adult social care.* LAC (DH) (2008) 1. London: Stationery Office.

Department of Health (2008b) *Refocusing the care programme approach: Policy and positive practice guidance.* London: Stationery Office.

Department of Health (2009) *Valuing people now: A new three year strategy for people with learning disabilities.* London: Stationery Office.

Department of Health (2010a) *A vision for adult social care: Capable communities and active citizens.* London: Department of Health.

Department of Health (2010c) *Equity and excellence: Liberating the NHS.* London: Department of Health.

Department of Health (2010d) *Healthy lives, healthy people.* London: Department of Health.

Department of Health (2011b) *No health without mental health: A cross government mental health outcomes strategy for people of all ages.* London: Department of Health.

Department of Health (2012) *Dementia 2012: A national challenge.* London: Department of Health.

Department of Health and Social Security (1971) *Better services for the mentally handicapped.* London: HMSO.

Department of Health and Social Security (1974) *Report of the committee of inquiry into the care and supervision provided in relation to Maria Colwell.* London: HMSO.

Department of Health and Social Security (1975) *Better services for the mentally ill.* London: HMSO.

Department of Health and Social Security (1981) *Growing older.* London: HMSO.

Department of Health and Social Security (1985) *Social work decisions in child care: Recent research findings and their implications.* London: HMSO.

Department of Health/Social Services Inspectorate (1989) *Homes are for living in.* London: HMSO.

Dockrell, J, Grove, N and Hasan, P (1999) People with learning disabilities, in D Messer and F Jones (eds) *Psychology and social care.* London: Jessica Kingsley.

Dominelli, L (1988) *Anti-racist social work.* Basingstoke: Macmillan.

Dominelli, L (1989) *Feminist social work.* Basingstoke: Macmillan.

Dominelli, L (1997) *Sociology for social work.* London: Macmillan.

Dominelli, L (2009) *Introducing social work.* Cambridge: Polity Press.

Douglas, A and Philpot, T (1998) *Caring and coping.* London: Routledge.

Drake, R (1996) A critique of the role of the traditional charities, in L Barton (ed.) *Disability and society: Emerging issues and insights.* Harlow: Longman.

Drakeford, M (2002) Poverty and the social services, in B Bytheway, V Baciqalupo, J Bornat, J Johnson and S Spurr (eds) *Understanding care, welfare and community*. London: Routledge.

Duffy, S (2011) *A fair society and the limits of personalisation*. Sheffield: Centre for Welfare Reform.

Evans, S and Huxley, P (2012) Social work and mental health, in M Davies (ed.) *Social Work with Adults*. Basingstoke: Palgrave Macmillan.

Fook, J (2002) *Social work: Critical theory and practice*. London: Sage.

Forsythe, B and Jordan, B (2002) The Victorian ethical foundation of social work in England – Continuity and contradiction. *British Journal of Social Work*, 32 (7), 847–62.

Foucault, M (1961) *Folie de deraison: histoire de la folie à l'age classique*. Paris: Plon.

Foucault, M (1977) *Discipline and punish*. London: Allen Lane.

Fox-Harding, L (1997) *Perspectives in child care policy*. 2nd edition. London: Longman.

Franklin, B and Parton, N (eds) (1991) *Social work, the media and public relations*. London: Routledge.

Frost, N (2002) Evaluating practice, in R Adams, L Dominelli and M Payne (eds) *Critical practice in social work*. Basingstoke: Palgrave.

General Social Care Council (2002) *Codes of practice for social care workers and employers*. London: GSCC.

General Social Care Council (2008a) *Social work at its best: A statement of social work roles and tasks for the 21st century*. London: GSCC.

General Social Care Council (2009) *Raising standards: Social work education in England 2007–08*. London: GSCC.

Gibbins, J (1988) Residential care for mentally ill adults, in I Sinclair (ed.) *Residential care: The research reviewed*. London: HMSO.

Glendinning, C and Arksey, H (2008) Informal care, in P Alcock, M May and K Rowlingson (eds) *Student's companion to social policy*. 3rd edition. Oxford: Blackwell.

Glouberman, S (1990) *Keepers: Inside stories from total institutions*. London: King Edward's Hospital Fund for London.

Godfrey, A (2000) What impact does training have on the care received by older people in residential homes? *Social Work Education,* 19 (1) 55–65.

Goemans, R (2012) A consideration of the nature and purpose of mental health social work, *Mental Health and Social Inclusion*, 16 (2), 69–73.

Goffman, E (1961) *Asylums: Essays on the social situation of mental patients and other inmates*. New York: Doubleday.

Golightley, M (2011) *Social work and mental health*. 4th edition. Exeter: Learning Matters.

Goodwin, S (1990) *Community care and the future of mental health service provision*. Aldershot: Avebury.

Griffiths, R (1988) *Community care: Agenda for action*. London: HMSO.

Guy, J (1990) *Tudor England*. Oxford: Oxford University Press.

Hadley, R and Clough, R (1998) Learning disability: A service in jeopardy, in M Allott and M Robb (eds) *Understanding health and social care*. London: Sage.

Halmos, P (1968) *The personal and the political*. London: Hutchinson.

Harris, J and White, V (eds) (2009) *Modernising social work*. Bristol: Policy Press.

Harris, R (1996) Telling tales: Probation in the contemporary social work formation, in N Parton (ed.) *Social theory, social change and social work*. London: Routledge.

Hayden, C, Goddard, S, Gorin, S and Van Der Spek, N (1999) *State child care: Looking after children*. London: Jessica Kingsley.

Health Service Circular/Local Authority Circular (2001) *Intermediate care*. London: Department of Health.

Hendrick, H (1994) *Child welfare: England 1872–1989*. London: Routledge.

Hendrick, H (2003) *Child welfare*. Bristol: The Policy Press.

Hibbert, C (1987) *The English: A social history 1066–1945*. London: Collins.

Holman, B (1988) *Putting children first: Prevention and child care – a study of prevention by statutory and voluntary agencies*. Basingstoke: Palgrave.

Holman, B (2001) *Champions for children*. Bristol: Policy Press.

Holman, B (2003) Social work in the neighbourhood, in V Cree (ed.) *Becoming a social worker*. London: Routledge.

Home Office (1945) *Report by Sir William Monckton on the circumstances which led to the boarding out of Dennis and Terence O'Neill at Bank Farm, Minsterly and the steps taken to supervise their welfare, etc.* Cmd 6636. London: Home Office.

Home Office (1997) *No more excuses*. White Paper. London: The Stationery Office.

Horner, N and Krawczyk, S (2006) *Social work in education and children's services*. Exeter: Learning Matters.

House of Commons (1984) *Second report from the Social Services Committee, Session 1983–84, children in care* (The Short Report). London: HMSO.

Hugman, R (1991) *Power in caring professions*. Basingstoke: Macmillan Education.

Illich, I (1977) *Disabling professions*. London: Boyars.

Jack, R (ed.) (1998) *Residential versus community care*. Basingstoke: Macmillan.

Jones, C (1983) *State social work and the working class*. London: Macmillan.

Jones, C (2002) Social work and Society, in R Adams, L Dominelli and M Payne (eds) *Social work: Themes, issues and critical debates*. Basingstoke: Palgrave.

Jones, K (1972) *A history of the mental health services*. London: Routledge and Kegan Paul.

Jordan, B (1984) *An invitation to social work*. Oxford: Robertson.

Jordan, B (1997) Social work and society, in M Davies (ed.) *Companion to social work*. Oxford: Blackwell.

Jordan, B and Jordan, C (2000) *Social work and the third way*. London: Sage.

Kendall, L and Harker, L (eds)/**IPPR** (2002) *From welfare to wellbeing*. London: Institute of Public Policy Research.

Kirkwood, A (1993) *The Leicestershire inquiry, 1992*. Leicester: Leicestershire County Council.

Konrad, G (1975) *The caseworker*. London: Hutchinson.

Laing, R and Esterson, A (1964) *Sanity, madness and the family*. London: Tavistock.

Langan, M (1993) The rise and fall of social work, in J Clarke (ed.) *A crisis in care?* London: Sage.

Levin, E, Sinclair, I and Gorbach, P (1994) *Families, services and confusion in old age*. Aldershot: Avebury.

Levy, A and Kahan, B (1991) *The pindown experience and the protection of children: The report of the Staffordshire Child Care Inquiry 1990*. Stafford: Staffordshire County Council.

Leyser, H (1995) *Medieval women*. London: Phoenix.

Lincolnshire County Council (2008) *'Lincolnshire is listening ...' Report on the development of a vision for adult social care 2008–2011*. Lincoln: Lincolnshire County, Council.

Lloyd, L, Calnan, M, Cameron, A, Seymour, J, Smith, R and White, K (2011) *Maintaining dignity in Later Life: A longitudinal qualitative study of older people's experiences of support and care*. NDA Findings 8. Sheffield: NDA Research Programme.

Lloyd, M (2002) Care management, in R Adams, L Dominelli and M Payne (eds) *Critical practice in social work*. Basingstoke: Palgrave.

London Borough of Brent (1985) *A child in trust: The report of the panel of inquiry into the circumstances surrounding the death of Jasmine Beckford*. London: Brent Council.

London Borough of Greenwich (1987) *A child in mind: The report of the inquiry into the circumstances surrounding the death of Kimberley Carlile*. London: London Borough of Greenwich.

London Borough of Lambeth (1986) *Whose child? The report of the public inquiry into the death of Tyra Henry*. London: London Borough of Lambeth.

Lymbery, M and Butler, S (eds) (2004) *Social work ideals and practice realities*. Basingstoke: Palgrave Macmillan.

Malin, N (ed.) (1994) *Services for people with learning disabilities*. London: Routledge.

Malin, N, Race, D and Jones, G (1980) *Services for the mentally handicapped in Britain*. London: Croom Helm.

Martyn, H (ed.) (2000) *Developing reflective practice*. Bristol: The Policy Press.

Marwick, A (1976) *The home front*. Edinburgh and London: Thames and Hudson.

McDonald, A (1999) *Understanding community care*. London: Macmillan.

Means, R and Smith, R (1994) *Community care: policy and practice*. 2nd edition. London: Macmillan.

Means, R and Smith, R (1998) *From poor law to community care*. 2nd edition. Bristol: The Policy Press.

Mencap (2001) *Behind closed doors*. London: Mencap.

Mental Health Foundation (1994) *Creating community care*. London: Mental Health Foundation.

Milburn, A (2002) *Reforming social services*, speech to the Annual Social Services Conference, Cardiff. www.doh.gov.uk/speeches

Miller, E and Gwynne, C (1972) *A life apart*. London: Tavistock.

Milner, J and O'Byrne, P (2002) *Assessment in social work*. 2nd edition. Basingstoke: Palgrave.

Ministry of Health (1957) *Mental illness and mental deficiency* (Report). London: HMSO.

Ministry of Health (1962) *A hospital plan for England and Wales*. Cmnd 1604. London: HMSO.

Mitchell, H (1998) The insider researcher, in M Allott and M Robb (eds) *Understanding health and social care: An introductory reader*. London: Sage.

Moncrieff, J (1997) *Psychiatric imperialism: the medicalisation of modern living. Soundings*, Issue 6.

Moriarty, J and Levin, E (1998) Respite care in homes and hospitals, in R Jack (ed.) *Residential versus community care*. London: Macmillan.

Moriarty, J, Levin, E and Gorbach, I (1993) *Respite care services for carers of confused elderly people*. London: National Institute for Social Work.

Morrison, T (1990) Emotionally competent child protection organisations: fallacy, fiction or necessity?, in R Pugh and N Thompson (eds) *Protecting children: Challenges and change*. London: Arena.

Moulin, L (1978) *La vie quotidienne des Religieux au Moyen Age, Xe–Xve siècle*. Paris: Hachette.

Munro, E (2000) Defending professional social work practice, in J Harris L, Froggett and I Paylor (eds) *Reclaiming social work: The Southport papers*. Birmingham: Venture Press.

Munro, E (2010) *The Munro review of child protection, Interim report. The child's journey*. London: Department for Education.

Munro, E (2011) *The Munro Report of child protection: Final report. A child-centred system*. London: Department for Education. http://www.education.gov.uk/publications/eOrderingDownload/Munro-Rewiew.pdf/.

Murphy, E (1991) *After the asylums: Community care for people with mental illness*. London: Faber and Faber.

National Development Team for Inclusion (2010) *Value people – What now?* www.ndti.org.uk/who-were-concerned-with/learning-disability/valuing-people-what-now4/

National Statistics (2005) *Adult social services statistics*. Leeds: NHS Health and Social Care Information Centre.

Newman, T, Roberts, H and Oakley, A (1996) Weighing up the evidence. *Guardian*, 10 January.

NISW and Rowntree Foundation (1998) *Shaping futures: Rights, welfare and personal social services*. London: NISW.

NISW and Rowntree Foundation (2001) *Shaping our lives*. London: NISW.

Nuffield Report (1946) *The hospital surveys: The Domesday Book of the hospital services*. Oxford: Provincial Hospitals Trust.

O'Brien, J (1981) *The principles of normalisation*. London: Campaign for Mental Health.

Office of the Deputy Prime Minister (2003) *Supporting people*. London: ODPM.

Oliver, C (2003) The care of the illegitimate child: The Coram experience 1900–45, in J Brannen and P Moss (eds) *Rethinking child care*. Buckingham: Open University Press.

Oliver, M (1990) *The politics of disablement*. Macmillan.

Oliver, M (1993) Struggling for independence. *Community Care*, 2 September: 13.

Oliver, M (1996) *Understanding disability: from theory to practice*. London: Macmillan.

Painter, B (2000) *Upon the parish rate*. Louth: Louth Naturalists', Antiquarian and Literacy Society.

Parker, R (1988) An historical background, in *Residential care: The research reviewed*, Vol 3 of the Wagner Report. London: HMSO.

Parker, R (1990) *Away from home: A history of child care*. Ilford, Essex: Barnardos.

Parker, J and Bradley, G (2007) *Social work practice: Assessment, planning, intervention and review*. 2nd edition. Exeter: Learning Matters.

Parton, N (1991) *Governing the family: Child care, child protection and the state*. London: Macmillan.

Quality Assurance Agency for Higher Education (2008) *Subject benchmark statement for social work*. Gloucester: QAA.

Rankin, J and Regan, J (2004) *Meeting complex needs: The future of social care*. London: Institute for Public Policy Research.

Ray, M and Phillips, J (2002) Older people, in R Adams, L Dominelli and M Payne (eds) *Critical practice in social work*. Basingstoke: Palgrave.

Read, J (1988) *The equal opportunities book*. London: Interchange Books.

Report of the Mental Deficiency Committee (1929) *Part III – The adult defective*. London: HMSO.

Residential Forum (1996) *A standards guide for residential care*. London: NISW.

Ridley, J (2002) *The Tudor age*. 3rd edition. London: Constable and Robinson.

Ritchie, J, Dick, D and Lingham, R (1994) *The report of the inquiry into the care and treatment of Christopher Clunis*. London: HMSO.

Robb, B (1967) *Sans everything: A case to answer*. London: Nelson.

Rogers, A and Pilgrim, D (1996) *Mental health policy in Britain*. Basingstoke: Macmillan.

Rose, M (1972) *The relief of poverty 1834–1914*. London: Macmillan.

Rowe, J and Lambert, L (1973) *Children who wait*. London: Association of British Adoption Agencies.

Royal Commision on Long Term Care of the Elderly (1999) *With respect to old age*, Cm 4192–1. London: Stationery Office.

Ryan, J and Thomas, F (1980) *The politics of mental handicap*. Harmondsworth: Penguin.

Sapey, B (2002) Physical disability, in R Adams, L Dominelli and M Payne (eds) *Critical practice in social work*. Basingstoke: Palgrave.

Sayce, L (1993) MIND's policy of user involvement www.mind.org.uk

Scottish Executive (2006) *Changing lives: Report of the 21st century social work review*. Edinburgh: The Scottish Executive.

Scull, A (1977) *Decarceration: community treatment and the deviant: A radical view*. Englewood Cliffs: Prentice-Hall.

Scull, A (1979) *Museums of madness: the social organisation of insanity in nineteenth century England*. Harmondsworth: Penguin.

Seebohm, F (1968) *Report of the committee on local authority and allied personal social services, Cmnd 3703*. London: HMSO.

Seed, P (1973) *The expansion of social work*. London: Routledge and Kegan Paul.

Shakespeare, T (2000) *Help*. Birmingham: Venture Press.

Shaping our Lives/P Beresford (2007) *The changing roles and tasks of social work from service users' perspectives*. London: Shaping our Lives/GSCC.

Shaw, G B (1911) *The Doctor's Dilemma*, Act 1.

Sheldon, J (1948) *The social medicine of old age. Report of an inquiry in Wolverhampton*. London: Nuffield Foundation.

Shrubsall, F and Williams, A (1932) *Mental deficiency practice*. London: University of London Press.

Parton, N (1997) Social theory, social change and social work: An introduction, in N Parton (ed.) *Social theory, change and social work*. London: Routledge.

Parton, N (2000) Preface to P Stepney and Ford (eds) *Social work models, methods and theories*. Lyme Regis: Russell House Publishing.

Parton, N (2001) Protecting children: A socio-historical analysis, in K Wilson and A James (eds) *The child protection handbook*. London: Bailliere Tindall.

Parton, N (2006) *Safeguarding childhood: Early intervention and surveillance in a late modern society*. Basingstoke: Palgrave/Macmillan.

Parton, N and O'Byrne, P (2000) *Constructive social work: Towards a new practice*. Basingstoke: Macmillan.

Payne, M (1998) *Social work and community care*. London: Macmillan.

Payne, M (2002) Management, in R Adams, L Dominelli and M Payne (eds) *Critical practice in social work*. Basingstoke: Palgrave.

Payne, M (2005) *The origins of social work*. Basingstoke: Palgrave Macmillian.

Peach, J and Horner, N (2007) Using supervision: support or surveillance? in M Lymbery and K Postle (eds) work: A companion to learning. London: Sage.

Pearson, G (1983) *Hooligan: A history of respectable fears*. London: Macmillan.

Penhale, B and Parker, J (2008) *Working with vulnerable adults*. Abingdon: Routledge.

People First Workers (1996) *Speaking out for equal rights workbook 2, Equal People Course Books*. Buckingham: Open University, People First and Mencap.

Perkins, R and Repper, J (1998) Principles of working with people who experience mental health problems, Brooker and J Repper (eds) *Serious mental health problems in the community. Policy practice and research*. London: Bailliere Tindall.

Phillips, J (1992) The future of social work with older people. *Generations Review*, 4, 12–15.

Philpot, T (2003) Everybody out. *Community Care*, 10–16 July.

Picard, L (2000) *Dr Johnson's London*. London: Weidenfeld and Nicolson.

Pierson, J (2002) *Tackling social exclusion*. London: Routledge.

Pilgrim, D and Rodgers, A (1999) *A sociology of mental health and illness*. Buckingham: Open University Press.

Pinker, R (1971) *Social theory and social policy*. London: Heinemann.

Pinker, R (1982) An alternative view, in *Barclay Committee, Social Workers*. London: Bedford Square Press.

Pitkeathley, J (1989) *It's my duty, isn't it? The plight of carers in our society*. London: Souvenir Press.

Platt, D (2005) The future of children's services. Keynote speech at the *Making Research Count National Conference*, 19 May 2005.

Porter, R (1991) *The Faber book of madness*. London: Faber.

Powell, F (2001) *The politics of social work*. London: Sage.

Priestley, M (2003) *Disability: A life course approach*. Cambridge: Polity Press.

Quality Assurance Agency for Higher Education (2000) *Benchmark statement for social policy and social work*. Gloucester: QAA.

Skills for Care (2008) *The state of the adult social care workforce, in England 2008*. Leeds: Skills for Care.

Smith, M (1965) *Professional education for social work in Britain*. London: George Allen and Unwin.

Social Care Institute for Excellence (2002) *Listening exercise: Summary of findings*. London: SCIE.

Social Exclusion Unit (2004) *Mental health and social exclusion: Social exclusion report*. London: Office of the Deputy Prime Minister.

Social Work Reform Board (2010) *Building a safe, confident future: Implementing the Recommendations of the Social Work Taskforce*. London: Department of Education.

Social Work Reform Board (2011) *Building a safe and confident future: One year on – detailed proposals*. London: Department of Education.

Social Work Taskforce (2009) *Building a safe and confident future*. London: Department for Education.

Spray, C and Jowitt, B (2012) *Social work practice with children and families*. London: Sage.

SSI/SWSG (1991) *Care management and assessment: Practitioners' guide*. London: Department of Health/SSI/SWSG.

Stainton, T (2002) Learning disability, in R Adams, L Dominelli and M Payne (eds) *Critical practice in social work*. Basingstoke: Palgrave.

Steadman-Jones, G (1976) *Outcast London: A study in the relationship between classes in Victorian society*. Harmondsworth: Penguin.

Stevenson, O and Parsloe, P (1993) *Community care and empowerment*. York: Joseph Rowntree Foundation.

Stroud, J (1960) *The shorn lamb*. London: Longman.

Sumner, K (ed.) (2002) *Our homes, our lives*. London: Centre for Policy on Ageing/The Housing Corporation.

Szasz, T (1971) *The manufacture of madness*. London: Routledge and Kegan Paul.

Szasz, T (1973) *The second sin*. Surbiton: Anchor Press.

Tew, J (ed.) (2007) *Social perspectives in mental health: developing social models to understand and work with mental distress*. London: Jessica Kingsley.

Tew, J (2011) *Social approaches to mental distress*. Basingstoke: Palgrave Macmillan.

Thomas, N and Pierson, J (2001) *Dictionary of social work*. London: Collins Educational.

Thompson, N (2000) *Understanding social work: Preparing for practice*. Basingstoke: Palgrave.

Thompson, N (2002a) *Building the future: Social work with children, young people and their families*. Lyme Regis: Russell House Publishing.

Thompson (2002b) Social work with adults, in R Adams, L Dominelli and M Payne (eds) *Social work: themes, issues and critical debates*. 2nd edition. Basingstoke: Palgrave.

Thompson, N (2005) *Understanding social work*. 2nd edition. Basingstoke: Palgrave.

Tilbury, D (2002) *Working with mental illness*. 2nd edition. Basingstoke: Palgrave.

Titmuss, R (1965) Goals of today's welfare state, in P Anderson and R Blackburn (eds) *Towards socialism*. London: Fontana.

Titmuss, R (1968) *Commitment to welfare*. London: Allen and Unwin.

Townsend, P (1962) *The last refuge*. London: Routledge and Kegan Paul.

Townsend, P (1979) *Poverty in the United Kingdom*. London: Allen Lane.

Training Organisation for the Personal Social Services (2002) *National occupational standards for social work*. London: TOPSS.

Tronto, J (1993) *Moral boundaries: A political argument for an ethic of care*. New York: Routledge.

Trotter, C (1999) *Working with involuntary clients*. London: Sage.

Twigg, J (1998) The medical/social boundary, in M Allott and M Rob (eds) *Understanding health and social care*. London: Sage.

Utting, W (1991) *Children in public care: A review of residential care*. London: HMSO.

Utting, W (2006) Conference address, Thomas Coram Unit, University of London.

Valuing People Support Team (2005) *Making things better*. The Government's annual report on learning disability. London: Stationery Office.

Vernon, A (2002) Multiple oppression, in B Bytheway, V Bacigalupo, J Bornat, J Johnson and S Spur (eds) *Understanding care, welfare and community*. London: Routledge.

Wagner, G (1988) *Residential care: A positive choice*. London: HMSO.

Walker, A (1984) *Social planning: A strategy for socialist welfare*. Oxford: Blackwell and Martin Robertson.

Walmsley, J and Rolph, S (2002) Community care for people with learning difficulties, in B Bytheway, V Bacigalupo, J Bornat, J Johnson and S Spur (eds) *Understanding care, welfare and community*. London: Routledge.

Walton, P (1999) Social work and mental health: Reforming the training agenda for ASWs. *Social Work Education*. 18 (4), 375–88.

Walvin, J (1987) *Victorian values*. London: Cardinal.

Warner, N (1992) *Choosing with care*. London: HMSO.

Webb, S and Webb, B (1911) *The prevention of destitution*. London: Longman.

Williams, P (2009) *Social work with people with learning difficulties*. 2nd edition. Exeter: Leaning Matters.

Willmott, P (1975) *Consumer's guide to the British social services*. 2nd edition. Harmondsworth: Penguin.

Wistow, G (2000) *The modernised personal social services: NHS handmaidens or partners in citizenship?* Leeds: Nuffield Institute for Health.

Younghusband, E (1947) *Report on the employment and training of social workers*. Carnegie: United Kingdom Trust.

Younghusband, E (1978) *Social work in Britain: 1950–1975: A follow-up study*. Vol 2. London: Allen and Unwin.

Younghusband, E (1981) *The newest profession*. Sutton: Community Care/IPC.

Index